Discovering Angus
and The Mearns

Other titles in this series

Discovering Angus and The Mearns

I.A.N. HENDERSON

JOHN DONALD PUBLISHERS LTD
EDINBURGH

To Prunella

Ki DS
136940

ISBN 0 85976 302 1

Phototypeset by Newtext Composition Ltd., Glasgow.
Printed & bound in Great Britain by Martin's of Berwick Ltd.

Acknowledgements

My thanks for assistance go to David Clark for his cover picture; Jack Morgan for the map; Colin Prior for the portrait; Gavin Drummond, Director of Libraries and Museums in Angus, for photographs – with a special word of thanks to his staff in Brechin Library; to D.C. Thomson, Dundee; to Charles Kerr and Mae Pitkethly for additional photographs; to Jean Dundas and Anne Findlay for advice; and a kiss to the little lady with the cow.

Introduction

This book is an amalgam of fact and opinion, blended with a little history. It is hoped that it will interest, inform and involve the reader with that part of Scotland that was Angus and the Mearns.

Contents

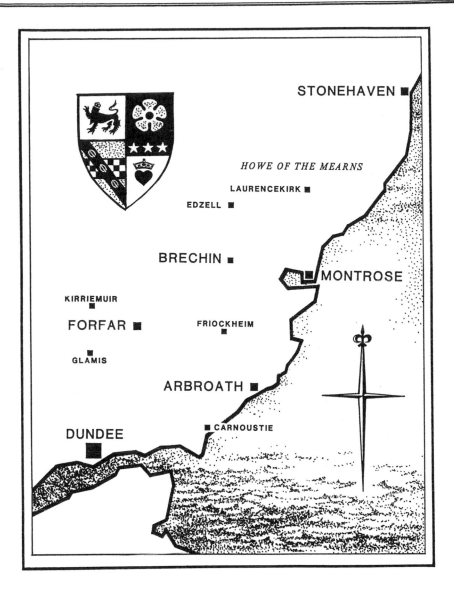

ANGUS AND THE MEARNS

'Left a bit . . .'

CHAPTER 1

Strath and Howe

Angus and the Mearns are taken together like gin and tonic. They may be enjoyed separately but they are better combined. They always have been. Strathmore and the Howe o' the Mearns, which together form the greater part of Angus and the Mearns, are simply adjoining segments of the same extended valley.

Old records bracket Angus and the Mearns together as far back as the year 993 although at that time they called Angus 'Angusia'. It was still 'Angusia' in 1675 but a document dated 1795 refers to 'the County of Forfar and the Shire of Angus'. Forfarshire it was from then on until a County Council meeting of May 1928 decided that the old name of Angus should be restored. The Local Government (Scotland) Act of 1947 (Section 127) finally confirmed this as official when it enacted that 'the County sometime known as the County of Forfar should henceforth be known as the County of Angus'. The Mearns has always been the Mearns and nobody knows where it came from although it has been suggested that it means 'border lands'. That could be said of a lot of places and names. The last reorganisation of local government in 1975 which imposed Tayside and Grampian on us and consigned Angus and Kincardineshire to limbo, is best ignored. We are dealing here with Angus and the Mearns as the geographic entity it has always been.

The Highland Boundary Fault, which effectively marks the end of the Highlands, also marks the western boundary of the Mearns/Strathmore Valley. The Highland Boundary Fault runs diagonally right across Scotland south-west from Stonehaven to the Clyde estuary. The south-east border of Angus and the Mearns is formed just north of Dundee by a spur of the Sidlaw Hills which extend from Perth up to Montrose. Add on the impressive alternation of sandy beach and rugged cliff bounding the coastal belt all the way from Carnoustie to Stonehaven, plus the Angus glens that penetrate the Highland Line and you have the land known to generations of east-

1

coasters as Angus and the Mearns. The area encompasses Highland and Lowland, fertile plain and barren mountain. The contrast of high summer on the golden sands of St. Cyrus and mid-winter on the north face of Craig Maskeldie is as marked as any this Earth offers. It would be invidious to suggest that Angus and the Mearns is better than any other part of Scotland, but fairly easy to prove.

The geologic structure of the glens of Esk, Lethnot, Clova, Prosen, Moy and Isla is of old, durable, metamorphic rock which fixes them firmly as part of the Highlands. The base rock of the big valley is Old Red Sandstone from the Strathmore syncline. When the last Ice Age melted and the remaining glaciers disappeared, between 8000 and 6000 years BC, the fertile soils of the valley were laid down. One great ice flow, the Strathmore glacier, joined up with the Tay glacier which extended right back to Rannoch moor. Lesser glaciers moved eastwards out of the Highlands, scouring out the glens as they came. The resultant run-off and residue – the 'till' – formed the basis of the rich alluvial soil that carpets Angus and the Mearns today.

The people of the area are as favourably mixed as their soil. Walk down Castle Street in Forfar any day and Picts, Scots, Romans, Danes and Saxons will greet you as you pass. On market day you will see La Tène and Beaker Folk as well. They come in from the Montrose direction. All these blood lines are clearly present in Angus and the Mearns today and we have the memorials, artefacts, relics, residue and folk to prove it.

The first traces of human habitation along the east coast from Fife to Aberdeen are of flint tools and midden deposits from Mesolithic tribes of hunter/fishermen immediately following the Ice Age. These people were followed by Neolithic folk who added farming and husbandry to the Mesolithic skills. Their hearth stones, dwelling places and middens have been identified. Some of these early settlers came across the sea from northern Europe and brought a more sophisticated lifestyle with them. They were experienced farmers, craft workers and traders. Evidence of their trading is seen in the numbers and types of stone implements we have found. Axes and tools that were made from stone from the north and west of the country have been found in Angus and the Mearns. A considerable

Angus . . .

trade must have been carried on and the people must have travelled extensively to conduct it.

As the Bronze Age gave way to the Iron Age, so the picture of primitive life becomes clearer; but not much. There are great hill-forts and settlements, souterrains and sculptured stones in Angus and the Mearns and very, very, little is known of them. With the developments of new techniques of aerial photography and radiocarbon dating, more is being discovered than the unaided eye could fathom and at last we may be near to unfolding some of the truth. Fresh evidence is being produced regularly to contradict existing theories and history is being re-written. That is nothing new. Historians exist by refuting existing theories and re-writing history. One hesitates to agree with the view expressed by the late Mr Henry Ford, the American automobile manufacturer, in his libel suit against the *Chicago Tribune* in July 1919. When referred to an historical precedent, Henry Ford replied in ringing tones

'History is bunk'. His opinion has been much quoted. Henry may have been a shade too sweeping in his condemnation but he had a point. We will accept the history of Angus and the Mearns with reservations. It was not until the Romans came to Britain in 55 BC and subsequently, that history was formally recorded. Even then it has to be suspect; it varies with the historian you read. Much of our early Scottish history comes from the great Roman historian, Gaius Cornelius Tacitus, who gave us the definitive biography of Agricola and detailed all his North British campaigns. If you recall that Tacitus was Agricola's son-in-law, you might just begin to question his total impartiality. It is probable that the Picts were not just the rabble of primitive savages he describes.

In the early centuries AD, the two great native tribes mentioned by the Romans were the Scotti, originally from Ireland, and the Caledonii or Picti, from the north. It has always been assumed that the Picti were so-called because they painted their bodies or tattooed them in some manner. It is much more likely to have been because of the beautiful art work they created in their carved stone monuments. The Celtic Scots were Christian, the native Picts were pagan. For centuries they fought each other and together they fought the Romans. That much we know. The Scotti left their own records, in which they refer to themselves as 'Gaels'. They used an elementary alphabet of straight and intersecting lines, the twenty-letter 'ogam' alphabet. The Picts left no written chronicles at all but a wealth of stone carved pictorial art work that showed them to be an artistic, structured, highly developed community. Few details of their lives are known.

The Pictish kingdom was divided into two separate entities, Northern Pictland and Southern Pictland, each with its own King. Angus and the Mearns was the heartland of the Southern Pictish kingdom. The facts are sparse. Research is called for to rehabilitate the Picts. They emerged from the dripping mists of Caledonia, decorated our landscape with refined examples of creative art and then disappeared into the maw of the Gaelic-Irish Celts. They deserve better. The term 'Picts' was coined by the Romans merely as a convenient collective label for what was in reality a group of separate and

... and the Mearns.

different native tribes, each of which merited at least a name of
its own. They have been ill-served by history.

When the Romans left in 406 AD and Christianity spread
slowly from the Scots to the Picts, the two became closer. They
still fought each other but with diminishing fervour. In 685 the
Northumbrian King Ecgfrith, who had conquered all of the
south and east of North Britain, was defeated in battle by King
Brude Maelchon of Southern Pictland. In 710, King Nechtan
of Southern Pictland was converted to Christianity, facilitating
the eventual union of Pict and Scot but it was a slow process. It
was not until the year 843 AD that King Kenneth McAlpin of
Dalriada was able to unite the two kingdoms of Dalriada and
Pictland into the composite 'Scotland'.

From the welter of myth and fable that survives from this
obscure period, few facts emerge but one at least is clear.
Angus and the Mearns has always been a centre of population
and a well-spring of cultural development for its people. The
physical and geographic structure of the land encouraged the
infiltration of migrants along the coastline from the south and

the arrival of voyagers from northern Europe across the sea.
The vast mass of the Highland Boundary Line contained these
tribes to the low lands of the coastal belt and to the big valley,
just as the western Highlands confined the Irish immigrants,
the Celts, to the islands and coastline of the west. Angus and
the Mearns has always provided a good living.

With an environment of rich alluvial soil and an ancestry of
cultivators and husbandmen stretching back to Neolithic times,
the Angus and the Mearns farmer walks tall today. Stooping
slightly just for today, possibly, but that is a purely politically
induced posture. The E.E.C. Common Agricultural Policy is
not working in the best interests of Angus and the Mearns
farmers just at present. It is to be hoped that soon it may be.
The farmers of Angus and the Mearns have always been in the
forefront of Scottish agriculture – though in fact it would be
more accurate to say 'Scotch' agriculture. 'Scottish' is a
modern intrusion into the language and the internationally
accepted adjective, particularly in farming circles, is Scotch.
'Scottish' is a weak, twentieth-century Anglicised quasi-
amelioration that lacks the force and direction of 'Scotch'.
Scotch cattle, Scotch lamb, Scotch potatoes, Scotch barley,
Scotch bluebells, Scotch thistles, Scotch whisky and Scotch men
are known to the world and all are produced in Angus and the
Mearns. The 'Scotch cattle' used to be known as 'Angus Blacks'
and Aberdeen was added largely because it made a more
syllabic sound. Aberdeen had little enough to do with the
establishment of the breed.

Despite the present unstable state of agriculture in Scotland
and the E.E.C. generally, the farms of Angus and the Mearns
are working to full capacity and efficiency. They are applying
traditional skills and hard graft to the rearing of crops and
stock and they have achieved a degree of efficiency that is
unsurpassed anywhere in the world today. If only the
politicians were as efficient as the farmers. Crop yields are
increasing in quantity, quality and diversity; animals are
being bred to the exact specification of the butcher; seeds and
breeding stock are being exported worldwide and the
politicians tell our farmers to cut production and diversify into
leisure complexes, guest houses and forestry.

The current cry to farmers is to take land out of production.

Grain mountains, milk lakes, potato piles and beef bings are to be removed only by stopping production whilst millions in the Third World die. With our temperate climate, fertile soil, incomparable food products and a benign and dedicated workforce, Angus and the Mearns should be a stockyard and granary for the world. Instead of that we are directed to tourism and leisure activities and told to plant trees on our arable acres.

Tourism is being promoted nationally as Scotland's economic salvation. Where heavy industry has suffered and farming is suffering now, tourism is seen as the great alternative. It will be a black day when Angus and the Mearns farmers are reduced to being lackeys in bed-and-breakfast houses or grooms in pony-trekking and rare breed establishments. The farmers will be the rarest breed. It is to be hoped, rather, that Angus and the Mearns will just accept and assimilate tourists as it has the Beaker Folk, the Picts, Scots and Romans before them. To speed things up, it might be an idea to hand the trade over to the gamekeepers rather than the farmers. The Angus gamie in his district checks and matching deerstalker is a formidable sight on the hill and he is well trained to handle tourists.

The essence of tourism is that it is a carefully structured, highly organised and totally cynical operation. Tourists are a well-researched migratory species. They come in on the same flight paths every year and fortunately their habits and patterns of behaviour are known. When the main flocks have landed they scatter quickly and the art of good tourist management is to get them to gather again in smaller coveys, easier for plucking. With a supply of adequate ground bait, good clean roosting points, a varied diet and easy access to watering holes, tourists can be made to flock anywhere. With the right bait and efficient traps you will always manage to part the tourist from his money – which is, of course, the sole object of the trade. Signpost every castle, kirk, natural feature, souterrain and Round Tower in the area and drive them gently and unsuspectingly towards your No. 1 trap. The No. 1 trap must always be the Distillery. There is nothing quite like the Distillery for attracting tourists. Once you have them cornered, hit them with all you have in the way of craft shops, tearooms, potteries, picture-postcard and tartan souvenir emporia, antique shoppes, haggis-hurling meets and the like before they migrate, severely peppered, back to their winter quarters. The gamies would fettle them, right enough, but there must be a more dignified role for us, farmer and gamekeeper alike. Genuine visitors are quite another matter. Folk who come to Angus and the Mearns because they like and respect the place are welcome. We have always had our quota of enlightened visitors and we hope they will continue to come. The visitor who is prepared to get out of his car and walk the hill and cliff paths or play on the sandy shores will always be welcome.

Angus and the Mearns abounds with natural treasures and historic monuments and as yet they remain unspoiled. There is no county that makes less fuss of its history. The Pictish sculptured stones at Aberlemno, the Round Tower and Cathedral of Brechin, Restenneth Priory, the Brown and White Caterthuns and a hundred other memorials still stand and you can wander around them at will and for nothing. At Dunnottar Castle and the House of Dun there is a small charge but these are restored properties and that is another story. Angus and the Mearns respects its ancient monuments and, thankfully, has so far refrained from over-commercialising them.

The historic castles of Glamis, Cortachy, Brechin, Kinnaird, Finavon and Guthrie are still inhabited. Brechin Castle, home of the Earl of Dalhousie, is one of the oldest inhabited dwellings in Scotland. Glamis Castle, the Queen Mother's family seat, is the birthplace of Princess Margaret and the present home of the Earl of Strathmore. The Earl of Southesk lives in Kinnaird Castle near Brechin and the Earl of Airlie in Cortachy Castle above Kirriemuir. The castles of Angus and the Mearns figure prominently in Scotland's history. Many are in ruins now – Edzell, Melgund, Redcastle, Dunnottar and a host of others – but Inverquharity, long a ruin, has now been refurbished as a dwelling house. One hopes that this might set a trend. Melgund Castle, once the home of Cardinal Beaton and Marion Ogilvie and lately the home of a million and a half pigeons, is ripe for·development. Provided it isn't developed into another Auld Scottische Ceilidh Center and tartan Touriste Trappe.

The history of Angus and the Mearns is rich and satisfying fare but we must condition ourselves to eat sparingly. Scottish history, after Tacitus, stems mainly from the Scoti-Chronicon of John of Fordoun the great chronicler of our early years. At the end of the fourteenth century, John Fordoun wrote five Chronicles and part of a sixth and this work was immediately adopted by the ecclesiastical authorities of the day as the definitive History of Scotland. Monasteries across the land immediately set about copying out the Scoti-Chronicon and various bits and pieces were slipped in by assorted monks with ideas of their own. Copies of John Fordoun's work made by different monasteries were therefore themselves different. When Hector Boece (1465-1536) came up with his 'History of Scotland' in 1527 he delved deeply into Fordoun and unearthed a wheen mooly tatties. Hector Boece's contribution was further qualified by his 'extreme credulity and much invention'. (*Dictionary of Scottish History* 1977: Donaldson & Morpeth.)

When we add Hector Boece to John of Fordoun we get Scotland's early story. If we bear in mind then that all history is merely an expedient interpretation of putative fact to satisfy contemporary prejudice, we may proceed together. Hand in hand and treading lightly we will venture circumspectly into Angus and the Mearns; for Angus and the Mearns is couthy country, still inhabited by couthy folk. Their speech is less debased than most these days and the Mearns accent rolls broad around the Howe and down Strathmore. You are near Scotland's roots in this land. The ferm loons live the life their grandfathers lived before them and the fishermen live as fishermen have since the tides began to flow.

I went last night, as I frequently do, to stand and muse and brood and pray on the rickle of Neolithic stonework that caps the White Caterthun. To the north and east Glen Lethnot and the Clash o' Wirren bounded the Strath and the Mearns. The sky was dark and slashed with red and the wind carried the perfume of heather and bog myrtle down the Whisky road and up from Craigendowie. No man moved in all the miles around and the only sound was the sigh of the wind and the bleat of the blackface sheep.

There is no more peaceful spot in all the world this day than Angus and the Mearns.

CHAPTER 2

Steer for the Red Light

It is an unfortunate fact that Dundee has overtaken and consumed both Broughty Ferry and Monifieth. Strangled cries are still occasionally heard from both townships insisting that they still exist but to no avail. They are now integral with Dundee, and Angus begins at Barry. The border lands of the Dundee complex on the shore road are not pretty. Monifieth eventually peters out attractively enough into its golf course but that is immediately followed by a shanty town of caravans and shacks. A riding school with all its attendant clutter of painted oil drums and coloured poles and mud succeeds the holiday caravan site before the eye finds rest in Barry.

Barry

The village of Barry is a small and unpretentious hamlet which could have enjoyed a happy anonymity but for its proximity to Buddon Ness and the Barry-Buddon Links. In 1868 the Forfarshire Rifle Volunteers 'conceived the idea of having an encampment and on 12th June a number took up their abode for the first time under canvas'. It was to Barry that they repaired. Little could these pioneers have known of what they were about. Thousands upon thousands of suffering soldiers have since passed through Barry-Buddon and their memories, in the main, are not of the happiest. For some years after 1868 it was used merely as a summer camp for the Volunteers but when the War Office decided to set up a permanent artillery range in Scotland in the 1880s, Barry was a front runner.

The South and West wanted Irvine, the North and East wanted Barry. Irvine had the immediate advantage of close proximity to Glasgow and the fleshpots, Barry had the advantage of space. There was much more space available at

10

Barry and with a permanent artillery camp in mind, space was what the War Office wanted above all else. After ponderous deliberation and much lobbying of politicians, the remote, invigorating bents of Barry were selected in preference to the accessible enclosures of Irvine. The decision was made that Barry should be the permanent artillery camp for Scotland.

To implement the decision, an immediate order was passed that 'Four 32 pounder smooth bore guns on standing carriages and four 7 inch breech-loading guns on platform carriages' were to be installed at Barry. 'The platforms to be built by the Royal Engineers.' An additional order decreed that 'The six 40-pounder Armstrong guns at present at Panmure Battery are to be placed at the disposal of the Forfarshire Artillery Volunteers but to be handed over to the Scottish National Artillery Association for their annual meetings'. Since then, Barry-Buddon has trained soldiers non-stop. Many's the old sweat today who started as a young sweat at Barry yesterday. The Boer War, the Great War and the Second World War were all rehearsed at Barry-Buddon and there are still old men who will show you callused thumb joints and burned forearms to prove it.

It seems strange that an area so renowned for peace and quiet as Angus and the Mearns should introduce itself with an artillery range but it is there. At least it provides a contrast. It impinges but lightly on the neighbourhood and the most that anyone sees of it is the bleak expanse of the field firing ranges with red flags fluttering or the huddled encampments of barrack buildings crouched protectively amongst the dunes as the Aberdeen-London train thunders by. On one such train recently, a grizzled Black Watch pensioner was heard to wonder how modern recruits with small bore automatic rifles manage to pass their marksmanship tests. He recalled that during the '39-'45 War, a fair proportion of his mates passed their S.M.L.E. .303 firing course only because a pencil wielded by a friendly marker and pushed through the target reasonably near to the bull, exactly simulated the passage of a .303 bullet. 'Maybe,' he added, 'they hae thinner pencils noo.'

That old soldier was from the Second World War. It would take an older soldier – in his 90s now – to recall an occurrence from the Great War at Barry. It was in 1914, at Barry, that the dreaded disease of horses now known simply as 'grass sickness' was first diagnosed and classified. There was a massive concentration of horses from cavalry regiments at Barry in 1914, heavy draught horses as well as chargers. The disease had been reported previously in Angus in 1907 and 1911 but the first definite diagnosis was in 1914 when it broke out at Barry camp. The rows and rows of bell tents were backed by picket lines of hundreds of horses and when the disease struck they were decimated.

Grass sickness is a wasting disease. The afflicted horse is unable to eat, suffers muscular spasms and eventually dies. Few cases are known to survive and recovery is never complete. There is no known treatment. When it was recorded and listed at Barry it was known for some time simply as the 'Barry disease'. As it became more generally identified and the Barry connection less relevant, the name 'grass sickness' was adopted. Painstaking research and the most detailed docimasy has so far failed to find a cause or a cure. Little more is known of it today than when it hit the remount lines at Barry in 1914.

It will probably not be long before the cause is discovered and no doubt the name of the discoverer will go down in history along with Fleming, Baird, Rutherford and a host of others whose names are associated with great discoveries. Whoever he is, I hope the name of James Guthrie M.R.C.V.S. will not be forgotten. Jim Guthrie is a vet who has spent every spare minute of his career doing research on grass sickness. He has now reached a point where he knows that the probable causes are a fungal toxin or a neural virus which produces a pathological change in the nervous system subsequently triggered by a secondary stimulus to produce the clinical disease. If that doesn't mean a lot, at least it means that Jim Guthrie has eliminated practically every cause that has so far been suggested for the disease. Most of his research has been done with horses in the strath and glens of the Mearns and Angus. It would be particularly apt if the Barry disease could be eradicated as well as identified in Angus.

Barry camp is not used to the same extent now. Fashions in war have changed and less emphasis is presently put on a rifleman's ability to perform the 'In-out-butt-stroke-on guard-pass through' routine. That was the bayonet drill that could

Barry Camp in former times.

split the thumb joint open on the safety catch and bring smiles to the faces of sadistic small-arms instructors. It is a more humane spot nowadays, used mainly for Combined Cadet Corps camps and Territorial manoeuvres. I understand they now have sheets.

Over the railway and the fence from Barry-Buddon the golfers of Barry practise – and practice – their art. When golf took off as a national craze in the mid-nineteenth century the men of Barry were amongst the pioneers, and the Panmure Golf Club, Barry, is a very select, private, golf club today. Golf had been played in a haphazard kind of a way for centuries along the east coast of Scotland but the nineteenth century saw it organised and developed and the end of the century saw mushrooms relegated to second place in the growth stakes.

The Panmure Golf Club

The Panmure Club started playing on a little six-hole course at Monifieth which they shared with several other Clubs.

Exclusive from the outset, the Panmure Club marked itself from the other Clubs by levying a 10/- entry fee and a 5/- annual subscription. Caddies were paid the inflationary sum of 2d per round. In 1871, when an incursion of Carnoustie counter-jumpers and Monifieth mechanics was feared, the annual subscription was raised to 10/-. In the same year they built a Clubhouse for £638.0.11. This building is now used by the Monifieth Panmure Ladies' Golf Club. Before this clubhouse was built there was a little local difficulty with the railway company. They refused to stop their trains conveniently by the first tee, at the request of the Panmure Golf Club, and the club was forced for a time to rent a waiting room from the railway company as a clubhouse.

These minor difficulties were easily overcome by the sahibs, tuans and tycoons who composed the Panmure and by 1898 they had bought their present course at Barry and settled down, happily bordered by the railway on one side, the sea on the other and the field firing ranges at the far end. The present clubhouse is an exact replica of the Calcutta Golf Club clubhouse as a result of the close association between Barry and the Calcutta jute trade and the large number of ex-India wallahs who have been Panmure members.

The resemblance is not merely in the building. The modes and mores of Panmure Golf Club are those of a grander age. The atmosphere is warm and friendly as you arrive; quiet conversation and efficient service greet you in the bar, deep leather armchairs and a welcoming fire meet you in the library. Panmure Golf Club has retained not only the appearance of the Calcutta Golf Club but a great measure of its Sybaritic style. When participating clubs in the Angus Senior Golfers' League entertain each other, the norm is for a cup of coffee and a sandwich to be offered. Panmure Golf Club sets higher standards. They entertain visiting seniors to a full and satisfying lunch in an elegant dining room with immaculate silver and napery – and very good claret. Panmure Golf Club, Barry, is one of the last strongholds of civilised living in Scotland. It may have been some time since the cry of 'Koi hai?' last rang through its halls but the influence of the old ex-India boys is still there and it is good. In the present age of iconoclasm and egalitarian nonsense it is reassuring to come across such a survival of culture.

Carnoustie

The uplifting influence of the Panmure Golf Club prepares one for the douce decency of Carnoustie. As you survey the neat little streets and tidy avenues of the town you have a feeling that this place is somehow different, and it is different. It is entirely suburban. There is no heart to the town. It lacks the focal point of a harbour or a cathedral or even a square. Carnoustie is a clean, respectable collection of desirable residences with large gardens and no history. It compensates for that by providing its own provenance in relating the tale of how it was founded – as recently as 1797 – by one Thomas Lawson.

It appears that Thos. Lawson, variously described as a 'cottar' and a 'wright', was returning from Inverpeffer to Dundee one night in 1797 when he fell asleep on the bents. Now if Tam Lowson wasna' fu' when he woke up, I'll wager he was when he fell asleep, but that is only my view and it is not my story. I'll give it to you as Carnoustie gives it.

When Thos. Lawson woke up he felt so refreshed by the pure air of the beach that he vowed to build himself a house on the spot. He sought out the owner of the land, a Major Wm. Phillips, and negotiated a lease of 'two Scotch acres' at 70/- per annum. It is significant that when he went to pay his first year's rent, Mrs Major Wm. Phillips gave him 5/- back. She thought he wasna' wyce. So, incidentally, did Mrs Thomas Lawson.

When people saw the house that Tam had built amongst the sand dunes and the rabbit warrens of the foreshore, they agreed with the wives, *nem. con.* Tammy had built his house on a bare, exposed, windswept sand hillock that no sensible man could ever have thought suitable for human habitation. But wait! Thomas Lawson, cottar and/or wright, had a whole series of last laughs. The folk who came to scoff saw the excellent crops that Tommy grew in his garden and the peace and calm of his sheltered abode amongst the friendly dunes, and remained to build. Soon there was a regular clachan around him with a smiddy and a school and a church and the wives giving each other afternoon teas. T. Lawson Esq., pioneer, then proceeded to see them all off one by one by living to be 95 years of age and being eventually buried in Panbride kirkyard, leaving Carnoustie as his memorial. That is why there are no mediaeval town dwellings or castles or cathedrals in Carnoustie. Thomas Lawson did it all by himself.

When Carnoustie did begin to establish itself in the early nineteenth century, it had two immediate claims to fame – golf and sea bathing. The most obvious of these was sea bathing. Golf was still a bit of an upstart pastime and not likely to last. Fortunately, Carnoustie is blessed with a most excellent sandy beach. When the sun shines in high summer and the wavelets lap the crescent beach of Carnoustie bay, one wonders why anyone would prefer to frequent the crowded confines of the Mediterranean. Then the wind whips in off the North Sea and one knows. Carnoustie is a sun-lover's paradise for very few days in any year. The rest of the time it demands fortitude and resolution, attributes which were much more common in the robust nineteenth rather than the effete twentieth century. As the nineteenth century and Carnoustie developed, so did the popularity of sea bathing as a therapeutic and recreational exercise. The example of Prinny, who came eventually to the throne as George IV, and who was advised to go sea bathing at Brighton to counter the ill effects of a lifetime of dissolute excess, set the fashion.

Carnoustie made full use of its beach. A strong local campaign was mounted to provide 'bathing carriages' and soon the smooth expanse of sand was ribbed by the heavy wheels of mobile changing rooms. A docile Clydesdale, enjoying pensioned ease, moved bathing coaches down and up along a beach whose only pace was set by the incoming tide. Into the twentieth century Carnoustie flourished. As well as a sea bathing resort it built up a flourishing boot and shoe manufacturing trade and an important light engineering industry.

Changing times and changing patterns of trade have outmoded Carnoustie's factories although there is still a thriving engineering business, and the changing social scene

Carnoustie Beach 1950s – the end of an era.

has overtaken Carnoustie's attraction as a holiday resort. Until the 1950s, the town was still a summer holiday venue for thousands of people coming mainly from the west of Scotland and Glasgow. The onset of cheap foreign holidays and air travel has diverted Carnoustie's visitors to the Costa Cheapo and left Carnoustie to the golfers.

Golf is the real life force of Carnoustie. It has been suggested – and is firmly believed in some quarters – that when Thomas Lawson fell asleep on the Carnoustie bents it was only after he had spent exhausting hours looking for a lost featherie. There is no doubt at all that golf has been played in the area since the dawn of reason. Records show that it was played on the very spot where Carnoustie is now in the year 1527. The Panmure Register records that in 1527 Sir Robert Maule 'exercisit the gowf' there, and who is to say that he was the first? By the nineteenth century there was a ten-hole course in use, oddly enough with only five greens, each being used for two holes. No doubt that is where St Andrews got the idea.

17

Carnoustie took golf to its heart then. When the War Office tried to buy up the Carnoustie links to extend the Barry-Buddon Artillery Range, Carnoustie Town Council stepped in and insisted on buying up the whole area for golf courses. The Town Council has now gone, sadly, along with so much of the old local administrative set-up, and a Links Trust has taken over the land. The oldest Golf Club in Carnoustie is the Carnoustie and Taymouth, founded in 1842. Next was the Dalhousie, named after its patron the Earl of Dalhousie, in 1868. The Caledonian is the upstart offspring of these two, having had its centenary no sooner than 1987.

Carnoustie has three courses now and although the Championship course has been quietly dropped from the Open circuit – ostensibly because of traffic and accommodation problems in 1975 – there are firm grounds for believing that the Open might soon return. It was held in Carnoustie in 1931, '37, '53, '68 and '75, and it could be back in the '90s. Some folk, of course, don't want it back. There are always some folk. Some folk objected when it was first proposed to put a telephone in the Starter's box on the Medal course. That was about ninety years ago. Some folk said that a telephone in the Starter's box would be the end of golf in Carnoustie as they knew it. The Dundee men would phone in and take up all the places in the ballot for starting times. A telephone was put in the Starter's box and some folk went out at night and cut the wires: repeatedly. Eventually a cable was put underground and the Dundee men did not monopolise all the ballot places. So life goes on. Change is imminent in Carnoustie right now. The Beach Hall is being refurbished and developed into a 'Sports Complex' and the Dalhousie Golf Club is in process of being taken over by an American group. Two American golf architects, an American travel agent and an American golf writer are presently negotiating to take over the Dalhousie. This powerful consortium operates under the ambiguous company name of 'Friends of Carnoustie'. Aye, weel, some folk . . .

It is a pleasant little place, Carnoustie, neat, trim and ordered. Thos. Lawson would be proud of it. He would also be a mite surprised, for as Dundee has swamped its neighbours, so Carnoustie has overtaken and consumed West Haven. The

Mobile changing room – and staff. A docile Clydesdale helps out on Carnoustie beach.

little fishing village is now choked with modern houses and holiday homes and no fishermen remain. Were it not for the railway which acts as a physical barrier, there would be nothing of West Haven left bar a few mutilated cottages with second storeys and dormer windows overlooking an overcrowded strip of soiled and littered sand.

East Haven and West Haven

East Haven, a couple of miles along the coast, is maintaining its individuality rather better. The little sandy cove is still relatively unspoiled even though traffic barriers have now been erected just through the railway bridge and a close-cropped picnic area and large adjacent car park established. That about sums it up. We are over-populated now and we all have cars.

People always want to go where other people go and that
means that on a sunny August Sunday now you will have
difficulty finding a place to picnic at East Haven, except on the
designated picnic zone with its wooden trestle tables and
shaved grass. To protect the householders on either side, their
access roads have been barred to cars and that further cuts
down the available space. It is one of the unfathomable
problems of the age. For my own part I prefer to go down to
East Haven in mid-week in mid-winter to walk along the rocky
shore towards West Haven and watch the wading birds. That
avoids the crowds. It also avoids transistor radios and most of
the litter – two more of the unfathomable problems of the age.

Until the Second World War, East and West Havens were
still active fishing villages. With no harbour or jetty, only creek
fishermen could operate with shallow draught boats but away
back in 1855 there were thirty-five fishermen with nineteen
boats between them working out of the villages. By 1929 the
number was reduced to nine fishermen with five small
sailboats. The Second War saw the end of full-time fishing and
only the part-timers remain. The trade is reduced to lobster
creeling now and a lorry picks up the catch and off go the
lobsters to holding tanks and eventually to Paris.

The creels that can be seen lying around East Haven are now
made by the last of the real fishermen, Eric Duncan and
Geordie Lyall, whose families have been fishing out of East
Haven for generations. George now fishes part-time but all the
creels used by the local hobby fishermen are made by him. His
creels are a good example of the adaptation of traditional
craftsmanship to fit the range of modern technological advance
– or vice versa, if you look at it that way. The creels used to be
made from string netting over cane supports bent on a curve
from the base and weighted down with flat stones. The salt
water used to rot the canes at the joint where they were set into
the base and so the creel disintegrated. Nowadays they are
made from nylon netting over curved pastic garden hosepipe
filled, if you can imagine it, with concrete. They give every
appearance of lasting for ever.

East Haven was originally two rows of fishermen's cottages,
the Long Row and the Shore Row. When the railway came in
the nineteenth century, it split the two rows and cut Long Row

Henry Cotton being presented with the Open trophy at Carnoustie in 1937.

completely off from the sea with a high embankment, leaving only two access underpass bridges. This caused an outcry immediately but at that time the railway companies were all-powerful and the fishermen just had to make do. Today, oddly enough, the railway is regarded with affection by the present inhabitants of Long Row because the embankment now cuts them off from the crowds on the beach. Mark you, the 'crowds on the beach' are there for only a very short part of any year but the current owner of No. 11 Long Row, my good friend Stanley Beattie, assures me that the railway successfully protects Long Row from intruders. The occasional intrepid traveller who penetrates the underpass and comes on Long Row invariably expresses astonishment. Most of them take it for Brigadoon. Were it not for the protecting railway embankment, the little enclave of fisher houses and their antique gardens would have been destroyed by now.

The houses on the west side of the bay are rather different. They are suburban villas and not indigenous to East Haven. The Long Row folk refer to the inhabitants of the western development as the nobility. The row of six houses which sit on the slope behind Long Row was built by Lord Panmure for fishermen and farm workers and they are now suffering the contemporary fate of 'improvement'. East Haven used to be a typically close-knit fisher community but inevitably it is less so nowadays. When Stan Beattie bought No. 11 Long Row in 1973, he was one of the first of the 'incomers'. Today only George Lyall and Eric Duncan are left of the old-timers.

East Haven is as far as the road runs along the shore line. It turns sharp left there and runs up to meet the A92 Dundee-Arbroath road past West Scryne farm. A mile or two back along that road, towards Dundee, through Muirdrum and Travebank, there is a side road on the right marked 'Carlungie' which takes you up to Carlungie farm and its souterrain. A souterrain is an underground passage or dwelling: or it might be an underground byre, a storehouse, a cellar or a hidey-hole.

Whatever a souterrain is, there is no shortage of opinions as to what it was. Plausible theories have been advanced for each of the above suggestions to be the definitive answer. The fact is that there is no definite answer: nothing is known about them. All we have is surmise and guesswork. That doesn't make them any less interesting. The very vagueness of their purpose adds to the fascination of their existence. There are souterrains at Carlungie, Ardestie, Tealing, Airlie and Arbroath, and Carlungie is the most scientific and expert excavation.

It is believed – and all historical reference should be required by law to start with a Government warning like that – that the souterrains were in use in the first few centuries AD by the Picts and long after that by their successors. Of all the theories that have been advanced as to their purpose, the most reasonable would appear to be that they were cellars attached to surface dwellings. The Ardestie souterrain has a model showing that this could have been the case and it seems to be quite probable. The Carlungie site has traces of about eight surface dwellings having existed and it seems that the stone-lined passages beneath could have served as extra storage space for the hut dwellers. The popular theory that they were byres or sheds for cattle seems highly unlikely. Even when the protagonists of the idea claim that cows in the Pictish period were much smaller than they are today, it is hard to imagine even a few present-day calves being housed in the restricted space of the souterrain. Over the centuries there are records of some forty-eight different souterrains in Tayside, the largest being at Pitcur, Kettins, just south of Dundee. Carlungie is 140 ft. long as opposed to Pitcur's 190. There is one main entrance at Carlungie and three smaller entrances, one of which leads into a space described as a workshop.

From studies of all the excavations it is apparent that a souterrain was a curved subterranean passage about six feet deep and with its roof at ground level. Its walls were lined with undressed stones which sloped in at the top to support large flat roofing slabs. The main passage inclined down from the entrance and side passages led off. Finds of flints and tools have led to the belief that parts of the souterrain were used as workshops. The end of the main passageway is usually extended and enlarged into a spoonbill shape. The Carlungie souterrain is readily accessible, just past Carlungie farm steading where a signpost at the roadside points the way over the field.

The site is fenced and tended and a noticeboard gives an outline of the history. It is well worth visiting, if only to stand and muse and ponder the lives of our forbears who must have known a very different environment from ours. The neat, carefully cultivated fields of Carlungie farm, Monikie parish and Angus generally must be vastly changed from the scrub jungle and waterlogged morass of Pictland. The biggest change will have been effected by drainage. The souterrains had central soak drains in some cases but it is only the art of the drainer with his baked clay drain tile that has made modern farming possible. With the latest advances with plastic drain pipes, there is no limit to the acreage that can be reclaimed.

If you look up from the souterrain, you will see, to the north-east of you, Monikie Hill and the Panmure Monument. It is worth pausing a minute to reflect. The Panmure Monument was built by the tenants of Lord Panmure as a gesture of thanks for his generosity to them. When their crops failed at the time of the great famine in the nineteenth century, Lord Panmure would not take the rents due to him from his farmers. 'Live and let live,' he said. The Panmure Monument was erected as soon as normal conditions returned and the tenants could show their appreciation. There cannot be many such monuments around. It is known locally by everyone as the 'Live and let live' monument.

The Aberdeen Angus Beef Breed

Angus is known above all for its farming. Potatoes, barley, oats, wheat, soft fruits, and now oilseed rape, are produced in great quantity and top quality but the best known export from Angus must be the Aberdeen Angus beef breed. There have always been black cattle in Scotland, they are mentioned in our earliest manuscripts and carved on our sculptured stones. Our earliest ancestors met black cattle peering at them through the mists in Angus and in Galloway. There were black cattle all over Scotland and some had no horns but it took an Angus man to select the right animals to give him the nucleus of the breed of black, hornless, compactly built beef beasts that we have today.

It is impossible to say when the strain originated or indeed when any breed or race or family ever started. You go back as far as you can and you end up with chickens and eggs. In this case we can go back to several collateral lines of native black cattle and the starting point is taken when we reckon the main characteristics of the breed to have been established. In the case of the Aberdeen Angus beef steer you could say that 1808 was the significant date. That was the year that Hugh Watson – who was breeding black hornless cattle even then – took the farm of Keillor near Newtyle. He went to Trinity Market at Brechin in that same year and bought a black polled bull and ten black polled heifers.

Before anyone had thought of dehorning cattle as an aid to animal husbandry, Hugh Watson had realised the advantage of having a naturally hornless breed and he kept only hornless stock. There were others in Angus who copied him at the time but it was Hugh Watson who bought up the best they had and developed the best strain. The bull that he bought at Trinity Tryst, and which he called Taranty Jock, turned out to be the great progenitor of the breed. The Aberdeen connection was slight. Willie McCombie of Tillyfour, Aberdeen, was interested in Hugh Watson's work and followed his lead, as did Sir George Macpherson-Grant of Ballindalloch, Banffshire. The name Aberdeen-Angus came conveniently off the tongue so Banff was quietly ignored. A better name would have been Angus Blacks because that is just what they are. In addition to his great Taranty Jock, Hugh Watson had the best stock of dams to breed off. The best of those, 'Old Granny', was calved in 1824 and lived to be 35 – and it took a flash of lightning to kill her then. She had twenty-five calves and founded one of the great dynasties of the Aberdeen Angus kingdom.

The main points that the early breeders had to eradicate were colour, horns and poor conformation, and it took time. In the early days the animals stood much higher off the ground because they had been bred for generations as draught animals and for walking long distances to market along the old drove roads. Gradually the breeders got them down till they achieved the desired 'beef to the knees' and the Aberdeen Angus bull was the pre-eminent crossing sire in world breeding. Unfortunately one has to use the past tense.

Fashions in animal breeding change with fashions in eating, and world politics dictate the actions of people far removed from the political scene. For a variety of such abstruse reasons the Aberdeen Angus breed is currently somewhat out of favour. The breeders followed the dictates of one market too slavishly and ended up as their Shorthorn brothers did before them, breeding small, compact, refined animals when the world demands huge ungainly slab-sided meat machines. That is the reason for the lush pastures of Angus – which used to support thousands of beautiful, black, naturally polled, barrel-bodied bullocks with well sprung ribs and broad, deep layered backs, whose small intelligent heads ran smoothly into the neck and shoulders, whose fat was evenly spread over the frame and marbled through the muscle – to be grubbed up for alien crops of oilseed rape to despoil their acres. I could greet.

The Aberdeen Angus men are now furiously breeding for size. Quality may be affected at first but the Aberdeen Angus will be back on top before long to repulse these Continental upstarts. You mark my words.

East Haven.

The A92 Route

The A92 runs flat from Carlungie road end through Muirdrum to Arbroath but it pays to wander from it. A turn down by West Scryne and round by the Hatton takes you past an historic country house and through a typical eighteenth-century farm steading. The whole area was laid out as an airfield for the war and the remains of huts, sheds and brick buildings still abound. Many of the farm buildings now were Nissen huts or barrack rooms then. It seems strange to look at the detritus and think of the hundreds of ex R.A.F. personnel who can think back to wartime at the Hatton. The bustle and urgency of the busy camp are now replaced by the timeless sough of the wind. Grass grows through concrete foundations and rusty sheets of corrugated iron flap feebly. The Hatton has seen many wars.

On the other side of the A92 a signpost indicates Balmirmer – and there's a word for the etymologists to produce an etymon – and the road climbs up the first rise of hills in from the coast. The farm and clachan of Balmirmer sit on the crest of the hill sheltered in the lee of protecting hardwoods. If anyone should question the necessity for preserving our remaining oaks, elms and chestnuts, just tell them to ask the good folk of Balmirmer. They would be sair exposed without them. The road runs over the hill there to Arbirlot or straight on back to the A92, and even this short loop off the A92 illustrates immediately one of the great charms of Angus and the Mearns. You need travel only yards off the main roads to find yourself a hundred years back in time. The land is still the same and the by-roads lead you round to cottages and farms where Angus folk still tend the Angus soil, bound only by the changing seasons of the year. The old farm buildings change but the earth is still the earth our forbears tilled and rural Angus keeps the contact close.

From the hill road running from Balmirmer along by Craigend to Arbirlot school, the view of the coastal strip is one of the finest in Angus. The rolling fields run flat and fertile down to the level coast where Viking and Danish invaders were wont to raid. Angus was a popular summer resort for the Danes in the first few centuries AD. They made several sorties into Angus and even sacked Brechin on one trip until they finally got their come-uppance at Barry (Battle of) in 1010.

It seems odd to have come on Arbirlot school about a mile before you have come to Arbirlot but there used to be two schools. The one in the village, which is now a dwelling-house, was the Church school and the existing one was the parish school, sited in the middle of the parish. There are still some twenty pupils in the present school with two permanent teachers and various visiting teachers of specialist subjects. At one time practically all the pupils were the children of farm workers from the neighbouring farms but now only a few of the present roll come from the farms. That is one of the great changes in contemporary rural economy. Farm mechanisation has drastically cut the number of farm workers. The few who remain are, increasingly, moving to the towns and travelling daily to work. Their children go to town schools.

Arbirlot school is still one of the old-style country schools where the children are given a sound, basic education and much, much more besides. They are given personal attention, individual tutoring and real community care. Arbirlot school keeps its pupils close to their Angus roots. There is even one

The best of Aberdeen Angus on parade at the Kirriemuir Show.

child in Arbirlot school today who is driven up daily from
Dundee simply because his parents appreciate the benefits
of a country school and realise just how much it will mean to
him in future years. Long may such schools continue. When a
rural school closes for good, its pupils are uprooted from the
rural environment and a taste for town life is developed. Even
if the town is no bigger than Arbroath or Stonehaven the
child is divorced from country life for all time.

Past the school, the road leads round and down to Arbirlot
village on the banks of the Elliot burn, or straight on to rejoin
the A92. Arbirlot village has an idyllic setting. At one time it
was the archetypal Scotch village with Church, school, smiddy,
Post Office and shop. Originally it even had handloom
weavers, a slaughterhouse and a meal mill, and in those days
everyone in Arbirlot knew everyone else in Arbirlot and the
village lived its own satisfying self-supporting life.

It still has its idyllic setting and it still has a very active social
life but the pattern of village life has changed. Villagers do not
work in their village any more. The cottages are now
modernised with Georgian-style doors and panes of imitation
bottle glass in the windows and practically every house has two
cars. By day, Oliver Goldsmith would have recognised the

place, it is sweet Auburn: deserted. By evening you won't find a place to park if the W.R.I., the Men's Club, the Youth Club, the Brownies or any combination or permutation therefrom is in session. The Elliot burn still wimples down but now a Nature Trail – what else? – extends from the bridge down the old Carmyllie railroad track to Elliot. It is different from the old days but it still maintains an active social life even if television, rather than the Old Testament, regulates the lives of the modern villagers.

The Arbroath Golf Club

Following the road past Arbirlot and back to the A92 you come almost immediately to the old Arbroath Golf Club clubhouse, which has just been bought as a private residence. It sits on a bit of Balcathie ground in a commanding position overlooking the golf course and the sea. You are never far from a golf course in Angus. Arbroath golf course is down the hill from the old clubhouse and is usually known as Elliot golf course these days, for Arbroath Golf Club has ceased to exist – and there's a bit of real history for you.

The Arbroath Golf Club started with a meeting in the Arbroath Burgh Court House on 19th November 1877. Arrangements were made to lease ground from Balcathie, Mains of Kelly and Inverpeffer and old Tom Morris himself was called in to advise on laying out the course. That part of the course that was leased from Inverpeffer may ring a bell. Inverpeffer was the place that Thomas Lawson had visited before he fell asleep on Carnoustie bents that night. There is not much doubt that there would have been a drop of the cratur given and taken in the course of the evening.

Arbroath Golf Club started up in the approved manner with all the local dignitaries joining immediately and soon the Club was established and successful. At first they rented a room in Elliot as a Clubhouse but soon they had to move out for some unspecified reason, and after a succession of rented rooms in Elliot they decided to build themselves a clubhouse. It was a modest enough affair of brick that cost them £28.6/- and served them well until 1903 when they built their more commodious and substantial premises up the hill and just off the Dundee road. By this time golf was permeating through the ranks to the lower orders. Conversation in gentlemen's clubs at the time deplored the degeneration of an age that saw labourers playing golf; especially since some of the bounders were good at it. 'How,' it was rhetorically demanded of the company, 'can a workman play golf all the hours of summer daylight and then give of his best to his employer, even for the mingy ten hours a day they are prepared to work now?' Riddle me that, my fine friend.

The labouring men of Arbroath did play golf. Eventually enough of them played golf to warrant starting their own Club and in 1903 the Arbroath Artisan Golf Club was founded and took over the old Arbroath Golf Club clubhouse. It is significant that in 1903, social division in Scotland was such that Arbroath men playing golf over the same bit of Arbroath ground, divided themselves naturally into Gentlemen and Artisans. The subscription to the Arbroath Golf Club was ten shillings to join and one pound per annum thereafter. For the Artisans it was three shillings and no joining fee but the money was incidental. The social division was absolute. For those with inherited wealth, the 'gentlemen', life was easy. For the labouring man, hard Cheddar. There was only one way to breach the walls of privilege in those days and that was through education.

When Arbroath Golf Club was founded, the idea first came from four teachers who had been playing golf at Carnoustie and were fed up waiting for the train home to Arbroath. Messrs. Corstorphine, Moodie, Crichton and Davidson thought that it was time Arbroath had its own golf course. Theirs was the suggestion to form a Club and they were instrumental in its foundation. They must have rated as gentlemen. No doubt that was one manifestation of the Scotch respect for education. In those days Scotch teachers were educated. A more relevant social comment today is that Arbroath Golf Club has now ceased to exist whilst the Artisans have taken over the course.

Elliot village is one row of houses and a disused bleaching works just short of Arbroath. It used to be known as Elliot Junction where the Carmyllie local railway joined up with the Dundee and Arbroath Joint Railway line and there was a small station building and a footbridge. The footbridge is still in use for access to the seafront. On 28th December 1906 at 3.30 p.m., a Caledonian Railway train was standing in Elliot Junction when the North British Railway special for Edinburgh ran into it. It was an afternoon of dreadful, blinding snow and sleet and visibility was nil. The two trains smashed together and twenty-two people died. It was the worst railway disaster since the Tay Bridge collapse and is still one of the worst railway accidents ever in Scotland.

From Elliot in to Arbroath the railway still runs alongside the road and blocks access to the shore, allowing Arbroath lads to play football undisturbed on the West Links pitches. On the other side of the road an Industrial Estate is growing. Ahead lies Arbroath. Now there's a town . . .

CHAPTER 3

Red Lichtie Reflections

The approach to Arbroath is screened largely by the railway line. Arbroath Infirmary sits imposingly on the hilltop ahead, an industrial estate and a huge caravan park sprawl on the left and only a last-minute right-angled turn under the railway bridge permits the visitor a glimpse of the real Arbroath with its seafront and harbour. It is the harbour that is the living heart of the town.

It used to be obligatory, when writing of Arbroath, to refer to the fact that Arbroath was the 'Fairport' of Sir Walter Scott's *Antiquary*. As no-one nowadays under the age of 67 appears to have read Scott's *Antiquary*, the obligation may be less compelling. It would be encouraging to think that such a reference might be sufficient stimulation for someone – anyone – to read Scott's *Antiquary* today.

Arbroath has never been a great seaport. It is a fishing port now as it always has been. The first landing place for boats was to the east of the present harbour where the east causeway was built by the Abbot of Arbroath in 1194. Taxes were immediately levied on the protesting townsfolk to pay for it. Subsequent development continued under Abbot Gedy in 1395, and then in 1725 a much bigger harbour was built to the west of the original jetty. Today's busy little fishing port has grown from that beginning.

The story of Arbroath is best divided, like all Gaul, into three parts: the fishing community, the manufacturing firms, and the Abbey. The fishing community of Arbroath is like all fishing communities, a close-knit, self-sufficient entity: the nature of fishing makes it so. There has always been a marked division between the Arbroath fisher folk from the 'fit o' the toon' and the merchants from the 'tap' but this old separation is changing. Wealthy fishing families now build homes 'up' the toon and mix with the landward folk. At one time the division was so marked that regular fights used to erupt between the fisher folk and the farming chiels. The idea of a bothy loon marrying a fisher lass then was about as likely as a Young Conservative marrying a Scottish Nationalist today. It didn't happen.

The form of fishing that evolved in Arbroath over the centuries was the same long-line technique that was practised all along the east coast with minor, regional, differences. In Arbroath until quite recently they worked two kinds of line, the 'sma' line' for haddock and the 'gretlin' or great line for cod, halibut and the bigger fish. The sma' line was the Arbroath speciality. It consisted of a 'back' or main line with 'snoods' or droppers running from it. To the snoods the hooks were attached by horsehair 'tippets' about a foot and a half long. Each hook was 'beat on' to the horsehair tippet with strong linen thread and the whole dropper from main line to hook was about three feet. Each line had fourteen hundred hooks with a mussel on every one so the line was 'sma' only in comparative terms. The great line was made to the same pattern but with heavier line and bigger hooks more widely spread. The great lines have not been fished from Arbroath since just after the war.

As the sma' line fishing developed and huge catches of haddock were regularly landed, the Arbroath folk experimented with methods of preserving them for sale before quietly pinching Auchmithie's methods. Their success gave us the far-famed Arbroath 'smokie', that erstwhile East Coast staple and present-day culinary cult. A line-caught haddock smoke cured over a pit of smouldering oaken chips, poached in milk and served with a knob of salted butter. Whaur's your sole bonne femme noo?

The old way was the best way but nowadays your smokie is liable to come to you as a mousse or a paté or en papillote or some such fancy dress but the smokie is still a classic dish however you serve it. Lobsters, crab, halibut and smokies are all dishes for the connoisseur and all come from Arbroath. The old ways are changing, nylon has replaced hemp and horsehair, plastic floats have taken over from pigs' bladders, and the lines themselves are going out of use as the line fishers die off. Modern methods of pair trawling, where two boats trawl a net along the sea bed between them, are taking over but there is no sign of the smokie going out of fashion as yet. The

The Inner Harbour, Arbroath.

back lots at the fit o' the toon still have their tarry sheds with
smoke pits to produce the traditional Arbroath smokie.

One Arbroath tradition that has, regrettably, gone for ever is
that of the fisher lassies who used to walk the Angus
countryside and sell fresh fish from pannier baskets.
Colourfully dressed in the picturesque Arbroath costume of
full skirt, striped blouse and kerchief headdress, these bonny
lassies – and some ould biddies among them – carried their
fish round the countryside calling on all the farms and
cottages. They were kenspeckle figures and welcome visitors
around the country districts but they have gone now, never to
return. Their place has been usurped by little windowless
motor vans that cover twice the area in a fraction of the time
and have turned a centuries old traditional way of life into an
impersonal, mechanised, cost effective trade.

Arbroath is still a busy little fishing port and although its
methods and materials have changed, the Arbroath men who
fish the wild North Sea in little boats are still the Arbroath men
of old. Cargills, Spinks, Smiths, Bruces, Scotts and Beatties are
line bred for the job. They are fishermen. They come from
Arbroath. Barring an influx of Auchmithie blood in the
nineteenth century, they have always come from Arbroath.

They have a pride of place and a spirit of community that is tribal in its intensity. Modern sociologists point to such people as having been the great example of the 'caring community' and bemoan the fact that they no longer exist. Modern sociologists should go down to the Commercial Bar on the Arbroath seafront, buy themselves a pint and listen to the chat.

The development of the harbour as a trading port started in the late eighteenth century. Before that, any trading was confined to small cargoes of timber and iron from the Baltic. With the advent of manufacturing industries in Arbroath, imports of raw materials and exports of finished products soon built the port into a major trading centre. In 1790, Francis Webster came into Arbroath from Carmyllie where his forbears had farmed for generations. His first enterprise was the weaving of linen. As his business boomed from the start, he advanced straightaway into rope and sail making. Other entrepreneurs followed his lead and in 1823 the Corsar family business was founded to process imported flax and make sailcloth and sails. The various stages of hackling, spinning, bleaching and weaving were all undertaken by the firm of D. Corsar & Sons in their Nursery Mills and Spring Garden factory. By the second half of the nineteenth century they had a thirteen-acre bleachfield and a workforce of six hundred people. Their great world-famous product was 'Reliance' brand sailcloth which was made into sails in the sail lofts of Arbroath to power the windjammers of the world.

Old salts sitting on sun-bleached planks by the Old Shorehead used to pause in their Bogey Roll cud-chewing to tell tales of Arbroath's bygone glory days. One tale was told every time. It was of the British man-o'-war that came through the Bay of Biscay in a hurricane when every sail bar one was stripped to ribbons. That one was a 'stysell' (staysail) that stood strong, stiff and sailing to keep her head-to and safe and that stysell was the only one of her rig that was woven and stitched in Arbroath. The name of the man-o'-war has been forgotten but the name *Cutty Sark* is still remembered. Every square inch of her sail pattern came from Arbroath.

As Arbroath established itself as a manufacturing town with its production of sailcloth and coarse linens (Osnaburgs), so other industries followed. Alexander Shanks was born in Arbroath in 1801. In 1825 he started his own engineering works making textile machinery. In 1835 he took out a patent for his own invention of a hemp dressing machine and in 1841 he had to move to bigger premises to cope with his success. In 1842, Alexander Shanks, having failed to note that slavery had been abolished in the British Empire in 1807, developed the lawnmower. A prototype had been produced by one Edwin Budding for Ransomes of Ipswich in 1830 but most of the blame lies with Alexander Shanks of Arbroath. He made the thing work and Shanks' Arbroath Lawnmowers soon became world famous. You have his name. His firm produced all kinds of machinery including ships' engines. The *E.L. Lawson*, a Montrose vessel of some 200 tons launched in 1906, was powered by a Shanks engine. That engine, along with a number of puffing billy shunting engines, was made in the last factory that Shanks had in Wardmill, Arbroath. Alexander Shanks died in 1845, his firm in the 1960s.

At the same time that Alexander Shanks was busy perfecting his infernal machine, one of his contemporaries was equally busy on a more honourable pursuit. John Chalmers, born Arbroath 2nd Feb. 1782, went down to Dundee to work with his brother George and took time off to invent the adhesive postage stamp. That compensates for Alex. Shanks.

All kinds of firms were starting up in Arbroath around this time. Engineering was widely based but there were many others. In 1815 Brown's Arbroath Tan Works was exporting tanned leather to England and the Continent for boot and shoe making. Colin Grant of Carmyllie took the hint and came into Arbroath and started a boot and shoe manufactory there. He was closely followed by Fairweather who set up another bootmaking business, and by the latter part of the 1800s Arbroath was the bootmaking capital of Scotland.

All this export trade of linen and jute products, lawnmowers, boots and shoes, machinery and fish was augmented when Frasers opened up their factory to make textile-processing machines and Keith Blackman for general engineering. Arbroath was a major manufacturing town then and Arbroath harbour at the peak of its importance as a trading port.

There was one more Red Licht export that demands

recognition. Where Carnoustie's proud boast is that they have exported over 300 golf professionals to teach the world to play golf, so Arbroath could boast that they have exported as many mariners to sail the world's seaways. Men like Captain Wm. Sim, born Arbroath 1836, who grew to be a legend and a criterion of excellence in seamanship whilst he was still sailing. His contemporary fame rested on his adherence to the highest possible standards of efficiency in his profession. 'Cap'n Sim' became the words for perfection in sailing ships.

Captain Sim was given his first command in Yokohama, which is not entirely surprising since he spent most of his seafaring days in remote foreign parts. As he sailed the world's sea routes, his reputation for the precision of his navigation, and the cleanliness and order of his ships, sailed before him. If the phrase 'shipshape and Bristol fashion' had not already been current, 'spick, span and Arbroath fashion' might well have been coined, for Captain William Sim of Arbroath was famous. He sailed regularly to Rio de Janeiro and the South American ports and his name was known and respected there. Once, when he was on the Far East tea run from China, he had to berth in Arbroath in the *Princess Alice* to load a cargo of flour, and he was a celebrity. Crowds gathered on the quayside to admire the immaculate condition of his ship and catch a glimpse of its celebrated master. When the Captain walked ashore the crowd parted to allow him free passage. Captain Sim was not alone. Many's the Arbroath man who sailed the China seas in those days, to build the reputation for sound seafaring that still points the Arbroath fleet out to the North Sea fishing grounds today.

Arbroath Abbey

Underlying and overplaying every aspect of Arbroath life is the Abbey. It was founded in 1178 by King William the Lion, who dedicated it to St Thomas à Becket with whom he had been at school and a 'sharer of his tribulations' in England. Whether the tribulations were shared at school or subsequently, King William did not specify. The building was

Hercules, Capt. Wm. R. Smart, from the heyday of Arbroath skippers.

completed and consecrated in 1233, and from then on it played a dominant part in the life of Arbroath – and far beyond. When he died, King William was buried in front of the High Altar.

One tends to think of Arbroath Abbey as no more than a church, a religious house, an ecclesiastical centre. In fact it was the centre of social and administrative life in the area. Matters spiritual and temporal were equally directed by the Abbey. It held lands and rights far beyond the confines of its precincts. Decisions on the interpretation of the most abstruse points of theologic law were made by the Abbey, as was the granting of permission to dig lugworms at Monifieth. Never a town kirk, it was a regional government. It dictated the form of religious observance, it conducted schools, it patronised arts and crafts, it promoted trade and industry.

Much of the verifiable history that we have of Scotland in the centuries after 1233 comes from the Arbroath Chartulary. This was a record of all the Abbey's activities and transactions kept by the monks as a daily record of their works. It is the kind of history that counts: a contemporary record of events as they happened, interspersed with an account of some of the more mundane details of local administration. Rights of land tenure, fishing, road and bridge building, agriculture and tree-felling were all vested in the Abbey and meticulous reports were kept. The picture of contemporary life given in the Arbroath Chartulary is invaluable.

The Abbey put Arbroath into the forefront of Scottish affairs. For a century after its foundation the Abbey prospered as the whole of Scotland did at that time. King William, and later, Kings Alexander the Second and Third, regularly visited the Abbey to stay on their periodic tours of the realm. On occasion the Abbey even loaned money to the King. There was a reciprocal benefit in lending money to Kings. Royal favours and benefits were always bestowed in return. It was good business.

As the events that are reckoned great in Scottish history unfolded, Arbroath Abbey played a decisive part. When John Balliol was obliged to renounce his allegiance to the English king, it was the Abbot of Aberbrothock who was entrusted to go down and inform the monarch. When the Abbot returned to Arbroath, he was closely followed by King Edward who came up to try and sort things out for himself. On 7th July 1296, King Edward I lodged in Arbroath Abbey and 'exacted homage' from the monks before going on to Brechin where he formally deposed John Balliol. From Brechin he proceeded to march north as far as Elgin to demonstrate his sovereignty and bring all Scotland under his rule. In 1298 King Edward won the battle of Falkirk and on 1st August 1303 he was back in Arbroath Abbey. The Abbey was always in the van of the action. After the defeat of the English at Bannockburn in 1314, the king – by this time Edward II – appealed to the Pope to do something about the harm that had been done by these Scotch upstarts. The Pope reacted by sending a Papal Bull to Robert Bruce, again at Arbroath Abbey. This directive threatened Bruce with excommunication if he continued to fight against English rule.

When the messenger arrived with the Papal missive, addressed to 'Robert Bruce, governing in Scotland', and handed it over, Bruce refused to accept it. 'No, no,' he said, 'probably not meant for me at all – there are several Robert

Bruces engaged in governing Scotland just now – I am the King. Take it back.' This was in 1317 when Bruce was still striving to be recognised as King of Scotland.

The Abbey's biggest contribution to Scottish history came on 6th April 1320 when the Scottish Declaration of Independence was drawn up there and despatched to the Pope at Avignon. This was followed by a further communication to Avignon in 1323, and by 1329 the Pope had acceded to all their demands. Authority was granted for Robert Bruce to be recognised officially and formally as King of Scotland. Unfortunately for Robert Bruce, he had just died before the acknowledgement was received.

Arbroath has been called Aberbrothock, Aberbrothwick, Aberbrothick and once – by the historian Buchanan in the First Book of his *History of Scotland* – Abrinca. Since 'Aber' means 'above' and the local burn is called the Brothock, so Aberbrothock or Aberbrothick would seem to make sense. 'Abrinca' is simply an attempt to give the place a Latin name and a Roman connection. The Antiquary himself couldn't have done it better. Buchanan was, of course, a historian. The inhabitants have had to live with the various spellings at various times but once, in 1841, they petitioned Parliament to have their town's name regularised. They asked for 'Arbroath' to be accepted as including 'Aberbrothock' and 'Aberbrothwick'. The petition failed so, presumably, if you feel like calling it Aberbrothock, go ahead.

The designation 'Red Lichtie' is the nickname by which Arbroath folk are generally known. It was first used against them as a jibe and an insult but Arbroathians appropriated it for themselves and now they are proud to be known as Red Lichties the world over. The name originated when an early Harbourmaster was instructed to display a red light at the end of the main breakwater and, being short of red glass at the time, he painted a clear glass lantern with red paint and hung it up. The fact that the light was entirely blacked out did not go unremarked by passing sailormen. Red Lichties who tell you that their soubriquet derives from a red light hung in the south window of the Abbey by a benign Abbot to succour ships at sea, are fantasising. As are the all-male parties of Oriental tourists who regularly alight at Arbroath station to visit its famous Red Light district.

That south window itself is a talisman and a shibboleth to the Arbroathian. Expatriate Red Lichties at dinner parties are wont to wax lyrical, if not indeed maudlin, at the invariable mention of 'the auld Roond O': the south window. The window gapes empty from the ruined south wall of the Abbey. It is a feature of the ruin but exactly what other kind of an 'O' the Arbroathians can visualise has never been specified.

The town today is a strange conglomerate of ancient and modern, auld farrant and new fangled, sense and nonsense, a mediaeval fishing village buried in through roads, multiple shopping centres, one-way traffic systems and pedestrian walkways. Old Arbroath is being destroyed and nothing is being done as yet to replace or conserve it. Arbroath today is a mess. The worst thing about it is the dual carriageway driven halfway through the town. When it was decided that the Aberdeen road should not by-pass Arbroath but go right through, as it always had, they effectively cut Arbroath in two. The error was compounded when the road was not bridged to allow the Arbroath folk to go about their daily business, but a crazy system of one-way traffic was imposed instead: nor was the dual carriageway ever completed. It peters out halfway up the Montrose road. Add on the industrial developments out towards Elliot and St Vigeans, the scabrous growth of bungaloid housing at Hospitalfield, the municipal estates engulfing St Vigeans, and the town is in a shameful state.

Fortunately it appears to have reached its nadir. The good folk of Arbroath are beginning to object to the mess that has been made of their town and plans are being discussed to change things. At last it seems that conservation is about to be accepted as an essential policy for the future. It is just a pity that the burghers of Arbroath had no thought of conservation when they carted the Abbey away to build houses in the eighteenth century – or when they knocked down the fisher cottages at the fit o' the toon a few years ago. The present generation of Arbroathians is just beginning to show more awareness of Abroath's heritage. The worst excesses of the planners and politicians seem to have been suffered. A start is being made with refurbishing and conserving. The old Town House/Olympia cinema area has been retained and old houses generally are being restored within their original framework.

Arbroath Abbey. Abbot's House, now museum, on right.

There is hope. When the middle High Street is altered and empty shops re-open for business, Arbroath may once again flourish.

The Abbey Theatre

There is no town with more right to flourish. Arbroath has the most active art-loving, musical, theatre-going, cultured populace of any town in Scotland. The standard of art, music and theatre in Arbroath is far beyond the usual run of small-town achievement. Arbroath sustains its Abbey Theatre, Choral Society, Black and White Minstrels, Musical Society, orchestras and Instrumental Band. Each is first-rate in its own right. They have the amply furnished Webster Theatre available for performances and festivals and it also plays host to professional companies in season. Hospitalfield House is run by the Hospitalfield Trust and is a focal point for the local artistic colony.

The Abbey Theatre of Arbroath is a phenomenon in itself. It started quietly enough in 1947 just like any other Amateur Dramatic Club, scraping the barrel at every performance to pay expenses. Two things marked it out from other dramatic clubs: the standard of acting ability of its members and the vision and cool confidence of its backers. After the rounds of church halls, works canteens, school classrooms and factory floors, when the members' spirits could well have been flagging, the late Gwen Williams, one of their founding mothers, came up with an idea. She suggested buying the old decaying superannuated hackle factory behind the gas works and starting up their own theatre. The idea was so absurd it was accepted.

The Abbey Theatre took off. It flourishes today but it flourishes only because of the consistently high standard of its performances. One would hesitate to recommend the usual run of provincial amateur dramatic presentations. Most of them get by on a commendable degree of enthusiasm from the players and a hard night's work from the prompter. The Abbey Theatre is different. It is entirely professional in every aspect of its operation, except for one small detail. None of its members is paid. How they continue to find the steady stream of new recruits to maintain their standards of excellence is amazing. For forty years the club has flourished as a first-rate repertory theatre. Their season runs from September to May and they rehearse for six weeks and play for two, which demands a very strenuous and sustained effort from the players. Appearing six nights a week for two weeks is far more than the usual dramatic club requires, but then the Abbey Club is no usual dramatic club. It is much, much closer to a professional repertory company than to an amateur dramatic club.

Their theatre is small by any standards, seating only seventy-two people when full, but of course the Abbey Theatre is always full. For the season 1987-8 they played to 98% of capacity and made a whacking great profit, as usual. For the first few years of their existence they ploughed back every penny of profit into fitting out a first-class theatre, and now they have one of the best-equipped little playhouses in the country. Playing to packed houses – and having a retired Bank Manager, T. Burns Mitchell, for a Treasurer – has built up their funds until their current bank balance shows a thirteen thousand pound credit.

Arbroath: pedestrian precinct by the old Olympia Cinema.

If there are any objective criteria for assessing success in a purely cultural activity, thirteen thousand pounds in the Bank must be considered as one.

The runaway success of the Abbey Theatre for forty years is not the only sign of Arbroath's patronage of the Arts. Other Arbroath clubs and societies are equally successful. Classical music is catered for by various choirs, orchestras and the Instrumental Band: light classical by the Musical Society and the Gilbert and Sullivan Society; popular entertainment by the Black and White Minstrels – and here the commercial criterion is valid. Since 1961 the Arbroath Black and White Minstrels have given an annual show for charity. It is an outstanding show. It is so well known that tickets are utterly unobtainable each year. It is unbelievably good. The proof of that is that since it started it has donated over one hundred thousand pounds to the Scottish Council for the Care of Spastics. That is not a printer's error. One hundred thousand pounds. That is the measure of the Arbroath folk and the degree of their artistic skill.

Hospitalfield House

Artistic skill of a more precise nature is catered for at Hospitalfield House, built on the site of the old Hospice of the Abbey. It was a subsidiary sanctuary of rest, retreat and recuperation for the monks on occasion and a place where visitors could be entertained: a Hospitium. When the Abbey ceased to function and the hospitium was no longer required, it became a private dwelling. At one stage Cardinal Beaton bought – or appropriated – it for his friend/mistress/wife, Marion Ogilvie. In 1665 it was bought by James Fraser and eventually passed down to Patrick Allan-Fraser, the Arbroath artist. In 1850 a major alteration and addition to the house was started. By 1880 the building had been completely rebuilt and very little of the old hospitium remained.

When Patrick Allan-Fraser died in 1890, the Hospitalfield Trust took over the running of the house and it was again enlarged. Studios were built on, adding a north wing to the house, and Hospitalfield was opened as a full-time Art College. Today it is used as a study centre for short-term residential courses run by universities, colleges and schools. In summer it hosts a Summer Scholarship for three students from each of the four Scottish Art Schools. Arbroath is actively concerned in the promotion of art. It has a large number of local artists, an art society, regular exhibitions, its own art college and a stream of visiting artists. Music, drama and art are all alive and well and living in Arbroath.

Remnants of Monastic Life

If the old hospitium is carrying on its traditional role of catering for pilgrims, however indirectly, the old Abbey has long ceased to perform any such service. It stands today a noble ruin, destroyed not by the vengeful hand of the paynim or the predator but quietly carted away by the douce burghers of Arbroath to build houses. All over the town you see shaped stones and carved lintels that were fashioned by the hands of devout and dedicated master masons glorifying their Lord. The Abbey has been reduced to a few gaunt remains. The west

Hospitalfield House, Arbroath.

doorway, which was the main processional entrance to the Abbey, is the most complete. If the west door is closed when you arrive, it comes as a shock to step through and find that little remains of the ornate building you expect, other than the west gate and its towers. Inside, there is only the truncated wall of the south aisle and parts of the south transept and presbytery. Despite its ruined state it is still an impressive edifice. The close carpet of grass, fitted to the walls and pillar bases of the nave and aisles, contrasts subtly with the raw red sandstone ruin.

To a believer the place must be sacred, even to an infidel it must be significant. The most casual of visitors, whether attired in the garish garb of the tourist or the sober suiting of the antiquarian (*pace* Sir Walter), must be stimulated by the implicit magnificence of the building. It is a place to pray, whatever the God. Standing in the vestigial Choir, be it a sunny spring morning or a blustery winter afternoon, one feels that centuries of prayer, of chanted Masses and Kyrie Eleisons, have imbued the precinct and been absorbed by the very stones. If there are holy places, the ruined Abbey of Arbroath is one.

On a more secular note, the Abbey is now maintained by the Ancient Monuments Division of the Scottish Development

Department on behalf of the Secretary of State for Scotland. A display of illustrated information and an outline of relevant history is mounted in a room on the first-floor level of the gatehouse wing. There is also a museum in the Abbot's House. The Abbot's House is in a better state of preservation than the Abbey proper because it was retained as a private dwelling long after the Abbey fell into disrepair. The final demise of the Abbey was signalled by a Charter dated 1608 from King James VI in favour of the Marquess of Hamilton, confirming the dissolution. From that date the Abbey was no more than a handy source of good, free, building stone for upwardly mobile Red Lichties scrambling to build houses up the Nolt Loan Road.

In all the years that the Abbey existed as an active religious centre, it never served as the parish church of Arbroath, odd though that may seem. Whilst the monks were chanting their matins, vespers and intermediate orisons, the good folk of Arbroath had to trek out to St Vigeans to go to the kirk. A study of monastic practice shows why. The Abbey had not been founded, nor did it exist, to serve Arbroath, but to serve God. Its occupants had elected to leave the outside world and dedicate themselves to worship. That dedication was total. The discipline of their application to prayer was rigorous beyond belief. It started daily, soon after midnight when the first call to prayer, the first task of the diurnal Opus Dei, summoned the individual monk from his pallet down to the choir. There, with his fellows, he proceeded to sing the first nocturn of the first of the seven canonical sequences. The light of dawn brought matins, followed immediately by Prime, then it was but a short time before morning Mass. When Mass had been celebrated, the monks left the choir for the chapter house where they would be addressed by the Abbot or his deputy and discuss tasks for the day. Each worked according to his ability. Some would illumine manuscripts, copy documents, bind books. Others would perform more mundane chores like building, brewing or beekeeping. The Abbey was a self-contained entity, and although it had patronage and jurisdiction over lands and fisheries and churches outside its walls, the work of the monks was to maintain their own community and to glorify God. With one frugal meal at midday and bare, minimal, sustenance morning and evening the monks passed their days in prayer and contemplation, mortifying the flesh and praising God. Each day ended after Collation – a public reading session so called because the reading was usually from the Collationes of Johannes Cassianus – and the singing of Compline, the last office of the day. Bed time varied with the season but came somewhere between six and nine, from winter to summer.

The only variation in the soul-strengthening monotony of the life came in the celebration of the annual Christian festivals. A procedural change in the way a ritual was observed, a different chant for a set prayer, even an extra stoup of home-brewed ale on rare occasions, were luxuries. These were the facts of monastic life to the Brethren. These are the facts to ponder as you walk the sombre ruins of the Abbey in the footsteps of the dedicated sons of the Benedictine Order. If the harbour is the beating heart of the town, the old Abbey is still its soul.

Other Attractions of Arbroath

Whilst the growth of housing and industrial development round its edges, added to the chaotic one-way street and pedestrian walkway systems in its centre, make present-day Arbroath a monument to modern urban mismanagement, its geographic location is ideal. The fishing fleet returning on a sun-splashed evening tide sees it at its best. The long, curving, strand of the south beach ends just short of the town, rocks pile up round the headland and the sea wall of the outer harbour shelters and protects the anchorage. From the harbour a narrow beach of rock and sand runs out to Whiting Ness where the cliffs begin. From that point the homing fleet sees a red band of sandstone cliff running north as far as the eye can see. Breaches appear in the rock wall at Auchmithie, Lunan Bay, Montrose, St Cyrus and Stonehaven but, to boats at sea, the thin red line is unbroken.

Arbroath nestles at the southern end of the cliffs with a shoreline of rolling sand dunes to the south. The town is best seen from the sea. The impressive building on the hill towards which the home-bound sailor steers is not, however, the

Bonny lassies howkin' tatties near Arbroath.

Abbey – with or without its 'round O'. It is an old Victorian water tower that dominates the Arbroath skyline and is presently posing a problem to the town. What to do with an old abandoned water tower that looks like a Norman keep dominating the neighbourhood? This one is in good but deteriorating condition, requires regular maintenance and is of no apparent use to anyone. Answers on a postcard, please, but not to me.

The problem of what to do with an earlier relic was suitably solved in Arbroath some years ago. Gravediggers in the Eastern cemetery dug down into an underground vault and saved themselves a power of further digging by utilising the handy, ready-made stone-lined trench they had unearthed. No-one had told them about souterrains. There is now a souterrain in Arbroath with two twentieth-century burials tucked neatly in at one end. Future historians should be worth hearing when they come on that lot.

The cliffs rate second only to the Abbey in the list of

Machines lifting potatoes . . . less backbreaking.

Arbroath's attractions. For as long as Arbroath or the cliffs
have been there, folk have been walking out and back along the
clifftop paths. One of Arbroath's more famous old boys,
Harry Lauder, always remembered the joys of walking and
playing on the cliff tops and spoke fondly of his boyhood ploys
'oot the cliffs'. Whatever the weather, you are sure to meet
someone up there. You get walkers, runners, bird spotters,
photographers, fishers and botanists in their season and
courting couples in any season. Marriages founded on a
courtship conducted in the face of the howling gales of the
Arbroath cliffs, are firmly based. A bracing walk out to
Dickmont Den, a coorie doon in the lee of a storm-sculpted
rock, and a slow saunter home through the deepening dark
forge links that are not readily broken. Subsequent marriages
are likely to last – ours certainly has.

In May 1971 the first Arbroath Nature Trail was opened by
the Dundee and Angus branch of the Scottish Wildlife Trust.
What had previously been no more than a rough path along
the cliff top was now elevated into a recognised nature trail
with view points, trail signs, little bits of tarmac and specially

designed trail furniture, whatever that may be. A trail guide was published to describe the various plants and birds to be seen along the way and to outline the geology of the area. It was excellent. People who had walked out along the cliffs for years were now able to recognise and name plants and birds and rocks that previously had been just plants and birds and rocks. In 1975 the Seaton Cliffs Nature Reserve was added to the Scottish Wildlife Trust's bit and in April 1984 a new Arbroath Cliffs Nature Trail Guide was published by the Scottish Wildlife Trust.

It is a cracker. It lists twenty viewing points along the cliff tops and down by the shore. It describes the wide variety of birds to be seen, from guillemots to corn buntings; the grasses, plants and flowers; the snails, crustacea and seaweeds and the various rock strata and intermingled conglomerate layers. It is excellent, but how far does it go? Any more will be too much. Safety fences, built-up paths, cement-based coin-operated telescopes, cliff top shelters, hot dog stands and such common appurtenances of seaside resorts must be resisted. Arbroath beach, on the south side of the town, is perilously near the limit of plastic, garishly painted. Disney-inspired trumpery – with one commendable exception. They have an amusement arcade. It is decently enclosed in a permanent building, walled and roofed, sound insulated and well maintained. Anyone who wants the amusement arcade can find it and the public is in no way encumbered. No-one objects to that. It is the insidious advance of those commercial interests whose sight and sound and residual litter are offensive that must be contained. Arbroath let itself down some years ago when it went all out to attract summer visitors and destroyed the fit o' the toon and half of the West Links in the process. Arbroath needs to be particularly careful in the future. The nature trail on the cliffs has gone just far enough.

Let us hope that the walk out to Carlingheugh, up Seaton Den and back along the Auchmithie road to Arbroath, will be preserved as it is for ever. The more usual, and shorter walk is to go out along the cliff top just as far as you feel inclined and wander slowly back again. More folk do that. Only the intrepid venture on from Carlingheugh Bay, up the cliff by the Dark Cave and on to Auchmithie. That way lie black snails to frighten young ladies and prickly bushes to snag their tights. Wise men avoid such hazards. In the old days wise men also avoided the many caves which penetrate the sandstone cliffs out to Carlingheugh. Things were reputed to happen in those caves: lost pipers played interminable coronachs, dead sailors were deposited by the tide, masons did the things that only masons do, in those caves.

Geologically, the caves are the result of fissure faults in the sandstone being chiselled and structured by the action of sea and wind. Mythologically, they are the haunts of mermaids, devils, dead seamen, peripatetic pipers, masons and lost souls generally and infinitely more interesting.

CHAPTER 4

On to Montrose

The last segment of the road from Arbroath to Auchmithie is a dead end but that is no way to describe the village itself. Certainly there is no through road and you have to come out by the way you went in, but Auchmithie and its new suburb of Kirkbank make quite a settlement. Auchmithie has been a fishing village since fish were first found to be edible, but there is no regular fishing there now. Only week-enders and part-timers go out and the harbour is fast falling into disrepair. A few boats do go out intermittently for lobster and crab but they pay no harbour dues and there is no money for repairs. With the advent of the new houses the village has become a dormitory for Arbroath.

It is easy to bemoan the old days and regret the passing of the Auchmithie fishing community, but it had to go. No-one in the latter days of the twentieth century is prepared to work like the Auchmithie fisher folk had to in the latter days of the nineteenth – nor should they. Particularly when you realise that it was the women who did most of that work. The geography of the place, with its harbour at the foot and its houses at the top of a cliff, did not lend itself to efficiency. The fishermen did the actual fishing and faced the ever-present dangers of the sea, but it was the women who did most of the hard graft. The amount of that graft defies reckoning.

Gathering bait, redding lines, baiting 1400 hooks per line, cooking, mending, darning, knitting, carrying lines down to the boats and fish back up from the boats, cleaning, smoking and on occasion selling the fish, helping to launch and beach the boats at all hours – frequently carrying their men on their backs in and out of the sea – and with unfailing regularity, bearing children. Ponder that lot. The men kept the lines and the boats in good order and fished. They had the easy end of the load. Auchmithie in the nineteenth century had a way of life that was peculiar to Auchmithie and its whole economy was founded and maintained on female labour. When you look

at the crumbling harbour wall, the sea-breached breakwater
and the unprofitable pleasure craft drawn up on the shingle
today, it is too easy to feel only regret. There is much more to
it. The Auchmithie folk were an anachronism in their own
time. They could not match the pace of change when change
became inevitable, so their way of life simply died.
Auchmithie just managed to eke out a bare living in the days
of oar and sail. It lost out with the advent of powered boats and
a rural bus service. The ready market of Arbroath failed when
Arbroath started to fish its own lines and to supply its own
market. Arbroath had tried for a long time to compete with
Auchmithie but it wasn't until the nineteenth century that they
managed it. Back in 1705 the first formal approach was made
when the Provost of Arbroath invited a number of Auchmithie
families to come round to Arbroath and start fishing from the
new jetty they had just built. It sounded a fair offer and two or
three Auchmithie fishers packed up their gear, collected their
families and sailed round to set up in business. Little did they
know. No sooner had they arrived and started to organise
things in their new location than they were all ordered back to
Auchmithie: *instanter.* The Earl of Northesk had applied to the
Lord Advocate on the grounds that these families were his
servitors, having been taken over with the fishing rights when
the Earl bought Auchmithie from the Abbot of Arbroath. It is
all there in the records. The Lord Advocate ruled in favour of
the Earl of Northesk and ordered the Auchmithie folk back to
Auchmithie. There was a stushie at first but back they had to
go.
    It all seems odd. Since 1320 Arbroath has prided itself on its
Declaration of Independence, conceived and submitted in the
name of freedom 'which no man doth surrender but with his
life' etc. etc. In 1705 the Earl of Northesk was still able to have
his vagrant fishermen returned to him like so many bonded
slaves or professional football players. No doubt the
Declaration of Independence was intended more for Earls than
fisher folk but one would have thought that someone might
have invoked it on the fishers' behalf at the time. As it was,
Arbroath had to continue buying their smokies from
Auchmithie for quite a time before a few Cargills, Beatties and
Swankies were able to move freely down the coast and sink

Old Auchmithie – all of the women and none of the men working.

their tar barrels in the Old Shorehead. Since then Arbroath has made a name for itself out of the Auchmithie smokie and never a cheep of gratitude do you hear.

The original Auchmithie smokie factory was an elementally simple structure. An old fish barrel was sunk into a hole in the ground and a fire of hardwood chips lit below it. When the flames were starting to lick up, they were damped down with oak sawdust until the fire simply smouldered, sending up a rich and aromatic smoke. The line-caught haddock were cleaned, gutted, topped and tailed and left in salted water for a couple of hours before being linked in pairs and suspended on rods over the barrel. The exact moment to remove them was the secret of the Auchmithie matron who owned the barrel – and she knew it to a millisecond. Arbroath matrons today continue to perform similar feats of haute cuisine by the same primitive method.

In 1890, a contemporary observer commenting on the scene at Auchmithie with its rows of smoke pits smouldering away and wisps of blue smoke spiralling up from the subterranean red glow, compared it to Vesuvius. He might well have compared it to that part of the *Divina Commedia* where Dante was on about Inferno – and getting pretty near the centre.

Such a comparison would have been particularly apt if one remembers the Auchmithie children hovering around in the mirk. They were children of nature, the Auchmithie bairns. In 1909 the Brechin Young Ladies' Choir held their annual picnic at Auchmithie. By train to Arbroath and out to the village by horse brake the intrepid travellers ventured, only to have their revels marred by the Auchmithie bairns. As the Brechin Young Ladies disported themselves on the silver sands of the beach, the Auchmithie juvenalia ringed them in a chanting, menacing, mob. No matter how the Young Ladies rang the changes from piggy backs to 'I dree I dree I drop't it', the Auchmithie juniors intruded. When tea was taken and the Young Ladies flopped, exhausted, on the ground, the sons of Auchmithie kept up their chorus and the leitmotif was 'Gie's a ha'pny, Gie's a ha'pny, Gie's a ha'pny . . .'

In later years, but still in the early days of this century, J. B. Salmond of Arbroath wrote a series of articles in the *Arbroath Herald*. His theme was the old way of life in Auchmithie. In one of his pieces he mentioned a visitor being greeted by an Auchmithie boy with 'I'll stand on ma heid for a penny'. Such facts of Auchmithie life might do more to portray the misery and grinding poverty of reality than the patronising sentiment of Musselcraig and the Mucklebackits did.

Whatever the opinion on Arcady, there is no doubt that life in Auchmithie was hard. The only recorded occasions for pleasure and enjoyment in the village were the celebrations associated with betrothal and marriage – and they seem serious enough. J.B. Salmond's description of the formalities of courting and marriage in Auchmithie reads like an ornithologist's description of the mating habits of exotic birds today. There was the initial contact period when acceptance and rejection alternated before an informal pair-bonding started. At this point the female began her nest-building and mate-attracting rituals, collecting pretty objects to decorate the nest. In Auchmithie's case it was 'dishes': clothes baskets full of crockery of all kinds to deck the kitchen dresser and walls. Next came the official declaration of intent when the swain and his father made a formal call at the girl's house and were ceremoniously rebuffed. Only the offer and acceptance of whisky from the male to the female families could overcome all apparent objection. This directly reflects the ritual posturing and display of birds in the wild. J. B. Salmond's description could have come straight from a bird book. The customs and habits of the Auchmithie fishers were as foreign to contemporary Scotland in the eighteenth and nineteenth centuries as the ornithological comparison is to us today. These are the facts to balance nostalgia: harsh conditions and grinding poverty were the staples of Auchmithie life.

There is a new Auchmithie today; new houses and old houses done up with double glazing and all mod. cons. Life is better for the Auchmithie folk and they no longer fear the rigours of the sea. They have television to dull their senses like the rest of us but 'way back in the brain, deep down in the subconscious, are we not all driven by the same atavistic compulsion to believe that life was better then? We have lost all contact with Nature and the elements. Old Auchmithie lived by them and their souls were the better for it.

St. Vigeans

Auchmithie village is in the parish of St. Vigeans and is still far enough from Arbroath to be safe. St. Vigeans village is too close to Arbroath. St. Vigeans is now in Arbroath. A pincer movement between the Industrial Estate to the west and the municipal housing estate to the east has closed on St. Vigeans. The quiet, idyllic little hamlet by the Brothock burn has been squeezed out of its independent existence. It used to consist of a kirk on a mound, a school on another mound and a winding street between. An old rustic bridge spanned the Brothock and there used to be a whole series of old mills by that particular stream. The Brothock was one of the most highly developed power sources in the area. Right down the Brothock Valley, power mills for all kinds of textile and industrial processes were operated from its flow. Today it trickles impotently down for most of its time and just occasionally roars down in spate to flood out Robin Fairweather's wholesale boot and shoe warehouse yet again. The bridge in St. Vigeans village is now blocked off from traffic and the village sleeps uneasily in the shadow of creeping urbanisation.

The charm of St. Vigeans lies in its long row of unspoilt cottages. No hideous extensions and monstrous dormer windows spoil their native charm as yet. Two of them have been modified internally to make a home for a collection of Pictish stones. These houses make a great setting. If Pictish stones have to be kept indoors there is no better place to put them than the cottages of St. Vigeans. They make a basic, plain, uncomplicated showcase and do not detract in any way from the stark appeal of the stones themselves. You are never very far from the Picts in Angus and the St. Vigeans Pictish museum is as good a place as any to study them.

Archaeologists have classified Pictish carved stones into three main groups. Group 1 they take to be the oldest, from the middle of the seventh to the middle of the eighth centuries AD. Group 2 carries on till the tenth century and they show the increasing religious influence as the Picts adopted Christianity. Group 3 is a smaller list of still later examples which are almost entirely Christian. All these groups share common symbols which have been recognised and given names which purport to describe them: 'V' rods and 'Z' rods are understandable – but why 'rods'? Why not 'lines' or 'letters' or 'marks'? That is the way of archaeologists, though; someone said 'Vrods' 'way back and V rod it is. Their comb and mirror are less convincing. Their elephant is not on. Donald Duck would be nearer the mark. Archaeologists, however, are conservative chiels and although they keep contradicting each other's theories, they hang on to their 'facts'.

The best example of Pictish carved stone art work in Angus and the most intricately carved of the St. Vigeans stones is the 'Drosten' stone, so called because the word Drosten appears on it. Books have been written about that stone. Palaeographers have researched and analysed and theorised and argued about it for centuries. Countless interpretations have been given of the writing which appears on a small panel at the bottom end of one of its edges but to no avail. The letters and words have been described variously as Latin, debased Latin, Gaelic, Erse, Anglo-Saxon or Welsh – each being confidently and fluently translated by its proponent.

The facts pertaining to the stone are few. It appears to have been first found standing over a grave in St. Vigeans kirkyard.

Auchmithie smokies: the original.

It was later removed and built into the floor of the kirk itself. When the Minister, the Rev. John Muir, wrote his piece on St. Vigeans for the *New Statistical Account* of 1842, he refers to the stone as standing, broken, over the grave of some 'unknown eminent person'. When Patrick Chalmers of Aldbar wrote his treatise on *The Sculptured Stones of Angus* published in 1848, he refers to the stone as having been found on the floor of the kirk with pieces broken off and one piece built into the adjoining wall. He also refers to the fact that the stone had been dug up and replaced in the kirkyard. In 1848 it was definitely outdoors but during the restoration of the kirk in 1870 the stone was again dug up, some broken fragments cemented back on and the refurbished stone put into the kirk porch for safe keeping. From there it was moved into its present position in the cottage museum where it stands today, proud, if somewhat enigmatic. The inscription on its edge, by the way, looks nothing like 'Drosten' to me.

The definitive work on the Drosten Stone has been written. Look for it on second-hand book barrows. If that fails, go you to Arbroath Public Library, ask for volume No. 67.913.031, *The Drosten Stone of St. Vigeans and its Inscription,* published by Wm. Smith of Aberdeen in 1928, and bathe yourself in its sensuous prose. Every theory is explored, every possible language discussed. The brief, comprehensive yet comprehensible tome is a work of inspired creation. Its erudition and ingenuity are a twin delight. There are thirty-one other bits of Pictish stone in the museum, six are Group 2, twenty-three are Group 3 and the rest are even later. Only the Drosten Stone merits a book to itself by a gifted, if anonymous, writer.

The quaint little kirk of St. Vigeans is an old and notable foundation. It is believed to have been founded by Irish missionaries during the great period of Celtic evangelism in Scotland in the fifth and sixth centuries. St. Vigean – or Vigian – is taken to be derived from the Latin name for St. Fechin, an Irish saint who died in 664 and who also gave his name to Ecclefechan. Just don't ask what 'Eccle' means. Whatever the origin of St. Vigeans, its kirk was certainly in existence and serving as the kirk of Arbroath long before William the Lion founded the Abbey in 1178. St. Vigeans kirk was actually given by William 'with all its belongings' to the Abbey.

In 1650 the Reformation required that the kirk building be modified to meet the demands of Presbyterian worship but apart from the removal of the altar and the installation of a pulpit, little was done. Local belief at the time, and for long before, was that the mound on which the kirk of St. Vigeans stood was a supernatural structure built by hobgoblins, shored up on columns rising from a subterranean lake. There is no evidence as to what prompted that idea. By the early eighteenth century at a time when the sacrament of Communion had not been celebrated for some time in the Kirk, a rumour arose that next time it was to be taken there, the whole building would crumble and sink back into the lake. On the due date an expectant congregation assembled and took up vantage positions on the adjoining knoll – where the manse is now – and sat down to enjoy the spectacle. No doubt somebody was selling them sandwiches and cups of tea. When the bell duly tolled and the Minister and his Elders entered the doomed Kirk a frisson of fear rippled through the crowd and that was that. For some unaccountable reason the Kirk stood fast. It is still there.

Up the hill from St. Vigeans, across the road from the Kirkton Industrial Estate, is H.M.S. Condor, a former Royal Naval Air Station now occupied by the Royal Marines. Since 1938 'the Condor' has been a good neighbour to Arbroath. Thousands of sailors and marines have been stationed there, local folk have had employment, many servicemen have married local girls and returned to settle in the area. One or two particularly fortunate local men have married W.R.N.S. from Condor. The supply has ceased now but marrying a Wren from the Condor was a privilege and a joy, believe me. A civilian glider club operates from the Condor airstrip now and the pleasing sight of these graceful, silent, ecologically acceptable machines is vastly better than the offensive obtrusion of the powered aircraft they used to have. The Condor also acts as a barrier and a stop to the Arbroath politicians who are hell-bent on spreading their town over the surrounding countryside like a creeping weed.

Recent relaxation of planning regulations and the present crisis in Scotch agriculture have permitted and encouraged the spread of town into country. The general state of the European agricultural economy has prompted a call for agricultural land to be taken out of production. All kinds of schemes for 'diversification' in farming and use of farm land are being touted but the worst scheme of all is the decision to build on good farm land. Some schemes for alternative uses can be reversed and the land is still available for farming. Build on it and you lose the land permanently. That and the death of St. Vigeans by strangulation is all part of the price the Angus folks are paying for failing to curb their local politicians.

The Red Head, Ethie Haven, Lunan Bay

Eastwards of the A92 the hinterland of the Angus coastline above Arbroath is still unspoiled. Up the coast from Auchmithie the red sandstone cliffs run on as far as the Red Head, an awesome precipice where seabirds scream above a seething sea. Round the headland of the Red Head lies Ethie Haven, an old fishing hamlet whose renovated cottages are now private holiday homes. Few folk know of their existence. Visitors at Lunan Bay sometimes ask what that place is opposite – just below the cliffs – and are told that it is an old fishing station but 'I don't know how you get there'. You get there with a little local knowledge, two farm tracks and a lot of brass neck. Ethie Haven is an idyllic retreat for the fortunate folk who have houses there. It has no sandy beach, no modern 'facilities' and absolutely no spare space. The last thing Ethie Haven needs, or wants, is a string of cars grinding down its track, turning round and grinding back up again. If you want to go to Ethie Haven, go on your own two feet and I'm sure no-one will object, but keep your cars out of it.

Ethie Haven was a thriving fishing village once, although its shingle beach is approached only by an L-shaped inlet through a dangerous barrier reef. Line fishers used to work out of Ethie Haven, then salmon netters, and now a local firm sometimes has a couple of men working there. No doubt Ethie Haven has always been a place where folk lived but it has never supported more than a handful of people at any one time. There are the remains of an old chapel at the south end of the bay and that probably marks the period of peak population, the seventeenth and eighteenth centuries.

The Ruined Red Castle

The Red Head and the Ethie_Haven coastline form the southern boundary of Lunan Bay, a long and gloriously unspoiled sandy beach. In its day, Lunan Bay has been much favoured by geologists, bird-watchers, choir outings and Viking marauders. Halfway along it there is a prominence on which the ruined Red Castle stands. The Red Castle was the last of a long line of fortifications on that spot. Its commanding position over the bay meant that from earliest times, anyone who wanted to command Lunan Bay took up position on the mound. There are traces of fortifications going back beyond recall. When the Beaker Folk and their La Tene successors left and the more recent Danes and Norsemen arrived, they were all met by whomsoever happened to be living there at the time, firmly entrenched on their mound. We can only guess at the kind of buildings they had, most likely wooden huts behind a stone wall. The present ruin consists of three sides of a four-storey tower and part of an enclosing wall, reputedly the remains of a castle built by William the First. Some say it was built by William the First, some say he used the existing castle when he visited Arbroath to check on the construction of his Abbey, some say the castle was built by Walter de Berkeley and given to William the First as a hunting lodge.

Whatever the facts were, the castle was certainly owned eventually by William de Berkeley and passed, by a Berkeley marriage, to Ingleram of Balliol, an ancestor of King John Balliol. Several other families owned it over the years until in 1367 it was owned by Sir Robert Stewart of Innermeath whose family retained it right up to the end of the sixteenth century. In 1579 the Red Castle was attacked and set on fire by Andrew Gray, the upstart son of Lord Gray of Dunninald, a local laird. When the castle was attacked, old Lady Innermeath and her daughter were in residence but they managed to survive the fire by retreating to the tower and shutting themselves in. Their lives were saved but unfortunately the young lass miscarried and lost a child. The whole episode arose from the cupidity and ambition of young Gray of Dunninald, and for that he was reprimanded and warned as to his future conduct by King James.

One would have thought that a Royal ticking-off would have been enough to curb Gray's actions, especially when he was specifically ordered to 'desist from his violence' in future, but not so. He had scouting parties out at Red Castle again before the embers were properly cold. When the King was apprised of this, he immediately ordered the Provost of Dundee to muster his forces and proceed to the Red Castle, picking up Erskine of Dun and his men on the way. That should have done it but as soon as the Dundee-Dun army withdrew again, Gray was at it once more. This time he stormed the castle, took it over, destroyed it and took all that he could carry back to Dunninald.

Somehow or other he got away with it, for the next time we read of Gray of Dunninald he was one of the jurors who tried Archibald Douglas, one of the conspirators in the murder of

Darnley. His sacking of the Red Castle and flouting of the
King's orders seem to have been quietly overlooked. No doubt
the King was quite happy to let the whole affair die down for
he was having the same kind of trouble all over Scotland at the
time. Jealous landlords were fighting amongst themselves for
power and King James had to spend a lot of his time in the
early part of his reign, trying to pacify or subdue them. Even
Erskine of Dun, after he had established himself in the Red
Castle, had to be evicted by a sharp reminder from the King.
Erskine had stayed on in the castle because the immediate
owners were minors and unable to look after their own
interests. It seemed an easy picking but enough jealous
neighbours objected strongly enough for the King to intercede
and have Erskine moved out.

After Gray's attack, nothing much is heard of the Red Castle
except that it continued to be occupied right up till the middle
of the eighteenth century. There is documentary proof that it
was 'roofed and in good repair' in 1770. The process of tracing
ownership and following family connections in such cases is
frequently confused by the intrusion of different people of the
same name at the same time. The reference to Gray's
involvement in the trial of Archibald Douglas is one such case.
We read that Gray the younger of Dunninald sacked the Red
Castle in 1579 and yet he served as a juror at the trial of
Archibald Douglas in 1581. That shows a pretty quick change
of fortune for him. It is further confused by the fact that there
were several prominent figures called Archibald Douglas
around that time. Archibald was a favourite Douglas name. It
takes time to establish that it was the same Archibald Douglas
who was involved in the murder of Rizzio in 1566 and the
murder of Darnley in 1567 but not brought to trial until 1581
and finally pardoned in 1586. History is a confused and
confusing pursuit.

A more rewarding pursuit is to visit the old Red Castle today
with the June sun beating down on it and the waves rolling
gently on to the sands below. Lunan Bay is a peaceful place
now, no matter how rumbustious it once was. Better to take the
kiddies to play on the beach below than bother about the
history of the Red Castle above. It is a favourite Angus picnic
spot now and even on a sunny summer Sunday there are miles

of empty beach. Given a shade higher temperature and guaranteed sun, Lunan Bay would lick any Continental 'paradise' into oblivion. As it is, there are days in June and July when the sun burnishes the golden strand, listless waves collapse exhausted on the shore and families of Angus folk relax and revel in the beauty and peace of their fortunate county.

Lunan Bay is one of the high spots of Angus – metaphorically speaking, of course – for physically it is low land. The whole of the east coast of Scotland from Berwick to Buchan is lowland and nowhere is there a more beautiful sandy beach than the three miles of unspoiled shore that is Lunan Bay. If the occasional chill breeze, the odd summer downpour and the sporadic North Sea haar are the price we pay for the absence of tourist throngs, then it is a bargain price. Scotland is still a blessed land of unspoiled beauty and we should be fighting to keep it so, not selling it out to Mammon. The Antonine Wall was not such a bad idea and damn the Tourist Board.

The Red Castle stands halfway along Lunan Bay and at the edge of Inverkeilor parish. The Lunan Burn is the boundary. The parish is contiguous with that of St. Vigeans and extends from just north of Auchmithie to Lunan Bay and inland to Friockheim. The name is fairly obvious: Inverkeillor – mouth of the Keillor – and there is a Keillor burn to prove it. The fact that the village is more than a mile from the mouth of the Keillor burn is incidental. Try to trace any other origin for the name and straightaway, in the *Statistical Account* for the parish, you come up against an alternative version of the name – 'Congschollis'. There is no way through that. Inverkeillor at least makes some kind of sense, even if the number of 'l's is optional and may be sprinkled to taste.

The village of Inverkeilor itself is of a singularly unimposing appearance. It used to be a one-horse town but it seems the horse died. Its most interesting feature now is the oddly designed little church on the hill, commanding the north road and the Lunan Valley. It is an asymmetric structure with a row of carved stone coats-of-arms embedded in the south wall. Inverkeilor kirkyard is as fascinating as all kirkyards, with its ornate tombs for the Lindsays, Raitts, Ramsays, Carnegies &

Bruce-Gardynes and a War Memorial for the Orrocks, Smiths, Shepherds, Taylors and Vannets. On the left of the old road through the village, lies the Chance Inn – so called because in the old days 'Chance' houses provided accommodation and coaches by chance – without booking. The most interesting feature of the present Chance Inn is a photograph in the transmogrified public bar of a troop of Scots Greys halted at the inn door on a ride from Aberdeen in 1902.

Cardinal Beaton

The parish of Inverkeilor loops south to meet the coast at Low Skelly and includes the estate of Ethie Castle in the loop. Ethie House – now Castle – is assumed by many authorities to have been built by Cardinal Beaton but this appears to be unlikely. It seems much more probable that the house was in existence before Cardinal Beaton came to the area and was merely occupied by him when he became Abbot of Arbroath in 1524, before his elevation to the Cardinalate in 1538.

Cardinal Beaton is one of the most striking and complex characters in the whole of Scottish history. At a time of violence, cupidity, carnality and licence he proved himself more than adequately violent, cupidinous, carnal and licentious. His career serves as a classic example of nepotism: having followed his uncle James as Commendator of St. Andrews in 1539, he was duly followed by his nephew, also James, as Commendator of Arbroath in 1543. His impact on Scotland, and the county of Angus in particular, was considerable.

Born David Bethune, in the year 1494, he was the son of John Bethune of Balfour and nephew of the aforementioned James. Educated at St. Andrews and Paris, he became Rector of Campsie and a regular visitor to the French court. His career led from Abbot of Arbroath in 1524 to Lord Privy Seal in 1528, serving as Ambassador to France in 1519, 1533 and 1538. All his life he was a noted Francophile and in 1537 he was Bishop of Mirepoix and became a French citizen. His election to the Cardinalate came in 1538 and he was made Archbishop of St. Andrews and Primate of all Scotland in 1539. By 1543 he was

Chancellor and conducting a powerfully anti-English and pro-French policy. He died in 1546: violently.

Other facts of Cardinal Beaton's life, less publicised and less flattering, are evidenced in his history of sexual promiscuity – although one of his mistresses, Marion Ogilvie, did subsequently become his wife – and in his impassioned persecution of heretics. This last obsession reached its apogee in 1546 when he watched with a positively pathological delight the torture and burning of George Wishart in St. Andrews. Seldom has retribution been so obviously and immediately enacted. Three months later Cardinal David Beaton was himself murdered on the same spot. John Knox, one of Wishart's associates, was tried and sentenced to death for his involvement in the murder but the sentence was commuted. Knox was sent to the galleys and subsequently went to Geneva before returning to Scotland in 1559. These historic facts serve to illustrate the barbarity of the era of Cardinal Beaton. They were robust times and he was a robust character.

This matter of Cardinal Beaton's association with Marion Ogilvie is particularly significant. Clerical celibacy was a tenet of faith for Catholics of the time, yet Beaton lived openly with Marion Ogilvie at Melgund Castle before they eventually married. If they did marry. Contemporary sources refer to Marion Ogilvie as his 'reputed' wife. Since Marion Ogilvie was the third child and only daughter of Sir James Ogilvie, later first Lord Ogilvie of Airlie, it is doubtful if such a liaison would have been tolerated without some form of official recognition. Whether married or not, there were several children of the union and it all serves to illustrate the laxity of observance in the Church of the time. It probably also explains the root cause of John Knox's personal hatred of Davie Bethune.

Despite his peccadilloes, the Cardinal is held in high esteem in Angus. To us he means Arbroath Abbey, Melgund Castle – which he built for Marion – Hospitalfield House – where Marion lived after his murder – and Ethie Castle. Ethie Castle has the strongest claim to his memory. Arbroath Abbey and Melgund Castle are in ruins. Hospitalfield House has been rebuilt. Only Ethie Castle remains in any way original. Ethie's claims to the Beaton connection are that they have a piece of furniture, which is known to have belonged to the blessed

Cardinal, built into one of their staircases and they have his ghost. It may be that only the more gullible will accept the latter claim but they do reinforce it with a wealth of circumstantial evidence. Folk who have met the Ethie House ghost have described it as being of 'a very small, fat, red-faced man in a red gown with a cord tied round his ample middle and with one foot wrapped up in flannel.' That was the Cardinal. Supplementary evidence from witnesses who have not actually seen the ghost but have heard him perambulate upstairs rooms in Ethie Castle, have described his tread as 'Thump – swiish, thump – swiish, thump – swiish . . .' At that the cognoscenti are wont to nod their heads and say 'Aye, he was badly bothered wi' the gout, ye ken. That's the Cardinal's leg ye're hearing'.' Such evidence is irrefutable.

Inverkeilor, Lunan and Craig

Cardinal Beaton may or may not have lived in Ethie House but the Carnegies certainly did. The Barony of Ethie formed the greater part of the parish of Ethie, now Inverkeilor, and it passed to the family of Carnegie. Both the first Earls of Northesk and Southesk were Carnegies, the brothers David and John Carnegie, sons of John de Carnegie. Ethie Castle became the seat of the Earl of Northesk and remained in Carnegie ownership for many years.

The little strip of land running up through the parishes of Inverkeilor, Lunan and Craig, bounded by the sea on one side and the A92 on the other, is quite unique. With all the traffic flowing past on its way north and south and the sea effectively restricting east-west passage, the area has all the attributes of an island. It is slower moving than the rest. It is less industrialised. It is a little, sheltered, isolated coign of old rural Scotland: and much cleaner.

North of Ethie you enter this unspoiled land. At Lunan, where the Kirk sits right by the road and the kirkyard runs down to the bank of the reed-bound river, the good Victoria herself could still be with us. The Lunan water swells out at the bridge pool there and on a summer's afternoon with dragonflies dancing on the still water and honey-heavy bees bumbling along the bank, you are a hundred years back in time. If Nature mirrors Art, this is a nineteenth-century watercolour.

Previous centuries would have painted a more lurid picture. Lunan Kirk was the kirk of Walter Mill the martyr. Walter Mill, minister of Lunan parish, adopted the Reformed Church teachings and opposed the doctrines of Popery. He was ordered to desist from such heresy and resume the Catholic creed. He refused. After repeated warnings as to the consequences, he was eventually arrested, taken to St. Andrews, tried and sentenced to be burned at the stake. The year was 1558 and that was the legal punishment for heretics.

Walter Mill had been the parish priest of Lunan for a long time. He was eighty-two years old when he was apprehended: a quiet, studious, much respected country priest. The revulsion of feeling when he was sentenced to be burned to death was so great that it seemed for a time that the people of St. Andrews were going to prevent the execution. After some attempts at interference, it went ahead. Walter Mill was publicly burned to death in St. Andrews in April 1558. His death was of tremendous significance. The public outcry against the heinous act was so great that the Reform movement within the Church grew rapidly and inexorably from then on. Walter Mill was the last Protestant martyr to be burned in Scotland. The peace and tranquillity of our Lunan Bay today were dearly bought. The quiet kirk, the sheltered home, the ruined Red Castle and all the couthy country scene were bought in blood. Think on that when next you lean over Lunan bridge and see the torpid trout lie drowsing in the dark, safe-shadowed, stream. If history can teach us anything at all, it must be the debt of gratitude we owe our forbears.

Behind the Kirk, Lunan House stands in its well-wooded grounds and walled garden beside the river. An older house was demolished and the present building erected in 1825. At that time the estate belonged to the family of Blair, subsequently Blair-Imrie, but more recently the house has been a hotel and now it is a home for handicapped people.

Up the hill from Lunan and over the railway bridge there is a Blair memorial. Just off the roadway there is a forty-five feet tall obelisk in memory of Lt. Col. James Blair of the Bengal

Army who died at sea on 12th August 1847. Contemplating the worthy Colonel's life and times reinforces the Victorian mood — despite the disreputable modern housing scheme around his memorial. Keeping one's back firmly to the housing development, the prospect over the Blair demesne to the south and east is of fair farming land, well wooded and contained, the dunes behind the bay of Lunan and the rough rocks of Ethie and the Red Head. The Blairs were weel tochered.

Still avoiding the A92 and taking the Ferryden road round past Nether Dysart farm with its substantial steading and custom-built cartsheds, you come to Dunninald. The estate of Dunninald House, Dunninald Mains farm and its attendant cottages and estate houses form quite a settlement, even more remote and distinctive than the rest. The original Dunninald Castle was built on a rocky headland down on the coast but nothing remains of that building. It was abandoned by the eighteenth century. Old books refer to the castle as 'Black Jack' and it has been surmised that maybe a Black Jack lived there at one time. It makes more sense when you find out that the precipitous rock on which the castle stood was the Black Jack. A castle called Black Jack is questionable; a rock called Black Jack is most appropriate. The present Dunninald House is sometimes called Dunninald Castle simply because there used to be a Dunninald Castle and the present house is built in a baronial style and looks a bit castle-like. It was built by a Mr Patrick Arklay in 1824, when a lot of local building was going on, and designed by Gillespie Graham.

James Gillespie Graham was a Perthshire man who lived from 1777 till 1855 and became a famous architect in his lifetime. The Steeple which serves as Montrose's landmark to the world was designed by Gillespie Graham. As was Edinburgh's Moray Place and its adjoining streets. His elaboration of an essentially simple concept of design gave his work a classic stamp that is instantly recognisable and turned Dunninald House into Dunninald Castle at first sight of its castellated frontage.

Over the way from Dunninald is Usan House, another old foundation regularly rebuilt over the centuries. In 1260, one Willelm de Lechten inscribed his name as witness to a Royal Charter of land given to Walter de Rossy and thereby listed

The Elephant Rock, St. Skae.

himself as the first recorded Leighton in Scotland. They are still here. In 1608 young John Layton did his bit by rebuilding the existing Usan House of his day. Some of his handiwork is still visible in the present house. The estate subsequently passed to families of Scotts and Keiths and is currently owned by Alstons. Down from the house on the coast at the rock of St. Skeoch, or St. Skae, there is a private burial ground where Arklays of Dunninald, Keiths of Usan and Scotts of Abbeythune are interred.

The rock of St. Skae is a notable feature. Its local name is the Elephant Rock and from the right angle, in the right light, with the right amount of whisky inside you, it looks exactly like an elephant. When all the conditions are scrupulously met and the red rock is tinged by the setting sun, the illusion is complete. The elephant is indubitably pink.

The coastline here is mainly Red Sandstone but there are veins of other rock, with limestone and puddingstone prominent. The beaches of Angus and the Mearns teem with agates and chalcedons washed out of the parent rocks by the sea. The formidable ladies with sensible hairstyles and little square hammers frequently to be seen chipping bits off the Usan landscape are gemmologists. When the agates have been tumbled, polished and mounted, they make beautiful jewellery.

The limestone strata were worked commercially in the early nineteenth century when it was discovered that calcium carbonate could be burned to produce lime which made a

Limekiln, Boddin.

valuable fertiliser. It is reckoned that Angus was the first place in Scotland where this process was developed. On the coast below Usan there is an old limekiln that serves to baffle a lot of visitors. Most of them take it to be the ruins of a castle. In its day it burned a lot of limestone, and the fertile state of the local farms illustrates its value. Modern crop rotation and the development of artificial fertilisers rendered limestone an uneconomic source and the kiln was left to moulder. Bits of it have been used as a storeroom by local fishermen but its days as a working kiln are long past.

Just north of the limekiln is the little old abandoned fishing port of Usan. Local authorities quote the name 'Usan' as having been Hulysham, Ulyssishaven and Ulishaven before becoming Usan. I hae ma doots. I canna imagine that Usan was ever called Ulyssishaven. Nor is there any record of Ulysses ever calling in at Usan. He negotiated the coast of the Sirens safely and managed to dodge Scylla and Charybdis successfully. Ithaca, Troy, Scyrus, Sicily and Aeolia, yes: Usan, no. I doubt if he ever had to take shelter in Usan. The name by which it was known positively until quite recently was 'Fishtown of Usan'. Now it is Usan.

In the days when Scotch kings used to visit Forfar and stay in its castle, around 1296 to 1309, they had their fish brought over from Usan. The track from Usan to Forfar across Montrimment moor was known as the 'King's Cadger's Road' for that reason. In more recent times Usan was a busy little fishing port, although its harbour is so restricted that boats have to be moored in line astern along a single fissure in the rocks. When you look at the harbour now, with only one man fishing out of it, you wonder how it could ever have been a thriving fishing port. Then you look up at the rows of old abandoned houses and you see that it has been a sizeable village. If you then make the effort to read its history, you find that when Miss Margaret Gardyne went to teach in Usan in the early days of the nineteenth century, there were sixty pupils in the school. That makes you think. If you read further, you may even unearth the fact that as late as the 1880s, Usan had a flute band of its own dressed in blue striped double-breasted vests with short reefer jackets and brass buttons, worn with white duck trousers. They were good enough to play, by request, on the lawn at Brechin Castle in July 1882 for the delectation of the Earl of Dalhousie. That should flabbergast you, as it did me. Usan today is derelict with one new bungalow built by the one remaining fisherman.

In the heyday of the port the Usan men fished haddock, cod, crab and lobster locally and went off to the herring fleet in July, the men to crew the boats, the girls to gut fish as freelance fisher lassies. It may be of biological interest to note that practically everyone in Usan was called Paton.

The A92 has served to isolate this corner of rural Angus but, on the other side, to the west, the area of Rossie and Upper Dysart is almost equally secluded. The whole area, along with much of Angus and the Mearns generally, has one notable phenomenon. You seldom see any people. Keep off the main roads, stick to the side roads and farm tracks and you scarcely see a single soul. This arises from the facts of modern life in Scotland. Farm workers are few in number. They tend to live in the towns and travel out to work each day. Those folk who do live in the reconditioned farm cottages are town workers who go in by car each morning: mother and father to work in business, trade or profession, shop, office or factory, and the children to go to school. They return in the evening to watch television and sleep.

By day these country homes are deserted, as is the countryside. A farm of two or three hundred acres that used to employ six or seven men full-time with all their dependent families, now has one or two regulars with intermittent part-time help. This means that as you walk around our country roads you do not meet any people, nor do you see them working in the fields. An occasional tractor driver, cocooned in his cab listening to stereo music above the roar of his machine, is the usual – except for seasonal tattie, raspberry or strawberry gangs. Even they are a diminishing band as machines are developed to replace them. It is a recent but definite result of a changing social pattern and quite surprising when one first realises it.

Up the hill, past Gightyburn and Mountboy, on the edge of Rossie Moor is Rossie School, known until recently as Rossie Reformatory. The original Reformatory was a house on the south slope of Kinnoul Hill which had been built as a dower house by the owners of Rossie Castle, now defunct. Rossie Reformatory was formally opened in May 1857 and was a pioneer institution in the rehabilitation of young offenders. Over the years it housed hundreds of boys who had committed serious crimes. Its record of reform was impressive. Extra buildings were erected as required and by the 1900s it was a large progressive institution for the detention and education of wayward juveniles. Just before the Second World War, in 1939, an entirely new custom-built school and Governor's house were erected to provide even better facilities. The outbreak of war effectively ended development in that direction.

This building, which is the main part of the Rossie school today, now stands empty and neglected. Only one wing of the establishment is in use to house a small number of inmates and the future of the main building is in doubt. It will be interesting to see what becomes of it. At present the place is a monument to 1930s architecture and should be preserved as such. It enjoys a superb setting on the upper slope of the hill with a glorious south-facing view. One can see it as a hotel, a school, a home for the disabled, a further education college or a time-share leisure complex. I suppose that there are those who will vouchsafe that already it is all of these.

Over the way from Rossie and overlooking the town of

Usan and its Coastguard Tower: now deserted.

Montrose is the hamlet of Craig or Kirkton of Craig. The Kirkton part is irrelevant now because the kirk has been deconsecrated and changed into a dwelling house. The original building remains but it is a sad sight with overgrown grounds and dilapidated driveway. Craig is as quiet as all our villages are now but in its way it symbolises the decay of one aspect of rural Scotland whilst illustrating the renaissance of another. The old working village has been replaced by the dormitory village and a new social pattern is evolving. Whilst one weeps for the demise of the village school, kirk, smiddy, shop and Post Office, one must reluctantly accept the end of an era. The old village way of life has gone. Craig parish runs into Ferryden and Montrose. The amalgamation and unification of these two contiguous territories and the total annihilation of Ferryden as a fishing port, mark the end of another era.

CHAPTER 5

Montrose and into The Mearns

Montrose is a refreshingly self-satisfied wee town; it always has been. The writer, Reid, in his *Picturesque Forfarshire*, observed that 'entre nous, Montrose has for generations, if not for centuries, posed aristocratically among its more plebeian compeers and still there hangs around it an indefinable atmosphere of "tone" and superiority'. Alan Reid, F.S.A. (Scot), F.E.I.S., was spot on. There is no doubt that Montrose has always rated itself a cut above its neighbours. 'Way back in the nineteenth century when the railway first linked Montrose and Brechin, it was a Montrose joke to call out as the Brechin train drew in, 'Tak in yer washin', the Brechiners are here'. The jibe was easily deflected by the Brechin riposte:

Here's the Basin, there's Montrose
Shut your een and haud your nose.

If the jingle lacked something in poetic inspiration, it did hold a measure of critical pertinence. The approach to Montrose from the Brechin direction is the least impressive entrance to the town and the Basin has been known, on occasion, to pong.

The Basin is a formidable feature: a landlocked lagoon of some 800 hectares or a vast malodorous swamp of mud and gunge, depending on time and tide. Officially, Montrose Tidal Basin is a listed Local Nature Reserve, which means that it is preserved by law in the public interest. The biggest part of it belongs to the Scottish Wildlife Trust and they employ a full-time ranger who supervises the running of the whole area. Under his management, volunteer parties help to build hides, plant trees, count birds and remove litter. The present incumbent is one Rick Goater, an eminently suitable individual. If his name seems somehow appropriate, his appearance is positively so. The tanned, bearded, wax-jacketed and green-wellied Rick Goater is the epitome of your classic contemporary ranger/naturalist. To the essential skills of his calling he adds a leavening sense of humour.

76

One hopes that his sense of humour is shared by the vast numbers of duck and geese that frequent the Basin. Their lot is not to be envied. One bit of the Basin welcomes their arrival, counts them in and hopes they will enjoy their stay. The other bit blasts them out of the sky. This apparent dichotomy arises from the sharing of facilities between the Scottish Wildlife Trust and the Montrose Wildfowlers' Association. The Wildfowlers have been there for a long time. One hopes they will be there for a long time to come. There is nothing wrong with potting a brace of duck on a winter's evening and having them stuffed with oatmeal and onions and ladled with rich aromatic sauces, as my old mother used to do when I was a shooter. Man does not live by bread sauce alone. Equally, something had to be done about the depredations of the Montrose cowboys who used to crowd the Basin and pop off at anything that flew, from whooper swans to bats. A balance has now been struck between the conflicting claims of the shooters and the bird watchers. Shooting is now by permit only, during restricted hours in the season from September to February. Access to the Basin is by certain specified and clearly defined entry points. Changed days from the time when the rustling reed-beds crawled with heavily armed Montrose bandits who had as lief blow your hat off as hit a windborne widgeon.

The ecology of the Basin itself is utterly fascinating. As the tide creeps in, hissing along imperceptible hollows in little rivulets, to merge and form islets and sand banks before submerging the whole estuary in one gurgling, slapping sheet of grey water, the nature of the whole place changes. Bivalves and molluscs, lamellibranchs, gasteropods, cephalopods and little slimy things with horns, come out to play. Creatures that have spent half a day deep-hidden in the mud now emerge to stretch their legs and fill their little lungs. Life returns to the mud banks. What appeared to be a barren expanse of glutinous goo turns out to be a rich and highly populated feeding ground. It was, of course, a rich and highly populated feeding ground all the time. When the tide was out, the Basin teemed with swimming, diving, wading, flying and perambulating birds that probed and pierced, ripped out and smashed open, their innocent prey. The unsavoury habits and stomach-turning cruelty of Nature revolt one.

For the less callous observer than your committed bird watcher, the appeal of the Basin could lie in its variety of colour, its waving reed beds, fringe trees and multi-coloured mud. There is beauty in its mud. The realism of Peter Scott and David Shepherd can be captured by the camera. The colour, texture and light-enhancing intensities of mud and sand and water need an artist. The boyhood joys of wallowing barefoot in Montrose mud are happy memories. They would fain be recaptured. James Morrison, the artist, has already painted a haunting picture of Montrose over the pale line of the Basin against a northern sky. *Picturesque Forfarshire* commented that 'The setting is of such charm that the title of "the Scottish Venice" seems not inaptly applied to the queen of this tidal expanse'. Aye, weel, Venice had its Canaletto – and young Canale did a lot for the town – who knows but James Morrison might do something of the same for Montrose.

At the south-west corner of the Basin there is an old jetty which used to be the mooring quay for Old Montrose. Before the arrival of the railway there was a revolving drawbridge at Ferryden to allow boats to sail up and down with cargoes for Old Montrose. The railway did away with the need for this facility and the bridge was rebuilt without its moveable section. It was finally removed in the recent demise of Ferryden, and Old Montrose is now just the mansion house and cottages of that name.

There have been many plans, at various times, to contain the water in the Basin and make it a permanent inland sea. The remains of the plans can be found dotted around the Basin. The most ambitious of these is still visible at low tide, running from the edge of the Stenshell burn westwards into mud and oblivion. On old maps it is marked 'Dronner's Dyke: remains of'. Local wise men tell you that Mynheer Dronner was a Dutch expert brought over to do the reclamation job until the raging east-coast storms defeated him and he retired to Holland to commit honourable suicide. Experts from Holland certainly were consulted but it seems more likely that 'Dronner' is simply the Dutch word for 'Drainer' and the scheme ended when the money ran out.

In addition to all its physical charms and fascinations, the Basin is a philologist's delight. It has a bit called the Lurgies.

What a picture that conjures up. The Lurgies. Imagine wandering off the path on a moonless night and ending up in the Lurgies. The camouflaged duck-hunters of Montrose would be the least of your worries. It would be the spike-tailed stoker from the infernal boiler room you'd be after meeting in there. If you missed him, you could cross the channel of the South Esk and land yourself in the Slunks. The Slunks. It doesn't help any to look it up and find that a slunk is just a wet, marshy hollow. You would have found that out when you sank into it. The Lurgies and the Slunks, contiguous sections of the Basin's perimeter; what a wealth of language.

The Town of Montrose

Montrose proper is a really delightful town. It has a glorious sandy beach, wide stretches of links and dunes, golf courses, parks and spacious gardens. Its buildings are classic and its streets wide beyond compare. From any aspect one has to admire Montrose. The main thoroughfare, the High Street, used to be so broad that they cut it in half with a central flower barrier to make two one-way streets out of it. In the old days it was a street of booths and stalls and hucksters. Over the years they became regularised into formal markets on prescribed days which gradually fined down to one market day on Friday. Now there is only one street trader operating on Fridays in front of the Town House. The cattle market continues down by the railway sidings.

The face of Montrose has changed greatly over the years and one of these changes has rendered the Montrose folks' old nickname 'Gable Enders' a shade meaningless. In the eighteenth and nineteenth centuries, Montrose houses sat gable end to the street. Neighbouring towns built their houses facing the street, as sane people tend to do, but Montrose has a tale about its gable ends that they claim makes sense. Apparently, in the eighteenth century when the High Street was an open market, it was much wider even than it is now. Crossing the street must have been a day trip. When such a large market was no longer required – no explanation is offered – the Town Council gave permission for the houses on both sides to be extended forward. It seems that adding a projection with a gable end was the easy way to do it. A likely story.

Whatever the reason, the old High Street houses were built end-on to the street. Photographs taken in the nineteenth century show them quite clearly. If the 'Gable Endies' nickname is less relevant now than formerly, it is still used by neighbouring communities when describing Montrose folk. A recent football match report in an Angus newspaper said that 'Two goals inside as many first-half minutes appeared to have put City on easy street in this first round tie but a brave fight back by the gutsy Gable Endies was thwarted only by some fine saves from David Lawrie in the home goal and a pressure-relieving Gordon Lees counter.' Angus folk know who was playing.

Partly because of its novel system of architecture, Montrose has been blessed with a myriad of little lanes or passages – 'closes' to the locals – which intersect the town centre. One can step a few paces from the main thoroughfare and find sheltered corners of old-world charm that are a delight to see. Many of the Montrose houses off the main streets have little secluded gardens and courtyards that are havens of peace in this frenetic age. Some are private property with gates to bar access; some are public ways and can be traversed. In either case one encounters nooks of ageless ease where time is warped out of context. There are flagged courtyards with cherry trees, slanting sunbeams, and sleeping cats, a hundred years removed from the modern world that thunders down the High Street. Wherever you wander in Montrose the town comes up with one surprise after another.

Down at the harbour there is all the bustle of a major port with ships berthed along a busy waterfront. You can walk around the timber yards and potato sheds and see great godowns filled with import and export cargoes. How many people realise that Montrose is a major trading port? Ever since the thirteenth century Montrose has been an active seaport and for long it was the main Scotch port trading with the Baltic. Over the years the trade has varied with flax, wine, tobacco and timber coming in and grain, malt, potatoes, salmon and whisky going out. Montrose ships sailed the world's seas and Montrose ships used to be built in Montrose. The shipbuilding trade has

The busy harbour, Montrose, now part of the North Sea oil era.

decreased but one yard still operates. Nowadays, Montrose and the built-over Ferryden function together as an important North Sea oil base.

Just uptown from the harbour, the huddle of sheds and warehouses gives way to the Mid Links. The Mid Links is one of those delights for which Montrose is famous. It is a public park divided up with grassy play areas, formal lawns, flower-beds and trees. Dignified private houses and imposing public buildings flank its perimeter. Near the south end, Montrose Academy stands across the whole width of the Links and the building is presently being extended further across into the Bow Butts. The façade of the existing Academy is an impressive neo-Greek front with steps up to the main doorway and three adjoining doors, with attractive fanlights, giving access. Two *trompe l'oeil* pillars flank the entrance and a rotunda clock tower with gilded dome surmounts the whole.

Montrose Academy has one rather unusual claim to fame. It enjoys the reputation of being the first establishment in Scotland to teach the Greek language. Erskine of Dun, that multi-faceted personality, was credited with bringing a Frenchman, one Monsieur Marsilliers, to teach Greek at the Grammar School in Montrose. It is an odds-on chance he found him in Marseilles, but whatever his origin, M. Marsilliers is claimed to have made Montrose Academy 'the cradle of the

81

Greek language in Scotland'. One wonders about that, but Montrose is adamant. Whether or not he was the first in Scotland, it is recorded that M. Marsilliers definitely did teach Greek in Montrose Academy – or Grammar School as it then was – and he was succeeded in that capacity by George Wishart. The same George Wishart who was subsequently burned at the stake in St. Andrews at the instigation of Cardinal Beaton. Wishart had become one of the 'heretics' who were campaigning for Church reform.

There is no doubt that in the sixteenth and seventeenth centuries, Montrose did have a widely renowned school. Another of its famous Old Boys of the period was Andrew Melville (1545-1622) who was educated and subsequently became a teacher in Montrose. He went on to study and to teach in Geneva before returning to Scotland in 1574 to be Principal of Glasgow University. In 1580 he was appointed Principal of St. Andrews University where he set new standards for higher education that were universally adopted. Of even greater significance at that time was his espousal of the Presbyterian cause and his advocacy of greater democratic control of the Church. For his pains he was exiled in 1585 and became a Professor of languages at Sedan where he died in 1622. If the Montrose folk do tend to blaw in their ain lugs about the Academy, they have sound reason.

All along the east flank of the Links, from the beautiful old Victorian buildings in Melville Gardens – built 1887, as the carving on the front proudly proclaims – past the Academy and Paton's Mill, that crumbling relic of the Industrial Age, through Union Place to Wellington Gardens, there are treasures of domestic architecture. The Georgian town houses of Union Place are still intact although the servants' quarters in the basements have now been modified into desirable flats in their own right. The whole line of the Mid Links holds Georgian, Victorian, Edwardian and later twentieth-century houses interspersed with older cottages which have been modernised.

On the western side in Panmure Place, is Montrose Museum, a small but effective building in classic style, modernised inside but untouched on the outer. Panmure Terrace is a row of dignified houses set back from the street with little front flower

Montrose Highland Games, Clydesdales being judged.

beds and basement flats. Opposite the Terrace, in the middle
of the Links, is the Episcopal Church of SS Mary and Peter.
This building was the original St. Peter's Church which
amalgamated with St. Mary's in 1920 to form the combined
charge. It has an interesting beamed roof and an impressive
side chapel with a beautiful triptych. The tranquil churchyard
is one of the hidden gems of Montrose.

The gates of SS Mary and Peter's church are simple iron
yetts of durable construction. They must be, they have been
there since they were presented to the church by an expatriate
Montrosian from Gothenburg in 1722. The link with
Scandinavia was forged by the trade in flax and timber but it
was productive of more than just money. A cultural and artistic
exchange ensued, and with the emigration of many Montrose
men to Scandinavia, a close bond was formed.

The Episcopal Church in Montrose was not the only church
in Montrose to benefit from Scandinavian generosity. The
Parish Kirk has its hearse, or chandelier, which was presented
even earlier in the seventeenth century by an Admiral of the
Swedish Navy who was, in fact, a Montrose lad called Clark. He
was one of the Montrose emigrants to Sweden who went on to
become famous in his adopted land. In the Stockholm Museum
today one of the treasures on display is a silver-gilt chalice
made by Donat Feiff. Donat Feiff was the son of a Montrose

silversmith called Donald Fyfe. Say Donald Fyfe with a Swedish accent and you get Donat Feiff.

The fact that Donat Feiff was a silversmith is significant in itself. Montrose was a famous centre of the silversmith's and goldsmith's art in the seventeenth century. The Tudor rose of the Montrose hallmark was a much-sought mark of quality in its day. Try to buy a seventeenth-century Montrose-marked silver chalice today – or even the odd Montrose spoon – and you'll find that it still is.

Down from the Mid Links the road runs to the sea front. A few years back, Montrose used to advertise itself at the main entrance to the town as possessing 'The finest beach in Scotland'. It no longer does so. It may have been the Trades Description Act, it may have been objections from other beach-owning towns, it may even have been a rush of atypical Montrose modesty which prevailed but the sign is no longer there. Truth has triumphed. Montrose beach is very, very good but the best beach in Scotland is at Oldshoremore.

The oil industry is the present boom trade in Montrose, and while Aberdeen and Peterhead grab the headlines as oil centres, Montrose is quietly beavering away for itself. Several ancillary enterprises – like the Offshore Fire Training Centre – are flourishing in their own right and keeping the Montrose economy buoyant. The Centre celebrated its tenth anniversary in 1988 and the firefighters gave a powerful display of the techniques they teach their trainees. They have facsimile production platforms and North Sea oil installations to work on, and every facet of fire control and prevention is covered. The Montrose Offshore Fire Training Centre is now a world leader in its sphere and is recognised internationally as such. Firemen come from all over the world on courses and to study the research and development of firefighting skills. As part of the training programme the Centre regularly sets off practice conflagrations of terrifying intensity. Vast clouds of thick black smoke from oil fires belch up from the mock-up rigs. Passing tourists invariably rush to the scene like so many moths.

On the landward side of the rolling sand dunes that line the famous beach, there are two golf courses. Until recently there were five different Golf Clubs using them but a recent rationalisation has cut that to three. The two courses run throuither, as though golf wasn't bad enough without that. About a hundred years ago, D.H. Edwards in his *Around the Ancient City* quoted an authority two hundred years before him who had rated Montrose golf course as 'next to St. Andrews in excellence'. D.H. then went on to say that 'recently a high authority declared it to be one of the three best in Scotland'. Dropping only one place in two hundred years is good going but the last hundred has seen it slide. You would be hard pushed to find a 'high authority' now who would list either the Medal or the Broomfield in the Top Twenty. Broomfield is one of the courses and Broomfield is also the site of Montrose Airfield.

Montrose airfield leads us into an area of turbulence. It is claimed, by Montrose, that Montrose aerodrome is the oldest in Britain. A copy of the *Dundee Courier* of August 1988 carries the report: 'To mark the seventy-fifth anniversary of Montrose Air Station, the oldest aerodrome in Britain, a programme of unusual events has been planned by Montrose Aerodrome Museum Society for next weekend'.

Research reveals that Lt. F. Waldron of No. 2 Squadron, Royal Flying Corps, flew a Box Type Pusher Biplane into a prepared landing strip at Upper Dysart farm on 26 February 1913. That is pretty far back in flying history. Lt. Waldron had flown from Farnborough, so presumably Farnborough must have had an older aerodrome. Lt. Waldron did the journey in stages, so presumably there were intermediate older aerodromes. Upper Dysart airfield was vacated in January 1914 for Broomfield, so Broomfield is, at most, second to Upper Dysart. Lt. Waldron was a member of No. 2 Squadron, R.F.C., so presumably No. 1 Squadron had been flying for some time previously, using airfields. One does not cavil but one wonders. Can it be that Montrose has 'posed aristocratically amongst its more plebeian compeers' yet again?

The Border between Angus and the Mearns

On leaving Montrose, with only the flicker of a smile on the lips, one sees the separate suburb of Hillside up on the left over the fire-fighting school. Hillside is a village in its own right as well as a residential adjunct to Montrose with the complex of Sunnyside Asylum dominating the whole. It is no longer called Sunnyside Asylum but it was opened as such in 1757 when it was a pioneer of its kind. In 1757 mental illness was regarded as a hopeless affliction and the only treatment, incarceration.

The opening of Sunnyside Asylum marked the beginning of a more enlightened approach. Ever since then, the various units of what is now Sunnyside Royal Hospital have catered for the treatment of different forms of behavioural and addictive disorders. The most advanced techniques are now researched and practised at Sunnyside and it is rated amongst the best. Many innovative developments have originated there, and the present climate of opinion towards the care and treatment of mental illness generally owes much to the work of Sunnyside Royal Hospital.

The road through Hillside from Montrose is the A937 which links up with the A94(T) on the Laurencekirk bypass. The main road from Montrose to Aberdeen is the A92 which eventually joins the A94(T) to form the A92(T) on the Stonehaven bypass. Such are the fancies of roadmakers.

The A92 out of Montrose crosses the North Esk at the Lower Northwater Bridge, and the North Esk is the boundary between Angus and the Mearns. The Lower Northwater Bridge is a long narrow structure with an imposing plaque built in at the Montrose end. It looks an important feature, that plaque, but passers-by are advised to keep on passing. There is no adequate parking area and any car left within half a mile of the Montrose end of the Lower Northwater Bridge is a hazard and a danger to passing traffic. Anyone attempting to read that plaque will be subjected to obloquy from passing lorry drivers, and rightly so. Anyone persevering and succeeding in reading the imposing plaque is doomed to disappointment. It carries no thrilling tale of derring-do; it bears no poignant picture of runaway son or thwarted lover; it is just a list of subscribers and a congratulatory message of typical Montrose self-satisfaction. (Things not to bother about in Angus and the Mearns: No. 2. The plaque on the Lower Northwater Bridge.)

A more interesting feature of the bridge is the railing which runs along the parapet on both sides as far as the middle of the

The glorious sweep of St Cyrus Bay. The Conservancy Council's National Nature Reserve is on the right.

bridge. The railing stops there. Whilst the old border of Angus and Kincardineshire was the river – and presumably the middle of the river – how can a railing running only halfway across any river be justified? Hours of constructive thinking can be spent working out answers to that one.

The North Esk at the Lower Northwater Bridge is a scene of great angling activity. Upstream, in season, the river is dotted with anglers practising their wiles trying to catch fish. If your visit coincides with the running of the finnock, you may even see them catch one. Finnock is the name given locally to the young of the sea trout. Gallovidians call them 'herling', other folk call them 'sewin'. Whatever the name, the young of the sea trout are periodically prone to rush up our rivers in shoals. Driven by an atavistic urge and a yen for excitement, they career up our river channels snapping indiscriminately at passing lepidopterae in a wanton *joie de vivre*. Sometimes the anglers are successful.

On such occasions, should you come upon such a North Esk

angler and ask him what lure he is using to catch his fish, the answer is, invariably, 'A wee blue flee' . . . Stuff, sir, and nonsense. I know these North Esk anglers. They deal in esoteric things and obfuscation is part of their craft. The North Esk angler declines to tell the stranger what he is using in case the stranger copies him and comes to stand next to him and takes all the fish. Hence the 'wee blue flee'. What your North Esk man really uses is a minute piece of yellow tubing body dressed with a wisp of hare's lug and mounted on a size sixteen treble. Just do not, for the life of me, tell him I told you.

Downstream from the Lower Northwater Bridge there is a salmon hatchery run by a local Montrose firm. They have sheds and tanks and all the impedimenta and scientific paraphernalia of modern pisciculture. Salmon are valuable chiels. Visitors are welcome only by prior appointment; if then. Below the bothy, the river rather loses itself. Side channels and backwaters appear and the old river course runs off to the left. In 1879 the river changed course here and cut a new channel through to the sea.

Approaching St. Cyrus from the Nature Reserve

This area, on the north side of the river, is the start of the Nature Conservancy Council's National Nature Reserve at St. Cyrus, and a fascinating area it is. The course of the old river bed is now – slunks again – a saltmarsh, which means that it supports plants which are capable of existing in a salt water environment. The sea used to flood this part regularly but a storm in 1967 shut off the marsh from the sea with a huge sand bar and the sea seldom penetrates now. Slowly the nature of the whole shoreline is changing.

The Nature Conservancy Council is the body appointed by the Government to promote nature conservation. At St. Cyrus it oversees 92 hectares of saltmarsh, dunes and cliffs by agreement with the owners, Tay Salmon Fishery Company, Perth, and Joseph Johnstone, Montrose. The Reserve is maintained for the benefit of the native plants, birds, butterflies and folk. The public is encouraged to visit and walk the area, except for a spell from May to August when there is no access to a designated sanctuary zone. Other than that, visitors are welcome to come at any time and enjoy the glorious beach, the dunes and the cliffs and all the myriad plant and bird life that proliferates around them. There is a permanent warden, assisted by local honorary and volunteer wardens. Anyone regretting the imposition of Nature Reserve status on St. Cyrus in 1965 should pause to consider what kind of a cesspit the place would be by now had it not been.

It is amazing how much one can learn, about things one should have known years ago, in a visit to St. Cyrus Nature Reserve. Birds, flowers and butterflies cease to be just birds, flowers and butterflies and become individual species. Stretches of wind-blown grassy shoreline classify into sand dunes, dune pastures and gorse land. A talk with any of the wardens can disclose that Nottingham catchfly is actually a plant, a whinchat is a bird and some painted ladies are butterflies. The cliffs are shown to vary from sea cliff and scree slope to inland cliff and grassland, each harbouring its own floral and avian population.

One has always known the joys of walking, running and playing on the unspoiled beach of St. Cyrus, but how reassuring it is to know that it is being retained and preserved for our children. Not in the artificial, neon-lit, plastic playground fashion of the age but naturally and correctly, as it should be; as it used to be. Go to St. Cyrus any time. In the dog days of summer it is the perfect play beach; in the mellow brown evenings of autumn it is a sanctuary; in the blustery, cloud-capped wind-blown mirk of winter it is an invigorating challenge and in the soft sweet rain of a spring morning it is the earthly promise of paradise to come. St. Cyrus is perfect.

St. Cyrus village is at the top of the cliff with the landmark of its kirk steeple visible for miles. Originally it was a scattered hamlet at the foot of the cliff on the shore. Until the seventeenth century the whole area was called Ecclesgreig and the remains of chapels built beside the old burying ground are all that now remain of the lower settlement. The salmon fishers have always had bothies along the shore, for salmon fishing has always been the staple of St. Cyrus. Fixed stake nets run out from the beach and tethered bag nets extend beyond them.

Salmon (*Salmo salar*) is a migratory species of fish which spawn in European rivers – fortunately including the North

A closer view of St Cyrus steeple which is a landmark for many miles around.

and South Esks – and grow to maturity at sea. After spawning, the ovae develop into 'smolts' which eventually drift down to the sea and set off on their migration. For centuries it was imagined that the young salmon simply swam around indiscriminately in the sea feeding and growing wherever they chose. Then the truth was discovered. All the salmon which are hatched in Scottish rivers head straight for the waters around Greenland where they feed voraciously on krill and sprats and grow rapidly. Some of them return after a year and retrace their journey right back to their native rivers and spawning grounds. These are called 'grilse'. Others stay longer at sea but all eventually return at some time to spawn in their own river. This predictability is their undoing. The path of salmon returning to the North and South Esks is down the east coast past St. Cyrus. The St. Cyrus men knew this long before it was discovered, by tagging, where they were coming from. The St. Cyrus men didn't much care where they were coming from. Experience had taught them that at certain times salmon in large numbers were to be found swimming resolutely past their doors. Further experience taught them that a returning salmon will always return and nothing will prevent it. They built barrier nets which stopped the salmon in their tracks. Faced with a wall of netting too small-meshed to go through, the salmon has two options: to go up and down or right and left. Up, the net extends out of the water; down, it is pegged to the bottom. Right, he runs out of sea; left, is the deep water he instinctively seeks. He goes left. The St. Cyrus men are one jump ahead. Nosing along the barrier net to the left, the salmon is led quietly into a trap. The barrier net leads into an ingenious system of double nets which ends in a closed pocket. As the tide drops the netted salmon is removed by one of the fishermen, aptly called a 'flyman', who uses a massive pole-net to scoop up the fish. The art of the flyman demands courage, dexterity, training, expertise, dedication and more luck on a dark night than one would care to count on. Should you chance upon a St. Cyrus flyman at work, take time to study his method – not least the single, wristy, blow with which he despatches the unsuspecting fish.

The *coupe de grâce* is delivered by a priest. This is not some kind of Scotch Presbyterian kosher: a priest is a club for killing fish. Why a club for killing fish should be called a priest, I wot not. Nor do I wot why salmon are known exclusively as 'fish' in Angus. An Angus angler will say he caught 'Two sea trout and a finnock but no fish'. When he says he caught 'a fish' he means a salmon. All very odd.

The name 'St. Cyrus' itself has been known to cause talk amongst etymologists. Some speak of Cyrus, a martyr in Antioch, others of Cyrus the Monothelite Bishop of Alexandria, whilst there are those who say that Cyrus was a local man from Ecclesgreig. This last bunch cite the presence of St. Cyrus' well and St. Cyrus, ward as conclusive proof. You may choose. You may choose further with Ecclesgreig. Ecclesgreig is derived from *Ecclesia Gregorii*, the church of St. Gregory, but which St. Gregory? There were several. The choice is yours.

Had we not approached St. Cyrus from the Nature Reserve below the cliff, we could have turned off the A92 just as it starts to climb up from the Lower Northwater Bridge. A sharp turn to the left off the main road there leads to Stone of Morphie and through to Marykirk. Over the hill the eponymous Stone of Morphie stands right by the road at the edge of the farm steading. A huge, ten-feet-high obelisk in the stackyard marks Stone of Morphie farm. No plaque disfigures that stone, no cement path vandalises it. The great primeval symbol stands firmly rooted in its parent rock although it was knocked over once, a few years ago. How it got there, no-one knows. If it was the Picts – any of them – they omitted to apply their distinctive carving. If it was the Romans, Agricola forgot to tell Tacitus to tell us that he was there. If it was the English, they would have broken it up before they left. It stands enigmatically alone. On its west flank there are three cusps as for cup and ring markings but no rings. Its beauty lies in its stark mystery.

Back on the A92 and farther up, past Commieston farm, it pays to stop and look back at the view. Behind and below, Montrose sits smugly in its bay, the land rises gently from the shoreline and the view over the mouth of the North Esk and up over Hillside is outstanding. All over Angus and the Mearns there are vantage points offering views of unparalleled beauty like this, but to appreciate them one has to quit the car to hear the sough of the wind, the skraich of the gull and feel the snell air of Angus on the cheek.

Through St. Cyrus, the B9120 leads off the A92 and up the hill right over by Laurencekirk to Fettercairn. This is a road that well repays the trip. At the start the shore lands of Angus and the Mearns lie open below with the coastline and sea adding a complementary contrast, but the B9120 holds a greater treasure. Over the crest of the hill past Smiddyhill and Garvock, the road drops steeply down to Laurencekirk. There is a viewpoint just there, at the corner of the road where it starts to drop down, with parking space provided, that offers one of the finest panoramas in all the land. The whole stretch of the Howe and the Strath unfolds below. The border of the Grampian hills forms a natural boundary to the long stretch of the glen, and all the wealth of Angus and the Mearns is contained in the intervening land. Field and stream, plough and pasture, cot and farm, all merge in a patchwork pattern of colour stretching from the uplands of the Mearns to the richly wooded low lands of Strathmore. The colours vary with the seasons and the most recent variation has come with the

The Stone of Morphie.

introduction of oilseed rape as a main crop. In June of each year now, the usual shades of green and brown are shattered by the vivid yellow of ripening oilseed. It is an exotic innovation in this land of douce folk and mellow landscape and brings a whiff of Continental abandon to our scene. A very little more will be too much. Other than that, the view is outstanding at any time and provides one of the best spots for a comprehensive view of the geographic entity that is Angus and the Mearns.

Onward to Johnshaven

Continuing on the A92 from St. Cyrus, one passes the roads down to Tangleha' and Burnfoot. Tangleha', of the delightful name, has a beach of banked pebbles to bring tears to the eyes of barefoot kiddies and send prospecting gemmologists ga-ga with delight. Sacks of semi-precious gemstones – agate, porphyry, crystal and the like – can be gathered at will. If you know which ones are agate, porphyry, crystal and the like. Burnfoot is a quiet little dell but presently an endangered area, from tourism.

The fishing village of Johnshaven is something of a relic now with only one man fishing regularly out of it and a few part-timers playing at it. The old houses are being done up, and done in, but no amount of modernisation can affect the crazy town plan of the original. Johnshaven looks as if it got there by falling over the cliff. The old houses were built just where the old fishermen fand a bit beild. Wherever a neuk offered a hint of shelter from the prevailing gales, up went a house. Where a cranny gave protection from the salt sea spray, down went a garden plot. There are lanes in old Johnshaven where fat wifies dursna venture. The modern Council houses have fair spoiled the character of the place.

In 1722 Johnshaven was reckoned to be 'amongst the first fishing towns of Scotland' (*Statistical Account*). It had twenty-six boats in all, thirteen engaged in the deep-sea fishing and thirteen inshore. In all there were about two hundred and fifty fishermen working out of Johnshaven. This number declined when disaster struck the fleet at sea in 1743 and two of their boats foundered with all hands. In 1756 the Seven Years' War began against Austria and France and the British Navy needed more sailors in a hurry. They got them by the process of 'impressment'. In the summer of 1756 a Naval tender intercepted the Johnshaven fleet and 'pressed' the best men from each boat into the Navy. The Government then passed a law saying that one in every five fishermen from every fishing port had to serve in the Navy. All these factors reduced the Johnshaven fleet to a handful and by 1775, the year when the American colonists ceased to appreciate what was good for them, the Johnshaven fleet was reduced to five boats and a

Johnshaven: rush hour.

struggle to find crews. Ultimately they ended up with one deep-sea boat at the summer fishing and four or five yawls crewed by old men and boys, working inshore in winter.

In the 1790s a Dundee firm set up a factory to make sailcloth in Johnshaven, employing about fifty men and women. This was a logical development of the traditional cottage industry of the area which had been practised all along the east coast for a century or more. Flax from the Baltic and Holland was brought in to Arbroath and Montrose and distributed to individual spinners around the area. The Dundee initiative in Johnshaven was simply the natural progression of the existing local trade.

In the eighteenth and early nineteenth centuries the spinning of thread for the linen and sailcloth factories of Brechin, Forfar, Montrose, Arbroath and Dundee was nearly all done in the Mearns. There were two great cottage industries – conducted mainly by the womenfolk – spinning thread from flax and knitting stockings from wool. The men worked the land and the fishing, or as tradesmen in the ancillary trades, but the women kept the home fires burning brighter by outworking for the factories. The Johnshaven and St. Cyrus women in particular. They were so adept at spinning thread from flax that they worked a two-handed system whereby they spun two threads at the same time with a boy winding them on to a wheel at the other end of the kitchen. Your present-day business efficiency consultants couldn't demand any better Unit Production/Cost Analysis ratio than that. The introduction of improved spinning machines led to the centralisation into factories and the wifies became factory hands.

The spinning mill has gone from Johnshaven now, along with the fishing, but one industry does remain. Murray McBay and Co., Shellfish Merchants, handle nearly all the lobster and crab that are landed around our coasts. The big shed on the left as you go down to the harbour is their headquarters and they have huge holding tanks there to keep the crustacea alive and nipping until they are exported. The more exclusive fish restaurants of Paris serve only Johnshaven lobsters. On the Richter scale of nightmares, falling into a McBay lobster tank rates second only to falling into one of these road tankers full of live eels that go to France; or so my wife says. The shed which has the tanks at Johnshaven is itself a relic of the old days for it was originally a herring curing shed. It is a long time since they cured herring in Johnshaven.

The McBays of Johnshaven are one of the oldest fisher families of the area. One of the boats that was lost in 1743 had a McBay father and his twelve-year-old youngest son aboard. That father was the great-great-great-great-great-grandfather of the present McBay brothers of Johnshaven. With a family history like that, it should be assumed that the McBays are accepted as natives of Johnshaven. Not so, say the McBay brothers. They are incomers, they came from Miltonhaven, just down the coast.

Miltonhaven, or Milton of Mathers, no longer exists. It was a fishing village built on a shingle beach behind a long bank of limestone rock. When the lime trade started up in the area the rock at Miltonhaven was quarried extensively. In 1795 a storm broke through the quarry workings and the whole bank was breached. The sea rushed in and carried away the entire village. The present village of Milton of Mathers, or Tangleha', was built just inland of the old site. McBays were among the people lost in that disaster but a branch of the family had

Gourdon, harbour and village.

already established itself in Johnshaven. Folk around Johnshaven tell you that Macbeth, Shakespeare's Macbeth, was sib to the McBays.

That Pretty Little Place, Gourdon

Before leaving Johnshaven it is always worth remembering to make a complimentary reference to Gourdon as you depart. It adds a little spice. It is not advisable to make complimentary references to Gourdon as you enter Johnshaven; that way lies trouble. A casual remark that one is now going on to visit 'that pretty little place, Gourdon' is usually enough. You will then be subjected to an impassioned critique of every human frailty, natural shortcoming and practical disadvantage of the neighbouring village. The common rivalry that affects adjacent communities is here elevated to Star Wars level. They are so close together, so alike physically and sharing an identical *modus vivendi* that they really do loathe each other. My last attempt to gauge the depth of local feeling ended with my elderly Johnshaven friend, hatred flaming from his eyes, destroying the last vestiges of Gourdon dignity with the

97

summing-up: 'Naethin', he spat, 'that was gude ever cam' oot o' Gurden'. His case rested.

Just out of Johnshaven, Lathallan School occupies the old Brotherton Castle – although Brotherton Castle is not so old as most castles tend to be. The building was erected by one Scott, a Dundee jute manufacturer, in 1850. The Scott family lived in · it until 1948 when it was sold to an Aberdeen haulage contractor who sold it, in turn, to Lathallan School in 1951. Lathallan is really in Fife but the original Fife school was burned down and when the school transferred to Brotherton in 1951 they kept the Lathallan name.

Lathallan school is a prep school for boys and girls aged seven to thirteen. It prepares them for the Common Entrance exam which admits them to secondary school. It does not prepare pupils for any specific secondary schools; Lathallan pupils go on to all the major Scottish and English schools. One mentions that fact simply because the similarity in the names Lathallan and Strathallan makes people imagine that there is some connection between the two. Now you know. There can be no better situation for the primary education of youngsters than Lathallan school. The spacious buildings, the tree-girt grounds, the extensive playing fields make up the best possible environment for the young. If you have to go to school, it must be better to go to a school like that.

Gourdon is not at all as Johnshaven says. Gourdon is a lovely little sun-splashed fishing village with fish houses and curing sheds along the quay and a flourishing jute factory tucked unobtrusively away at the far end. Gourdon is the archetypal fishing port, less active than it once was but still maintaining a fishing industry. Only Gourdon and Stonehaven fish the sma' lines now and only three Gourdon boats and two Stonehaven keep the lines going at all; the other boats fish cod nets.

Most casual visitors to Gourdon seem, simply, to drive down to the harbour, park their cars, wander out and back along the jetty and hurry off to find ice cream and crisps. They peer uncomprehendingly into the boats, smile condescendingly at the men mending nets, marvel at the size of the gulls on the harbour wall and get in the way of Jim Lownie's and Doug Welsh's workers. That is tourism in action. It brings profit to the sellers of ice cream and crisps.

A more penetrating study of Gourdon would enlighten the visitor and inform him that there are eleven boats fishing regularly out of the port. Five are trawling for sole, plaice, cod and haddock; three are sma' lining for haddock and cod; three are gill-netting for cod. Thirty full-time fishermen crew the boats. It is Gourdon's good fortune that her young men still want to go to sea. When the fish are landed they are laid out on the quay for Gordon Lownie, the auctioneer, to sell. Most of the catch is bought by the local, Gourdon, curers and fish merchants. Any surplus is sent off to be sold in Aberdeen. The Gourdon men clean, gut, fillet and process their fish in fish houses along the quayside and eight little vans cart them off to sell around the countryside. The only 'processing' that is done is to smoke some of them over oak chips in the traditional way. The vans cover the whole of Angus and the Mearns and some go as far north as Inverurie and some as far south as Perth. Wherever they go, they sell fresh, clean, hygienically handled fish at reasonable prices. Would you believe that the E.E.C. is now going to insist that all these vans must be replaced with 'mobile shops' having walk-in customer access and hot and cold running water? That will kill off the present Gourdon trade in a wanny.

It might, on the other hand, make not a whit of difference. Disaster has a way of looming a lot but striking seldom. One new line fisher is going out this year and who knows what may happen in the future. Some years ago, in the '60s, Gourdon struck lucky for a time and it is always possible that something similar could happen again. This time it need be no more than a change in E.E.C. regulations.

The last time the Gourdon men hit the jackpot it was the salmon. New methods of drift netting with mono-filament nylon nets gave them a short time bonanza. They still recall it on the harbour wall of a summer's evening. The salmon were taken in lorry loads. Big, strong, broad-shouldered, deep-bellied salmon worth a fortune. The sma' lines were out and the gill nets were in. For a season or two – no more – the Gourdon men could scarcely believe their luck. They made more money in one year at the salmon than they did in a decade at the haddock.

It was much too good to be true. Vested interests,

conservationists, fishery protection officers and income tax men girded their respective loins and waded in. A stop was put. For a time it was the stuff of thriller writers. Boats creeping in and out of harbour at dead of night, spies lying along cliff tops with telescopes by day, flashing lights, Court injunctions and writs and even, at the height of the action, a private gunboat. The only thing they appear to have lacked was muffled oars. Every other ingredient of your ripping yarn for boys was there but no-one seems to have thought of muffling an oar. It seems a pity. The Mearns press had almost as big a boom as the fishermen. The national dailies were quoting the local weeklies. It was heady stuff for Gourdon until the Law ended the trade and the Gourdon men were left with a lot of surplus mono-filament netting and some very happy memories. It still seems a pity, though, that they forgot to muffle the oars. It might have helped.

If your visitor to Gourdon is really interested in the place, he might consider wandering as far along as the factory at the far end of the village. This is Sidlaw Yarns' spinning factory which makes high-grade yarns for the top end of the jute trade. Jute is second only to cotton in present-day fabric usage. It appears as carpet backing, car upholstery, suit linings and the skips of ploughmen's bonnets. Except that ploughmen are now wearing damned baseball caps. The Gourdon factory produces yarns to the highest specifications of the trade and its product goes worldwide. This factory, and one in Bervie, are the last bastions of the traditional local thread industry.

Jute followed flax in the east of Scotland, and jute came in with the old 'John Company' of India. It was they who sent specimens of 'India Grass' back to Britain to see what could be done with it. The Indians had been using it for centuries. All sorts of folk all over the land had a go at finding a use for the stuff but only Dundee came up with a sensible answer. Dundee had been given a sample because Dundee already had a great flax industry. Dundee was also a great whaling port and one bright Dundee lad had the brilliant idea of soaking jute in whale oil to see if that would make it more pliable, less frangible and possibly suitable for spinning and weaving. The world's jute industry stemmed from that inspired experiment in Dundee when dry, crackling, jute fibre from India was first soaked in greasy, emollient whale oil from the Arctic.

The jute trade has gone from Scotland now and only a few surviving speciality firms remain. Sidlaw Yarns' factory in Gourdon is such a one. They continue to exist by maintaining their top-quality standard. They produce the best and there is always a market for the best. This pursuit of excellence in its jute and fishing industries has imbued Gourdon with a decent sense of dignity. Not for Gourdon the internecine passions of Johnshaven. Mention Johnshaven in Gourdon and you are met with patronising smiles. 'They Johnner lads' are regarded with amused tolerance in Gourdon. Is it possible – 'way back somewhere – could there be?, a drop of Montrose blood in Gourdon?

If there is just a tinge of self-satisfaction in Gourdon's attitude, it is certainly justified. Gourdon is a thriving, flourishing community whose success is based on traditional industries. When the rest of the country lies around bemoaning the fact that the old days have gone and harbours and jute mills stand idle and neglected, Gourdon just spits on its hands and yokes in. Gourdon isn't blessed with the best anchorage on the east coast, it makes the most of what it has. Jute spinning has no reason for continuing in Gourdon other than the hard graft and expertise of Gourdon folk.

'Bervie' and Lewis Grassic Gibbon

Round the Doolie Ness from Gourdon you come on to Bervie Bay and the town of Inverbervie. The map says 'Inverbervie' but it is seldom referred to as any more than 'Bervie' by the locals. The burn is called the Bervie water and the town is Bervie. It is an inoffensive little town, conforming adequately to the general requirements of contemporary society, and that's about it. Bervie's claim to fame, if ever it thought of claiming any, was that on the 4th of May, 1342, the eighteen-year-old King David II of Scotland and his sixteen-year-old French wife, Johanna, were driven ashore on Bervie beach. They were returning from France at the time and had been harried by English warships before being forced to run aground. In gratitude for his safe deliverance the young King bestowed a Royal Charter on the town. For most towns that would have been enough, but not for Bervie; Bervie lost its Charter – literally, lost – mislaid, missed, misplaced, deprived itself of and had to apply for a replacement. In 1595 the borough bailies rather shamefacedly approached the Court authorities and in due course King James VI was pleased to renew Bervie's Charter. That is fame of a kind.

Fame of another kind was accorded to Bervie by James Leslie Mitchell, *alias* Lewis Grassic Gibbon. When Leslie Mitchell wrote of 'Segget', everyone knew it was Bervie. He didn't say it was but everybody knew. Lewis Grassic Gibbon was the greatest prose writer Scotland ever produced – and if you recite his prose as it demands to be recited you will find he was also the greatest poet Scotland ever produced – but he was hard on Bervie. We can see the political case he was making, we know he was a committed reformer and an inspired writer, but he was hard on Bervie: nearly as hard as he was on Stonehaven.

James Leslie Mitchell was born in Aberdeenshire on 13 February 1901. His father was a crofter at Hillhead of Segget and in 1909 he moved down to Bloomfield in the Mearns, just above Bervie. When young Leslie Mitchell first went to Arbuthnot school he was 'paired', as was the custom, with one of the older girls. This was the method they had for helping the younger children with their reading and writing. Young Leslie was paired with Margaret Milne, the niece of the farmer at Drumyocher.

'He was a braw reader,' said Meg Milne to me, 'and a richt nice bairn he was, but an awfu' wee nuisance for asking questions.'

It seems that he asked the right questions. Lewis Grassic Gibbon is the man to read if you want the sound and smell and taste of the Mearns. *Sunset Song,* the first of his *Scots Quair* trilogy, is the best descriptive prose piece that has ever been written about rural Scotland. Any man who has ever yoked a horse on a sleet-slashed winter's morning to cart neeps from the rainsodden sheughs of the Mearns will vouchsafe the accuracy of his pen. The majority of men, who have not, will savour the essence of the experience from Mitchell. His struggle to balance the harshness of Nature and the sustained torture of repetitive manual labour with the spiritual yearnings of the human soul, precluded his ever being the crofter he was born to be. The conflict of academic and peasant in James Leslie Mitchell's fertile brain generated his literary genius. Mitchell was an intellectual and an accomplished historian, far beyond the recognition of the Mearns. His research and study of the Maya people of South America, published in *The Conquest of the Maya,* established him as a leading anthropologist in his day. He was a prolific writer on a wide range of subjects before writing ten novels. Read Professor Douglas F. Young's study of James Leslie Mitchell, *Beyond the Sunset,* for a true assessment of the man. The one thing not to do is to judge Leslie Mitchell on the televised adaptation of *A Scots Quair.* The laboured acting and stilted speech of the cast gave a poor interpretation of Mitchell's genius. His words must be read to be appreciated. His introduction of Scotch words to English sentences emphasises the parochial application of universal experience. Who else could encapsulate so much feeling in so few words as 'the pringling smell of a new-ploughed park' or 'the summer hills gurling in summer heat'? Read Lewis Grassic Gibbon – and read bits aloud to yourself – but spare Bervie.

Bervie's most famous son was Hercules Linton, and Bervie has commemorated him in a pretty little rose garden with seats and terraces, just off the main road at the north end of the town. Hercules Linton was the designer of the famous clipper ship *Cutty Sark.* He was a celebrity in his day and Bervie recognises his contribution to British ship design. The memorial is a facsimile of the *Cutty Sark* figurehead with Burns's wanton wee witch depicted in avant-garde T-shirt with plain round neckline, cap sleeves and abbreviated skirt: very fetching. The inscription says:

> In memory of Hercules Linton of Inverbervie 1836-1900, designer of the Clipper Ship 'Cutty Sark' launched at Dumbarton 22 Nov. 1869, and now preserved at Greenwich.
> Erected by the Royal Borough of Inverbervie and the Cutty Sark Society. Unveiled by Sir Francis Chichester 23 Oct. 1969

Right beside the memorial garden the bridge over the Bervie water starts. This bridge, which replaced the old single-span narrow structure still standing upstream, is impressive. It curves in a near semicircle over the ravine of the Bervie water with the actual stream trickling insignificantly through one of its many arches. The bridge was opened by the Rt. Hon. the Viscount of Arbuthnott on 21st August in 'The twenty-fifth year of the reign of H.M. King George V' which was, of course, 1935. The memorial plaque goes on to remind us that the Provost of Inverbervie, the Rev. Neil McGill, was present.

Bervie used to be a thriving industrial town with mills and weaving sheds for flax and jute but these are now reduced to one flax spinning works. This has just been bought over by Sidlaw Yarns, the company that operates the Gourdon mill. Bervie is awaiting the outcome with a degree of trepidation. There is no fishing industry in Bervie for there is no anchorage. The seafront is a shingle beach contained behind man-made barriers of concrete and wire mesh, and a uniformly unattractive picture it presents.

Over the years, writers on Bervie have always found themselves a bit short of factual subject matter, so they have tended to repeat whatever apocrypha they could find. The most quoted apocryphon is the most ridiculous. It is the Bervie version of the origin of the name 'Guthrie'. I offer it to you.

It happened when King David had just been driven ashore at Craig David. As he was being tended on shore after the ordeal, one of his courtiers called to a passing fishwife, 'Gut a fish for His Majesty's supper', whereupon the hungry King intruded, 'Gut twa'. 'Ah'll gut three,' replied the loyal subject and the King delivered the memorable punch-line, 'Then Gutthrie forever shalt thou be'. I ask you.

Arbuthnott and its Kirk

Over the Bervie bridge and up the hill on the Stonehaven road there is a turn-off to Arbuthnott which well repays a visit. Past Pitcarry and Mains of Allardice farms, there is a narrow, single-track road signposted 'Arbuthnott Church'. This takes you down the Den of the Bervie water to Arbuthnott Church, or the Kirk of Sanct Ternan Arbuthnott, as it used to be known. It is a most interesting little church, taking its name from Saint Ternan, a Pict of the fifth century AD, about whom little is known. The building has been altered, inevitably, over the centuries as it has been in continual use as a site of Christian worship since pre-Reformation times. Today's kirk is a mish-mash of architectural compromises that have resulted in a very pleasing little building. The nave is a long, narrow, plain structure mostly nineteenth century with the chancel, dedicated in 1242, incorporating most of the original, thirteenth-century remains. The Arbuthnott Aisle was added in 1500 by Sir Robert Arbuthnott of that Ilk and was developed from the old Lady Chapel which stood on the site. The bell tower at the west end of the nave was also built by Sir Robert at this time and it gives the church a distinguished, original look as you approach from the main gate. The whole building has an original look and any visitor should be sure to look for the wooden door on the right, inside the Arbuthnott Aisle, which gives access to a spiral stone stair and the room above. This room was built for the use of the priest and gives an insight into the practical working of the kirk, with its wee keek-hole for him to spy through before going down for the service.

Arbuthnott Kirk sits on a shelf just above the Bervie Water, it is a place of utter tranquillity. You can go down to Arbuthnott kirk on a bright spring morning, a hot summer's day, a mellow afternoon of autumn or in the snows of winter and you will find peace. It should be a place of pilgrimage: fortunately it is not. The spirit is refreshed by Arbuthnott Kirk. Two miles away on the A92 a steady stream of traffic thunders by; heavy lorries run nose to tail, private cars leapfrog the line. Every one going lickety split to save time and the occupants not knowing if they are reaching the Mearns or racing to ultima Thule. If mankind would just remember to keep contact with Nature, mankind would be spared a heap of trouble. Nature shows us, teaches us, leads and directs us and all we have to do is follow.

In a corner of the kirkyard of Arbuthnott, tucked in behind the dyke, is the grave of James Leslie Mitchell. Leslie Mitchell died on 7th February 1935 in Welwyn Garden City in Hertfordshire. The only instruction he left regarding his death was that he should be cremated. This was done at Golders Green Crematorium on 11th February, two days before his thirty-fourth birthday. Only a few of his friends were present and the simple ceremony was enhanced only by a brief eulogy from Ivor Brown, the writer and critic, one of Leslie's closest friends. It was his wife, Ray, née Rebecca Middleton, who felt that he should lie in the Mearns and it was Ray who arranged the simple ceremony of interment in Arbuthnott.

The burial of Lewis Grassic Gibbon's ashes was performed on 23rd February at two o'clock in the afternoon. It was a cold, sharp, day with a snell wind blowing off the hills but a bright warm sun shining from a pale blue sky. A day that held the razor chill of winter in the warm hand of spring. The bruised snowdrops that the mourners trampled so thoughtlessly underfoot, fairly marked that day. The mourners themselves were in ambivalent mood. They were there to support James and Lilias Mitchell in the loss of their son, forgetting for the moment the shame of his works, and they were there out of curiosity to see who else would be there. They were the country folk of the Mearns, and the country folk of the Mearns had never liked Leslie Mitchell.

James and Lilias, his parents, held themselves in dignified silence. Ray Middleton was in charge and Ray Middleton said a few valedictory words in lieu of a proper burial service. The mourners looked sideways and watched and shuffled nearer and added up the number of famous faces and enjoyed it all. The Mearns folk had never liked James Leslie Mitchell since he had written such disgusting things about them. Decent, clean-living folk they knew themselves to be and yet young Leslie Mitchell had made a name for himself writing dishonest – and downright dirty – stories about them. They saw through his Kinraddie and his Blawearie. They knew who he meant. Black affronted they had been. It was only right that the librarians were refusing to stock his books. Just a pity that he had made all that money out of them and been back up from London a month or two before showing off his new motor car and all his orders. Who did he think he was? Not even a decent Christian burial.

Whatever the day you visit Arbuthnott, it is appropriate. Lewis Grassic Gibbon belongs here: it is his home. Maybe his stark realism would seem to demand a grave in a bleaker setting: the bare braes o' Bervie or whaup-haunted Kinraddie moor, but he deserves his coothie corner. In his short and colourful life he achieved more than all the ploughmen and the lairds who lie around him. James Leslie Mitchell was one man who never forgot his umbilical link with Nature.

Back up on the A92, the road runs a mile or two along the coastline to Stonehaven. This is all good farming land. The sea winds crop the trees and drive the cattle into protective huddles in the field corners, but the land is rich. This is the country of the progressive landlords of the eighteenth and nineteenth centuries who changed Scotch agriculture from Stone Age simplicity to modern efficiency. The much publicised 'Turnip' Townshend and Jethro Tull – he of 'Horse-hoeing Husbandry' fame – in England in the 1730s, were equalled and surpassed by the men of the Mearns. Over the years such men as Graham of Morphie, Allardyce of Allardyce, Barclay of Urie, Keith of Benholm and Arbuthnott of that Ilk, all Mearns men, vied with each other to be better farmers and landlords. The great advances came with the change to the horse from the ox as a draught animal which allowed better ploughs to be used and when the old, free-range system ended in the eighteenth century and farms were enclosed, drained, manured, crop rotated and planted out with new crops. Clover, turnips, beans and potatoes were introduced and new strains of grain developed. Graham of Morphie was a pioneer of heavy horse breeding and Barclay of Urie was an improver of beef cattle. There was no aspect of farm management or animal husbandry that these men did not advance.

The land of the Mearns reflects this excellence. Where the rolling braes of the Mearns subside into the geometric precision of the fields of Angus, the whole area is a fertile stockyard. It needs only one crackpot academic to write a thesis saying that this was the original and only Garden of Eden and no-one is going to argue. Angus and the Mearns is a braw land.

Catterline and Crawton

Along the coast, just north of Bervie, cliff and rock and cove supplant each other until the next fishing village is reached at Catterline. There is no regular fishing from Catterline now, only the odd part-timer with a few creels. The village sits on top of the cliff above a lovely, sheltered, anchorage but few Catterline folk live there. All our villages are the same now. The locals can't get away to the towns quick enough and incomers buy their houses. It's a fact of present-day life.

Catterline is known now, not for the excellence of its fish or the appeal of its resident seals, but for the name of Miss Joan Eardley. Joan Eardley settled in Catterline and made a name for herself as an artist. She painted in two distinct genres – Glasgow street scenes and Catterline shoreline studies – and is equally effective in each. Her name now causes something of a conditioned reflex when Catterline is mentioned – 'Catterline': 'Joan Eardley' – and it is interesting to remember that Catterline and Joan Eardley originally existed very successfully quite independently of each other.

Catterline used to be a thriving fishing village on the clifftop above a sheltered anchorage. It is a scattered hamlet now with its two main rows of cottages but the scene of much alteration and development. Fortunately, Catterline is limited in its spread by the Den restricting it to the clifftop. The road into the village is narrow and twisting and the shoreline littered. The best thing about Catterline for years past has been the Creel Inn. Thirty years ago this was simply a fisherman's cottage that had one room for a bar and the living room doubled as restaurant. It was famous for its fresh lobster and crab dishes.

It has changed hands since then and been monstrously altered but lunch, set in front of a roaring fire on a blustery day recently, was better than ever. The present landlord is the inevitable incomer from the south of England but this one had the good grace to marry a Catterline lass and bring her home. He was a chef in one of London's more prestigious hotels before coming up to Catterline and the meal I had, a fresh haddock served with a lobster – yes – lobster sauce, was memorable. There was more but I mention it only because it was so unexpected in the circumstances. Just do not rush down on my recommendation. I doubt if Catterline can retain such another artist until you get there.

A couple of miles up the coast from Catterline is Crawton, another of these once flourishing fishing villages, now

The fortress castle of Dunnottar.

deserted. The ruins of cottages line the clifftop above the shingle beach and the natural rock bank where the boats used to be moored. In 1850, Crawton was a thriving community of twenty-three houses and a school. Thirty Crawton men fished twelve boats at the lines and creels and by 1870 they even had their own fish merchant. The decline of Crawton started in the 1880s and by the time of the First World War the fishing was nearly finished. The village lasted until 1927 when the last inhabitant left and the houses fell into decay. Only the ruins of the village remain with the houses of Crawton farm still occupied. Etymologists tell us that the name Crawton is derived from the Celtic *crobh*, a tree, and *ton*, ridge. That may well be but there can never have been many trees around Crawton at the best of times.

The next inlet to Crawton Bay is the Trollachy where the Crawton Burn tumbles over the cliff into the sea. The place was a known haunt of smugglers, like every other little inlet along the coast, but the Crawton men were rather better organised than most – and they didn't blame their neighbours like the Bervie men did. The Trollachy is at the start of the Fowlsheugh – how appropriate – Bird Sanctuary. The R.S.P.B.

has a two-mile stretch of cliff here which includes one of the great breeding sites for kittiwakes. The multitude of birds nesting at Fowlsheugh every Spring make a sight and sound not to be missed.

Dunnottar Castle to Stonehaven

From Crawton to Stonehaven the coast is rocky, steep and dangerous. The most notable feature of this section is the ruined castle of Dunnottar, but before reaching Dunnottar one pauses to remark on the number of secluded little gullies among the rocks and the apparently Cornish influence in the place names. Hope Cove, Trelung, Wine Cove, Tremuda. It might be that the Mearns and Cornwall shared a common interest: whatever could it have been?

Dunnottar Castle is one of the most important fortified sites in Scotland. It sits on a huge rock projecting as a peninsula from the mainland and its prime attraction as a fort was the extreme difficulty of access. With sheer cliffs rising from the sea in an almost complete circle, the only way on to the rock is by a narrow ravine and a rocky path rising from sea level. Even before it was fortified, it was the site of old Pictish temples. Carved Pictish stones found at Dunnottar have been carted around the countryside; some of them can now be seen at Banchory House. It is believed to have been one of the oldest settlements in the country. It obviously would be: anyone looking for a place to found a religious cell in a secluded spot away from the crowds couldn't hope for better than Dunnottar. There is no record of the first fortification of the rock but it is clear that, from the beginning, kirk and king competed for occupancy of such an ideal site.

The first known fully Christian settlement on Dunnottar was that of St. Ninian, around the fifth century AD. Ninian was one of the great evangelists of the early Christian faith and he founded churches from Whithorn on the south coast, right across lowland Scotland and up the east coast as far as, and far beyond, Dunnottar. That much is known. How the conflict of orthodox Christianity with Pictish primitivism was contained or conducted, we know not, except that there was the absorption of a degree of Pictish mythology into the Christian message. However that conversion was achieved, we know that Christianity superseded Pictish paganism on the rock of Dunnottar the same as it did at every other Pictish settlement. After Ninian's demise, there is no mention of Dunnottar for centuries. Many guesses have been made and every reference to any place with a name remotely like 'Dunnottar' has been taken to refer to the rock. Fact is lacking. The first positive history of Dunnottar, after the identification of Ninian's cell, comes in the twelfth century when William the Lion was engaged in founding the great Abbey of Aberbrothock (Arbroath). From then on, Dunnottar Castle figures regularly in the mélange of fact and fable that we call Scottish history.

The castle, which was by now a regular defensive emplacement, existed alongside the surviving chapel of St. Ninian, and along with the quarters for priests, acolytes, soldiers and followers, Dunnottar rock held quite a settlement. It became a focal point in any civil or military upheaval in the area and so it was duly captured by Edward I as part of his attempt to subdue Scotland. In 1297 William Wallace was leading the resistance to Edward and he successfully stormed Dunnottar and defeated the English garrison. The remnants of the English soldiery sought sanctuary in the chapel of the rock but Wallace paid scant heed to Christian principles and burned chapel and soldiers together. Not the kind of gallant act we like to attribute to our heroes.

In 1336 the English were back in Dunnottar Castle and on Wednesday 24th July of that year, King Edward III of England visited the castle on a triumphal tour of the region. Whether or not this visit was taken by the Scots as an added insult, we are not told, but as soon as he left, the castle was re-taken and held. In 1390 it came into the possession of Sir William Keith, Earl Marischal of Scotland, and he set about building a proper castle. The chapel which had been torched by William Wallace was now dismantled and replaced by one built a mile or so up-country. No doubt the priests realised the inconvenience of sharing a prime site with a battleground and were quite happy to move. The Bishop of St. Andrews was not happy. He arranged for Sir Wm. Keith to be excommunicated for desecrating the holy ground by building barracks on it. The matter was resolved in 1395 when the Pope restored the Earl Marischal to full membership and the rebuilding of Dunnottar Castle continued apace.

Successive Earls Marischal of the same Keith family inherited Dunnottar and continued to develop it over the centuries. It figures prominently when Mary Queen of Scots returned from France in 1561 and made several visits to Dunnottar between 1562 and 1564. Mary was followed there by King James VI in 1580, 1589 and 1594. Half a century later, King Charles II was there to visit the 7th Earl Marischal. These visits show the importance of the place. Its strength as a fortress is reflected in the fact that many national treasures and valuables were stored there for safety including the Crown, Sword and Sceptre, the Honours of Scotland.

In 1651, Cromwell's Roundhead army besieged and captured the castle but most of the valuables and State papers had already been removed. The story of how the Honours of Scotland were smuggled out by Mrs Grainger, the wife of the Reverend James Grainger of Kinneff, is one of the great romantic sagas of Scottish history. It is also almost entirely fictitious. The Regalia were indeed removed secretly from the castle and were buried in Kinneff Kirk, but the tales of 'the valour and initiative of one woman' who 'pushed Scotland's Crown up under her skirts' are total fabrication.

No-one knows how the Regalia were removed; it was done secretly. The Mrs Grainger story is only one of many and its sole foundation is that a grant was subsequently made to the Rev. Grainger for his part in concealing the Regalia. Around that fact a fantasy has been created. Another tale, no doubt equally spurious, is that the State papers were smuggled out by being 'carefully stitched into a flat belt round her middle' by Anne Lindsay, a kinswoman of the Governor, whilst the Regalia were simultaneously lowered down the rock to a serving wench who was there 'on pretence of gathering dulse and tangles'. The provenance of such tales is impossible to trace but fascinating to study.

History is an amalgam of fact, fiction, surmise, hearsay and prejudice, but it's all we have. We're stuck with it. Voltaire described history as 'no more than accepted fiction', and you can accept whatever fiction you like about the Honours of Scotland. It becomes history as soon as you accept it. The most interesting thing about it all is the way the tale becomes embellished in the telling. Mrs Grainger started off simply as the wife of the man who was rewarded for looking after the Regalia. She was then introduced to the actual removal from the castle. We next hear her appeal to Cromwell's Commander for permission to visit the Governor's wife 'since she was sure that English gentlemen did not make war on women'. Bits were added at every telling until the present version has General Morgan, O.C. Garrison, helping her on to her horse – with the crown of Scotland stuffed up her skirt – and quite failing to notice that 'she must have looked a great deal more pregnant than when she arrived'. You silly General!

However you care to view the story of the Scottish Regalia and their removal from Dunnottar Castle, there is no doubt that it's all good tourist stuff. Every tourist attraction must have its essential element of romance. Dunnottar Castle drips with it. One of the most attractive features for the tourist is the part restored in 1925 by Lady Cowdray. It is a pleasant surprise to open a door in a ruined castle and walk into a refurbished sitting room. Even if the Sovereign's initials on the ceiling are those of King George V and his Queen Mary. At least the commemorative notice shows that Lady Cowdray did not subscribe to the Mrs Grainger myth. Lady Cowdray obviously supported the Governor and Mrs Ogilvie myth.

Beyond Dunnottar lies Stonehaven, but before arriving there one sees, and most probably passes, a tomb-like Grecian temple up on the right-hand side of the road above the cliff. This is Stonehaven War Memorial. There, are written the real facts of history. Stonehaven War Memorial sits out of the town on the hilltop overlooking the bay. It is a stone circle of pillars round a rectangular obelisk with the names of the Stonehaven men who died in two World Wars engraved on the walls. It is a lonely place; a weather-beaten, wind-blown prominence, most appropriate to its purpose. It takes a conscious effort to climb up to the Stonehaven War Memorial and that in itself is significant. You do not pass it idly. The people who make the effort to climb up to visit the Memorial do so on a pilgrimage.

The names on that Memorial are the names of Stonehaven men. Young Stonehaven men who went to war because it was expected of them to go to war and to die for their country and they did. They had no other cause to die so young. They answered the call of duty and they died for it. They are the stark statistics of history.

CHAPTER 6

Stonehaven and a New Direction

Stonehaven is a busy little town with a good harbour, a spacious beach, a thriving shopping centre and just about everything your busy little town could ask for. The Stonehaven folk reflect the wellbeing of their town. There are no more friendly folk than the good burghers of Stonehaven.

The original settlement at Stonehaven was no more than the small fishing village tucked in behind Downie Point, where the harbour is now, and bounded by the Carron Burn. A rival village, Cowie, existed farther up north of the Cowie Burn and the expanse of Stonehaven Bay divided them. They are all one now and Stonehaven is spreading like every other little town, spreading over the farm lands of its perimeter. The good burghers of Stonehaven are now about 82.4% incomers.

In 1781 the first proper bridge was built over the Carron and the New Town of Stonehaven dates from then. The 'New Town', 'Old Town' and 'Cowie' names are still used by the locals to distinguish the separate areas. The most recent improvement has been the construction of the bypass road which has restored a measure of order to the town's traffic.

The story of the Old Town of Stonehaven is inextricably bound up with the story of Dunnottar Castle. The little harbour of Stonehaven, round the corner from the Castle – two corners if you count Strathlethan Bay – was claimed by all the warring factions who disputed ownership of the rock. It was hard enough for the simple fisher folk of the Carron shore to wrest a living from the sea without having to cope with the demands and orders of all the upstarts who kept chasing each other away and changing the rules, but cope they did. Whether it was Picts, Scots, Scotch, English, Priest, King or avenging army, Stonehaven took the brunt of the action. James Graham, Marquess of Montrose, laid waste to Stonehaven in 1644. Cromwell laid waste to Stonehaven in 1651. General Monk laid waste to Stonehaven in 1657. Butcher Cumberland laid waste to Stonehaven in 1746, and when these boys laid waste, they

Stonehaven Bay and town.

laid waste. Houses, boats, churches, crops and even trees were burned. Nothing of any worth was left. The marvel is that there was always a Stonehaven to lay waste.

In 1600 Stonehaven had been created the County Town of Kincardineshire when the seat of the Sheriffdom of Kincardine was transferred there from the old Kincardine township at Kincardine Castle. Stonehaven was a more active and useful centre because of its harbour trade. When this had been done, the old Kincardine town simply faded away until there is no trace of it left today other than the ruins of Kincardine Castle near Fettercairn. The Mercat Cross which stands today in Fettercairn is the old Kincardine Cross.

When Stonehaven became the administrative centre of the County, it was essential to have a municipal building and there was only one suitable building in the town – the storehouse belonging to the Earl Marischal on the north side of the harbour. This building was rapidly modified to make a courthouse and a prison. It still stands today, restored and renovated, as the Tolbooth Museum and Tea Room, opened by the Queen Mother in 1963. The rest of the Old Town developed along the sea front towards Downie Point and inwards from that line.

When Robert Barclay of Ury built his bridge over the Carron in 1781, it was not built entirely out of the goodness of his heart for the people of Stonehaven. It certainly was an act of some degree of benevolence but qualified by the fact that he was then able to advertise desirable building sites for sale on the north bank. The New Town of Stonehaven stems from the benevolence or the astute business sense of Robert Barclay of Ury in 1781. The New Town was designed around a central market square called – who could have guessed? – Barclay Square. Local ornithologists having reported no sightings of nightingales, the name was changed to Market Square. A Market House was built in the square and later, in 1857, a clock tower was added. Around this nucleus of the Square and its perimeter streets, Stonehaven grew up. The railway reached the town in 1848 but the topography of the area necessitated the siting of the station up the hill from the town. This made for more building up the hill and a prosperous suburbia soon linked Stonehaven and its railway station.

The railway brought holidaymakers to Stonehaven, and with a good beach and most of the attractions that nineteenth-century holidaymakers craved, the place prospered. All the fun of the fair was laid on for the visitors and a makeshift promenade was extended out to Cowie. In 1895 a proper promenade was constructed with money donated by Mr William Mowat. Wull Mowat was a Stonehaven cobbler who set up a tannery and hit the jackpot. His little tannery flourished and he opened a bigger tannery. Wull Mowat's business acumen led him to expand and open branches all over Britain and he prospered. His tanneries became the mainstay of Stonehaven industry, his workforce was the biggest in the town and he became Mr William Mowat. Think of that when you walk out Cowie way today.

Cowie was inevitably assimilated into Stonehaven. As the Old Town usurped Cowie's fishing trade, so the New Town quietly ingested Cowie itself. Cowie today is a right angle of two streets, Boatie Row and Amy Row, hemmed in by a monstrous caravan park. Cowie residents complain about the intrusion, and letters to the local Press cite problems of winter parking, but to no avail: it is there. The fishermen's houses of old have now been modernised. Fishers no longer live in Cowie. The

Stonehaven, old town and harbour.

foreshore now sports a notice board bearing the ominous warning, in red letters on a white ground, 'Shellfish found on these shores are unfit for human consumption'. Say nae mair.

Any story of Stonehaven must record the name of Robert William Thomson, the Stonehaven man who invented the pneumatic tyre. Robert Thomson, the son of a Stonehaven mill owner, was born in 1822 and became a civil engineer of great distinction. In addition to the pneumatic tyre he had many other equally advanced inventions as diverse as a glass self-filling fountain pen and a locomotive, road-running, steam engine with solid rubber tyres. Thomson's inventions were so far ahead of contemporary engineering achievement that he failed to find backers to develop his ideas. Fortunately he patented his pneumatic tyre so all the credit must go to him. The Irish vet who subsequently developed tubed tyres was able to do so only because he had Thomson's pioneering work to help him.

Had it not been for the patents, it is unlikely that Thomson's work would ever have been fully realised and recognised. It was many years before his inventions were generally accepted and more before they were developed and the developers took all the credit. It is the aim of the Robert William Thomson Memorial Fellowship now, to publicise the genius of the man. Too little has been heard of him. It is reassuring to know that the Fellowship is concerned to bring his work to public notice and to keep his memory alive. There is a bronze plaque, unveiled in 1982, on the wall of the building which now stands on the site of his birthplace. This plaque was presented by the Royal Scottish Automobile Club to mark the centenary of his birth. An annual veteran and vintage vehicle rally which started in 1968 is held in Stonehaven in June in memory of Robert Thomson. Long may it continue.

Another annual Stonehaven rally, with much less historic justification, is the Fireball affair at New Year. On the stroke of midnight a procession of fireball swingers sets off from the Mercat Cross in the Old Town to walk along as far as the cannon – an upended cannon stuck in the pavement by Arbuthnott Court. As they go they swing fireballs. Fireballs are bunches of 'combustible materials' with the exception of petrol, oil, tar and certain other specified ingredients, encased in wire netting and suspended from a wire rope. It is believed – by very few – that this ritual has somehow survived and been observed since pre-Christian times. In fact it is a modern invention: much younger than Robert Thomson's pneumatic tyre.

According to Miss Elizabeth Christie, who wrote the definitive work on Stonehaven, *The Haven under the Hill,* it all started in 1910. Until then on New Year's Eve, the Old Town folk just met under the clock, had their dram, shook each other's hands and went off to bed. In 1910 a few young fisher lads started the fireball lark and it caught on. Miss Christie's meticulous research could find no previous reference: there is none.

It is probable that the young fisher lads had been up in Shetland the year before and seen the Up Helly A pyrotechnics there. Whatever the reason, it all began in 1910. A lot of folk think it should end in the 1990s. Its putative origin, in pre-Christian, Zoroastrian, mythology gives the purpose of such ceremonies as warding off evil spirits. Unfortunately the Stonehaven frolics are attracting evil spirits. Young drunks and hooligans have infiltrated the proceedings and are bringing

Stonehaven into disrepute. Maybe it should be quietly dropped now before it goes too far.

Just north of Stonehaven, up the hill, Stonehaven Golf Club beckons from the cliff top but not too enticingly. The course is an assault course carved from the native rock and swept by every wind that blows. The old men you see playing on Stonehaven golf course are quite young men when you get close to them. North of that, one leaves the Mearns. No-one can define the boundary: there is none to define. Since the name 'Mearns' was first coined it has had only the vaguest geographical reference and the present and surviving 'Howe o' the Mearns' represents the Mearns today. Stonehaven is generally accepted as the capital and the Mearns lies almost entirely to the south.

Immediately south and west of Stonehaven the soil begins to change from the thin black topsoil of the hills to the thick red loam of the Howe. The obtrusive rocks of the Highland Boundary Fault skirt the Howe and the Strath to the west whilst the sea is cordoned off to the east by the long ridge of high ground running up through Garvock and Bruxie to the Black Hill of Stonehaven. The diminishing undulations of the rolling green hills between, lead one gradually down into the Howe.

Drumlithie and Glenbervie

In this foothill area, just off the A94 and about six miles from Stonehaven, lies the village of Drumlithie; a village of great and original charm. Drumlithie is the archetypal Scotch village, a chip off the old block of time, a totally unplanned original. The houses of Drumlithie sit where the folk of Drumlithie wanted them. Its High Street is a lane of handbarrow width and aimless direction. The problem of cars in Drumlithie High Street should never arise. There is no room for them so keep your cars out of it.

Many people, of course, drive up to Drumlithie, drive right through Drumlithie and never ever see Drumlithie. The main road skirts the village so that the council houses on the left and the shanty town of gimcrack bungalows on the right of the

Glenbervie road give the impression that you are in Drumlithie. You are, in a sense, but to find the secret village of Drumlithie you have to get out of your car and ramble the roads. The High Street is the spinal cord of the place and from it little nerve centres radiate: houses and sheds, front gardens and back greens, cottages and crofts. Old Drumlithie was the perfect place for boys to grow up in. Its countless corners, stone dykes and patches of grass were bloodstained battlefields where generations of gijins and bajins resolved their tribal rivalries. Memories of being young lads in Drumlithie and the primeval joy of moonlit December nights when the frost crisp air of the Mearns caught the throat and swam in dragon's breath puffs to the sky, bring tears to the eyes of old Drumlithie men today.

These are memories that cannot be created anew. Our way of life has changed and the free play of children has been stopped. The old men may weep their tears of regret but the old way of life has gone. The old men always said it had: now it has. The entire way of life of Scotch folk has changed utterly in fifty years. Improved communication, cheap travel, mobility of workers and, above all, television, have changed permanently and irrevocably the centuries-old customs, habits, interests and speech of the native Scot. There is no point in bemoaning the fact, one must simply accept it with no more than a grimace and a nostalgic glance over the shoulder to the old halcyon days. The only difficulty is in realising that the trials of one's adulthood are coincidental with the halcyon days of another's childhood.

It is Drumlithie that occasions the cracker-barrel philosophy. The sight of real old houses with kailyairds and loom sheds does things to the race memory. Old Drumlithie is a permanent reminder of imagined Golden Ages. The facts, as usual, are somewhat different. The village was a centre of handloom weaving and a handloom weaver's life held little spare time for the weaving of Golden Ages. In 1777 there were so many handloom weavers in the village that a bell tower was built to regulate their working hours. The bell rang the hours for rising, starting, finishing and going to bed. The tower is free-standing at the junction of the High Street, and when you think of it, a bell ringing from a tower at set times is a lot more use to most folk than a clock. The folk of Drumlithie were one jump ahead with their bell tower.

Inevitably, the neighbouring villages were jealous. One young smart-Alec from the Auchenblae direction came up with the witticism that the Drumlithie folk were so proud of their bell tower that they took it indoors when it rained. A singularly inane and fatuous joke it was, but how it stuck! Everyone writing about Drumlithie now rushes to include the tale to show that he knows his Drumlithie. One feels for the Drumlithie folk . . .

Glenbervie is a mere mile along the road and consists of little more than a 'Big Hoose', a factory and a church. The big hoose is Glenbervie House, an imposing building when seen from the higher ground to the west but an odd mixture when approached. There is no saying how long a house has stood on that spot but the present building is partly seventeenth century with later additions which themselves are reproductions of an earlier age. Apparently the result is reckoned to be an architectural disaster though it looks good enough to me: especially from up Hawkhill way with the setting sun striking it. The immediate neighbourhood of Glenbervie House used to be the most secluded and peaceful place you could imagine. The old ruined kirk and graveyard by the den of the Bervie Water made it a fit retreat from the worries of the world. It was a totally unspoiled corner of the land until they opened a factory in the middle of it. Now there is a thriving manufacturing operation right by the road on the corner opposite the church. Row upon row of cars fill the car parks, lights blaze at midday; through endless windows office workers tap electronic pulses across the world to other office workers and busy little men hasten from one cup of coffee to another cup of coffee. Occasionally a figure in a white coat and matching trilby hat comes out and crosses the courtyard carrying a cup of coffee in his hand. He must be an executive.

The mind seizes up trying to fathom what all these folk can be doing in their hi-tech laboratory in the middle of Glenbervie. Nor does it look safe to ask. Secret processes and classified information seem more than probable, things that go bang and destroy all forms of life on the planet. It was a considerable relief to be met with a beaming smile and an open invitation from the charming girl in the office 'We make,' she informed me without cavil, let or hindrance, 'ingredients for the baking trade and non-dairy cream'. She could have knocked me down with a plastic feather. All that ultra-modern, state-of-the-art technology just to turn out ingredients for the baking trade and non-dairy cream. A herd of Ayrshires could surely do it better with less bother, and real dairy cream. Across the road from the factory, Glenbervie church sits by the roadside; a plain building with a formal kirkyaird beside it. The church was built in 1826 and has no great feature to commend it other than the war memorial which stands outside its west wall. Unlike most World War memorials this one is in the form of an old mercat cross, a plain column with an armorial head. It is most appropriate as a mark of remembrance. The names on it mark the personal tragedies of the parents, wives, sweethearts and families of Glenbervie. That is the tragedy of war; the agony of the survivor, not the oblivion of the slain.

The Road to Auchenblae

The road branches by the church. The main road to Auchenblae dips down to the left while the side road runs up over the hill to join the back road between Auchenblae and Stonehaven at Brae school. Brae school is a sorry sight today with the detritus of a car-breaking business fouling the old building and spilling over into the weed-bound playground. The school was one of the invaluable old rural schools now written off and closed in the cause of centralisation and standardisation. Generations of country children were educated at Brae school and it served them well. They were the children of the local community, their education was basic and it was sound. The closer a school can stay to the community it serves, the better social structure it creates.

Last time I was up Brae way the bus from Stonehaven pulled up at the road end and an old man got off and walked down towards me. 'Aye, aye,' says I. 'That's an affa-like day,' says he.

Our greetings met in mid air, indicating our willingness to

talk and we settled down to crack. The weather, the state of farming, the cattle beasts and the closure of rural schools were all covered and direct questions were asked. My name – my business – what I was doing at Brae school on a bleak November day – where did I come from? That is the way of country folk. We like to set a foundation on which we can build. There is no use trying to talk until you have established the parameters on which you will orientate. Our crack went famously.

It was the kind of conversation you can have only occasionally and with a stranger. After we had discussed the bulk of the world's worries I said, 'And did you work on the farms hereabouts in your young days?' He nodded. 'Aye . . . weel . . . I wis the fermer upbye.' He nodded up by the Bogtons. 'What's your name then?' I asked. 'Aitken,' he replied 'Aitken?' says I. 'There used to be an Aitken from up this way that used to go round the Games, he was a richt athlete, he came from the Auchenblae direction.' 'My loon,' said the stranger proudly and it turned out that I was talking to a man of some considerable standing in the Mearns. His father had gone into a Mearns farm in 1910 and this was an only son. He didn't say whether or not he had been lonely as an only son but when he grew up and got married himself, he and Mrs Aitken had four sons and four daughters. There are now Aitkens at Bogton, West Bogton, Tipperty and Chapelton and married daughters everywhere.

These are the real folk of the Mearns. Theirs are the families that form the Mearns community. Every facet of Mearns social life depends on the effort of folk like the Aitkens. Whether it be the kirk, the W.R.I., the Young Farmers, Fettercairn Show or a whist drive and dance in Auchenblae Hall the quality of Mearns life is set by the Mearns folk and the Aitkens are a Mearns dynasty. I was proud to have spoken to the dynast.

From Brae school the road to the left leads down through Dellavaird by Glenfarquhar to Auchenblae. An interesting little place, Auchenblae, built on the slope of a hill. Its main street runs down one hill, its kirk and school are on top of another. The main street is broad and spacious but the bit labelled 'Market Place' is so small as to be indistinguishable from the rest. It would seem that the market must have been held in the road. Changed days for Auchenblae when one remembers that Auchenblae was the site of the famous, and infamous, Paddy Fair. Paddy Fair was actually Paldy Fair, and Paldy was a contraction of Palladius, and Palladius was an early saint whose bones and relics were brought to Auchenblae by St. Ternan. St. Ternan was the Mearns man turned missionary and eventually raised to sainthood whose church we visited at Arbuthnott. Paldy Fair was an Auchenblae festival originally held in front of Fordoun Kirk then transferred about a mile out of the village up to the start of Glen Farquhar. Like all these mediaeval fairs, Paldy was a three-day riot of legitimate business, honest fun and downright depravity. You would hardly credit that, looking at Auchenblae today.

For the stranger to the district, a few words of explanation might not come amiss. The parish of Fordoun is a large parish and the present village of Fordoun (NO 750759) has little to do with it. The original Fordoun or 'Fotherdun' was created a burgh of barony by Mary, Queen of Scots in 1554. It was a settlement near Laurencekirk and has disappeared. Its parish kirk is now the kirk built in Auchenblae in 1829 on the site of St. Palladius's chapel so the visitor to Auchenblae must not be surprised to see that Auchenblae Kirk is in fact Fordoun Kirk. Across the den from the kirk the school that is patently Auchenblae school was, until recently, Fordoun school. Go down to Fordoun (NO 750759) and the school there is Redmyres school. If you find nothing odd in any of that, go back up to Drumlithie and you will find that the school in Drumlithie village is Glenbervie school. Do not then attempt to tell me that any of it makes sense.

There is an interesting point in there with Mary, Queen of Scots. Why always Mary, Queen of Scots? Why not Queen Mary? Queen Mary of Scotland? Queen Mary the First? I know why. It was all explained to me by Charlie Setz, Music Master at Kirkcudbright Academy many, many years ago – and he wasn't on about Mary, Queen of Scots. It is just the rhythm of it, it has a pleasing rhythm. It comes well off the tongue, Mary, Queen of Scots – or as Charlie put it 'Tiffy, ta-te-ta'. Say it over once or twice and you're hooked. O.K.; why else?

Drumtochty to Clatterin' Brig and the Deer Dyke

From Auchenblae the discerning visitor heads for Drumtochty Glen, the wooded valley that links Auchenblae with Clatterin' Brig. The Glen of Drumtochty leads into Strath Finella, eventually skirting Loch Saugh and the Hill of Strathfinella. The glen is about five miles long and is a beautiful, soft, green wooded valley well worth a visit. This is one of the terminal outcrops of the Grampians and the transition to the Old Red Sandstone of the Mearns in Drumtochty is marked by copious fluvioglacial deposits of sand and gravel. So say the geologists and who is to argue? It may be the last obtrusion of old, durable, metamorphic rock as they say, but it is still as bonny a wee glen as you will find and largely because it comes as such a contrast to the land on either side. The high ground of Herscha to the east and the Cairn o' Mount to the west make the thickly wooded valley the more distinct.

Drumtochty Castle is sited halfway through the glen and is a relatively new building, being a Gillespie Graham creation of the nineteenth century. Despite its youth the castellated neo-Gothic pile has weathered well into the surrounding landscape and is an imposing sight today. It has served as a home, a hostel, a school and a hotel over the years and has recently changed hands again. When it was a school they laid out rugby pitches down by the old cricket pavilion and it was a stirring sight to see the little lads play their rugby. Never were games played with greater partisanship. These same little lads must have happy memories today, of mellow autumn afternoons when the game was the thing and the ecstasy of total physical exhaustion was first enjoyed. The intrusion of sadistic games masters is not possible on such idyllic scenes.

One of the features of Drumtochty grounds and policies is their wealth of beautiful hardwood trees, somewhat emphasised now by the profusion of quick maturing softwoods planted around them. The Forestry Commission has a huge forest plantation starting on Finella Hill and extending in bits and pieces right up to the old Kincardineshire county boundary. One of my friends, a dedicated shooting man, claims that a fox can go from Fettercairn to Aberdeen without coming out of the trees. If your reaction to that is simply 'Good on you, foxy', you miss the point. Shooting men do not like foxes. Shooting men blame the Forestry Commission for turning Scotland into one great big fox covert. I suppose if you spend a lot of money rearing pheasants and a fox slaughters them before you do, you are entitled to moan but personally I like to see the odd fox. It is just a pity that the fox shares with man the habit of killing simply for the hell of it. Not all foxes do and not all men but it is in the nature of the beasts. The sight of a hen ree after a fox has been through it is equalled only by the sight of man's habitual butchery of every living species on the planet; including his own. The fox doesn't come out of the comparison too badly.

The Forestry Commission suffers a lot of criticism from several sources but no-one criticises their policy of free access to woodlands. Wherever you see a Forestry Commission wood, you will find access paths and woodland walkways clearly signposted. In Drumtochty Glen the Forest Walk offers a pleasant stroll through a conifer wood that is a joy to visit at any time of the year. The idea that outdoor activities can be enjoyed only in bright sunshine is a nonsense. So many people in Scotland refuse to venture out unless the sun is shining that you find Forestry Commission walks quite unused most of the time. I must say it suits me fine.

The Forest Walk is at the point where the Glen of Drumtochty leads into Strath Finella, of the lovely name, on the edge of Strathfinella Hill. There is also a Den of Finella or Den Finella over by St. Cyrus, just off the A92. Finella was the daughter of the Maermor of Angus, or Earl of Angus, and one wonders if her name would have been used quite so generally if she had been a Jean or a Maggie or anything at all less romantic than Finella. Her husband was Maermor of the Mearns, as her father was Maermor of Angus, and the King was doubtful of their loyalty. When Finella's son became involved in some sharp political practice, the King had him killed. If Finella's fame rests on anything more than her mellifluous name it is that she then killed the King. The year was 994.

The 'facts' are scarce, as always, and a tapestry of fancy has been woven from the thin threads of truth. It seems that if

Loch Saugh.

Finella didn't actually kill King Kenneth, she wasn't far away when it happened. The fancy comes in the tales that are told of how she killed him. One version has the king being killed by an ingenious machine which showered arrows on him when he touched, by invitation, the trigger. This was supposed to have happened in Kincardine Castle. Another story has Finella inviting the king to a *fête champêtre* at Stracathro and hiring a gang of ruffians to murder him there.

We will never know the truth of Finella but no matter, her strath is a picturesque tree-lined path to the more rugged highland area to the north and west. As the road climbs up to Loch Saugh the trees thin out and the fertile fields of the south run into the high ground through the strath. Loch Saugh itself is a long narrow man-made dam, much used by Brechin Angling Club in season. Out of season it is a gem of scenic beauty where all kinds of aquatic birds can be seen from the road. It is not often that you can pass Loch Saugh without wanting to pull in to the little parking area to watch the water fowl.

Past the Loch, the road bends round the hill and drops down to Clatterin' Brig, but before that, one passes Glensaugh Research Station, known locally as the Deer Farm. The official terms of remit for the Glensaugh Research Station are 'To study Food Production and Land Use in upland areas' and that is what they do; comprehensively. The passing tourist who assumes that raising a few red deer is the entire function of the station is far from the mark. Glensaugh Research Station is a world leader in developing techniques and new methods for hill farming. The herd of 700 red deer, split into constituent groups with 350 adult breeding females and 20 prime stags, is but one aspect of its work. The 'oohs' and 'aahs' of car borne families who spot the 'wild animals' from the road are not exactly echoed by the men who handle them. They see them more as a source of food for a hungry world.

The veterinary scientists' current and immediate concern is the prospect of bovine tuberculosis infecting red deer herds, both farmed and wild. Such is the romance of deer farming. Red deer popularity is more firmly based on an ability to produce high-quality, high-protein, low-fat meat from a natural low-grade pasture. The fact that they are beautiful creatures to look at, that deer horn sells for large sums to Oriental gentlemen who set great store by it, are bonus points. Glensaugh is a highly efficient, scientific, commercial research unit and if its experiments soon result in red deer being farmed as cattle are today, that will be a justification for its existence. It will also mean that romantics like myself will sigh deep sighs when they pass farmed fields of deer and the market value of Edwin Landseer's 'Monarch of the Glen' will probably plummet. Now they have started research on a herd of llamas, which can also be seen from the road, so there is no end to the possibilities.

The road drops down from the Research Station to cross the Burn of Slack at Clatterin' Brig, which must have been a misnomer in the old days for there was no brig, just a ford. A foot bridge was first built, then more recently a proper road bridge beside the ford. The name has no immediate bearing on the condition of the bridgeworks. Clatterin' is derived from the Old English 'Klettr', a cliff, and the fact that there is no cliff at Clatterin' Brig is not the kind of detail to deter your dedicated etymologist. There are wee kinds of cliffs all round it if you look carefully. Similar derivations are offered for Clatterin' Briggs near Longforgan in Perthshire, Clatteringshaws near

New Galloway in the Stewartry and Clatterbridge near Neston in Cheshire.

Should all that weight of evidence fail to convince you, there are alternatives. Clatterin' Brig is derived from the Gaelic *clacheran*, stepping stones. That could be nearer the truth but there isn't as much Gaelic left in the Mearns as could confirm it. The latest theory is that the first bridge was made of bog-oak trunks dug out of the adjoining marsh and they made a peculiar clattering noise when carts passed over them. You may have your own choice of derivative. I made the last one up for myself.

Just over the Clatterin' Brig, or ford, the road joins up with the B974 road over the Cairn o' Mounth. This is basically the old track road linking the Mearns and Deeside which was made up into a military road by General Wade between the '15 and '45 uprisings. Hard by the junction there are old lime workings and the remains of kilns, for this was a lime quarrying and burning centre in the early eighteenth century. Limestone outcrops are found from Clatterin' Brig right down through the foothills as far as Milton of Mathers and the coast.

Facing the road, on the first hill opposite, is a Tyrolean-type restaurant and crafte shoppe opened in 1958 by Prince Georg of Denmark for his wife, Princess Anne of Denmark, whose shoppe it was. The old quarry is now a car park and the shoppe sells all the things that such shoppes sell – tartan scarves, pottery mugs, silver-coloured brooches with pebble inserts and sticks with sheep's horn handles. Here be tourists.

The road up to the Cairn rises steeply from Clatterin' Brig and half a mile up on the left-hand side of the road is the gable end and broken wall of the old inn of Knowegreens. These walls were built in 1789 but there must always have been some kind of an inn on that spot. It marks the beginning and the end of the great Mounth road that saw Pict, Roman, Celt, Viking, Saxon, Dane, Northumbrian and Hanoverian pass in procession. Over the centuries every pacifying saint or invading infidel came or left by that route. It was the connecting pass between the lush land of the Mearns and the green saughs of the Feugh and the Dee. Knowegreens saw them all and it was a welcome spot to slocken the thirst of the prancing captain or the footsore private soldier of the line. When they had gone, the drovers followed and the seasonal gangs of Hielan' hairst lassies bound for the farms of Angus. Then was the time of hay and harvest and hochmagandie.

Knowegreens lasted until the beginning of the twentieth century when the temperance laws killed it off as an inn. It became a lowly 'Porter and Ale' house then until it was finally left empty and stripped of its roof to fall into the neglected ruin we see today. The visitors who pull their cars off the road at Knowegreens now, to refresh themselves with prepacked convenience foods and jumbo vacuum flasks, are totally unaware of the mass of memory that lies around their very feet. Knowegreens knows it all.

From there the road climbs to the summit of Cairn o' Mounth at 1488 ft. It is named Cairn o' Mounth and it seems that there must always have been some kind of a cairn there. The present rickle of stones is about twelve feet high and fifty feet across and takes a bit of climbing up even after you have climbed to it. The top of Cairn o' Mounth is the best of all viewpoints in Angus and the Mearns. Its height allows an uninterrupted view down the Mearns and through Angus to the south, with the sea to the east and the craggy top of Clachnaben up behind. There is always a feeling of freedom and space up on the Mounth and unless you strike a day of rain and hill mist, the view is unparalleled. From the vantage point of the Mounth you see why all the invading forces heading north took the Angus and Mearns route. The long broad valley, separated from the coast by the Sidlaw extension, offers an easy path round the Grampian barrier to the west.

About half a mile back down from the summit – for no-one really wants to go any further – there is a memorial well with a stone trough and a surround bearing the inscription 'This fountain was erected in memory of Captain J.N. Gladstone R.N., who died in 1863, by his grateful friend, Sandy Junor'. It is a substantial memorial and when the said Sandy himself died soon after, the Gladstone family reciprocated by having a memorial stone placed over his grave in Fetteresso churchyard.

Still farther down and over on the right behind Clatterin' Brig cafe, the remains of the old Deer Dyke can be seen leading over Arnbarrow hill. This Deer Dyke, or King's Dyke, was built by the lords of Kincardine Castle to enclose about five

Knowegreens Inn – what memories!

square miles of wood and park land in which Royal visitors could hunt wild animals. A closer study of the Deer Dyke shows the purpose it served and the method of its use. It was built a long, long time ago and old chroniclers who wrote of the murder of King Kenneth III by Finella in 994 mention his 'forest full of all manner of wild beasts'. It is not known when this forest was first enclosed within the Deer Dyke but it was certainly before King David I gave hunting parties there in the twelfth century. It is well documented from then on and any subsequent mention of visiting Royalty at Kincardine Castle invariably includes a reference to their having hunted in the Deer Park.

Originally the Deer Dyke was most probably just a boundary fence to mark the edge of the park but over the years it became an enclosure in which game could be confined. The Dyke itself was modified from being a mere marking fence into a full restraining barrier. A wide, open ditch was dug on the inner side, a drystone and turf rampart erected along it and a wood and wattle palisade built on top of that. Animals loosed inside it were not able to get out. When the current king fancied a morning's hunting, the venerers and huntsmen were then able to provide the required sport without too much trouble. It was a bit like the put-and-take fishing that goes on today.

Not much is left of the dyke now but it has been traced round the length of its perimeter and aerial photographs show most of it quite clearly. It is one of the relics of the old days when Kincardine Castle and the town around it was the county seat and administrative centre of the Mearns. The whole district of Glensaugh, Strathfinella, Clatterin' Brig, Lammas Muir and Green Castle was an important legislative and trading area supporting a considerable population. The town and castle of Kincardine had existed for centuries and was firmly established and recognised as the county town but it always had one significant drawback. It was too near the hills. The Mounth road into the Grampians allowed all manner of uncouth persons to descend on the low lands, perform their acts of villainy and withdraw to the hills with impunity. The crime rate around Kincardine town was infinitely greater than in the rest of the county and that was bad for morale. During the sixteenth century, due to a combination of audacious caterans, lax officials and eventually a sovereign – Mary, Q. of S., – who didn't want to hunt, the status of Kincardine had diminished. When the leading local family, the Keiths, applied for the transference of local government facilities from Kincardine to Stonehaven, it was readily granted. An Act of Parliament of 1607 finally recognised and recorded the change.

From that date the whole community right up to Clatterin' Brig began to melt away. It had been bad enough when Kincardine Castle had maintained a garrison to protect them, now it was too dangerous for comfort. Over the years the populace simply drifted off and what had been a thriving town for centuries past became a totally deserted site. Nothing remains today except the traces of a main street, a town cross, sites of the east and west ports and the old burial ground of St. Catherine's chapel. Of the town itself nothing exists but the line of its foundations. The Ozymandias syndrome applies. What was a vast battlemented commodious castle is now a scarcely detectable ruin on a tree-girt hillock. It is hard to visualise the size and strength of the great defensive fortification that stood there for centuries. Archaeologists have explored and excavated, measured and estimated and announced their findings. The castle was a square building of 38¼-yard sides. Its outer walls were 30ft high and 8ft thick, it had watch towers and curtain walls, moat, drawbridge and portcullis. The great Castell of Kincardyne, garrisoned and stocked to dominate and protect the Mearns, developed and maintained as a hunting lodge for the diversion of kings, now overcome by the nettles that grow from its foundation. It is hard to imagine.

Even further from our comprehension is the history of the ancient fortification of Green Castle. Green Castle lies about a mile and a half short of Kincardine Castle on the east bank of the Devilly Burn up towards Clatterin' Brig. It is a Pictish fort of unknown antiquity which has been used by succeeding generations as a fort, a homestead and possibly even a castle. Historians make poor attempts at defining it. They reckon its origin to be dated 'between 400 BC and 125 AD, during the Iron Age', and suggest that it was subsequently used by the Romans. Folk tales label it 'Finella's Castle' and locate the murder of King Kenneth III there in 994. We know where other folk tales locate King Kenneth's murder and, of the alternatives, Green Castle would seem to be the least likely.

Green Castle today is no more than an elevated earthwork on the slope above the burn, a natural defensive position and a typical Pictish hill fort. How much it was ever subsequently used by the Romans, the English, Queen Finella or the Girl Guides from Auchenblae, is open to question. It is an impressive place, anyhow, that commands respect for the Pict and induces moods of deep, deep, meditation in the contemplative visitor.

Great Houses: Phesdo, Fasque and Fettercairn

South again towards Kincardine Castle there are two notable country houses lying east and west of the old castle itself; Phesdo and Fasque. The present Phesdo House is a nineteenth-century mansion sitting in well-wooded policies just north of the old, original house of Phesdo. The original Phesdo was an important estate that figures frequently in Scotland's history. William the Lion knew Phesdo, and Robert the Bruce;

Phesdo paid revenues to Arbroath Abbey and Phesdo flourished until it was incorporated with Fasque in 1845 when it was bought by the Gladstone family.

Fasque House is best known because it was the childhood home of William Ewart Gladstone, four times Prime Minister. Before that it belonged to the Ramsay family and the present Fasque House was built by Sir Alexander Ramsay in 1809. Like Phesdo, there was a much older Fasque House but nothing remains of that building now. By the time the 1809 house was built, the Ramsays were already renowned for their pioneering work in agriculture and they had been leaders in the progressive use of fertilisers, enclosures, crop rotation, improved stock breeding and seed selection over the years. When the new Fasque House was built in 1809, it was set in existing grounds already laid out with formal gardens and mature hardwood trees. The Ramsays had a penchant for trees.

In 1829 the estate was bought by Sir John Gladstone, a businessman who had made a fortune as a grain broker before entering Parliament in 1820 and being knighted in 1846. Sir John was a dedicated improver who followed the Ramsay lead and continued the development of Fasque. He added extensions to the house, built roads and bridges in the grounds, added an artificial lake and planted trees everywhere. Fasque is still renowned for its trees. Sir John had four sons and the youngest was William Ewart Gladstone, the Prime Minister.

From May to September now, Fasque House is open to the public and it is a stately home well worth a visit. Less grand than some of its counterparts, it is a perfectly preserved example of how the affluent landowner lived in the Victorian era. The house itself has many attractive features, particularly the entrance hall and staircase. Entrance for the paying public is by a side door and the servants' quarters but the main entrance from the front door gives an immediate impression of the symmetry and balance of the architecture. The perfect form of the hallway, the double cantilever staircase with its free-flowing banister against the curved window lights and architraves, is an artistic triumph. That staircase is a visual joy and an engineering masterpiece. The soaring beauty of the double flight is achieved by a cantilever construction where the load on each step is transmitted through the steps below. Not only is the stairway an artistic gem, it is an example of the craftsmanship of a period when manual skills had reached their apogee in Scotland. Workmanship like that of Fasque House is not matched by the machine-turned prefabrications of today. The immediate appeal of Fasque to the visitor is that it shows the house exactly as young W.E. Gladstone knew it. The kitchen is laid out as the Gladstone family cook would have had it and the bedrooms are as the upstairs maids could have left them. All the impedimenta of daily life are laid out for use. Modern housewives are usually amazed to see how little their modern appliances have advanced from the Fasque models. Labour-saving devices that we assume to be the products of twentieth-century invention turn out to have been used for centuries. The big difference is in the basic power supply: we use electricity, our forefathers used solid fuel, natural ice and human labour. The kitchen of Fasque has cooking ranges, hot rings, baking ovens, browning ovens, roasting spits and turning jacks that can certainly equal the best that any modern kitchen can produce. The larder at Fasque is a dark, cool, stone-shelved repository fitted with deep lead-lined ice-boxes. Cool drinks with ice cubes, in the middle of summer, are not a modern prerogative. The Fasque folk had underground ice houses from which ice blocks were taken, packed between layers of straw in ice-chests and available for use all through the year. Refrigeration is nothing new. Fasque had Argyll gravy pots with hot water jackets to keep gravy hot at table, hot air circulated from open coal fires, double glazing on some windows and great wooden shutters on the insides of others. The house is full of innumerable bits and bobs of ingenious contraption to make life easy. Above all they had the greatest labour-saving device of all time: money.

They didn't have electric light but they had plenty of lamps with plenty of servants to trim them. They had no vacuum cleaners but they had plenty of housemaids, with knees, to crawl around with dustpans. They had no cars but they had elegantly equipped carriages and beautifully caparisoned horses with liveried coachmen to drive them. Their grounds and policies, rose gardens and vegetable plots were tended by armies of workers. Fasque House was served by farms and dairies, gardens and fishponds, apiaries and game larders. The most sophisticated structure existed to support the landed gentry of the day and Fasque House was well underpinned. They lacked nothing to maintain a standard of living that cannot be exceeded today. Provided they had the money. Whether the servants were as happy with their lot is a question for the philosopher, not the economist, and certainly not for us.

Fasque estate is on the right-hand side of the road into Fettercairn. Fettercairn House is on the left. Where Phesdo is a newish house on an old foundation and Fasque is a newish house on an older foundation, Fettercairn is a conglomerate construction of the new, the old and the ancient, continually modified and extended over the centuries. It was for long the seat of the Earls of Middleton and figures in old charters of the Abbey of Aberbrothock (Arbroath). It is now owned by relatives of the royal family and is not open to the public.

Apart from being one of the oldest and most important historical sites of the Mearns, Fettercairn House is renowned for romantic and literary connections of much wider significance. Sir Walter Scott, when he was plain Wattie Scott the law apprentice, visited the Stuart family in Fettercairn House and immediately fell deeply in love. His inamorata was Miss Williamina Stuart, daughter of the house and a belle of repute, even at that time when she was only fifteen years old. Walter Scott professed his love for her and to her and courted the demoiselle passionately in the gardens and grounds of Fettercairn House, but the lady loved another. When Walter Scott left, with or without his heart, the lass was soon engaged and married to William Forbes who duly became Sir William Forbes (Bart.) and eventually Sir William Stuart Forbes (Bart.) of Pitsligo and Fettercairn. No-one knows whether or not she ever regretted turning down the wee Waverley novelist.

Sir William never made the impact that Sir Walter subsequently made but he did achieve a measure of fame in his way. It came because Sir William Stuart Forbes was a close friend of James Boswell of Auchinleck, the biographer of Samuel Johnson, and was nominated as one of Boswell's three executors. When Boswell died, in 1795, Sir William removed chests full of personal papers from Boswell's London house and brought them up to Fettercairn. The intention was to go through them at leisure and sort them out. Unfortunately, Sir William himself died only three months later and the other two executors, Edward Malone and W.J. Temple, wound up Boswell's estate without knowing that a significant part of it lay in Fettercairn House.

We all know how easy it is for a few leather trunks to lie around one's country house without being noticed and Boswell's kists lay for one hundred and thirty-five years in Fettercairn House before a visiting academic from Aberdeen University chanced upon them in 1930. His reaction may be imagined. To come upon such a treasure trove of literary gems would be a triumph for anyone; for a visiting professor from Aberdeen University it was a passport to fame. Professor Claude Collier Abbott is now famous.

The 'Fettercairn Papers', as they are known in literary circles, provided a whole bunch of keys to Boswell's life and times. There are over one thousand letters, besides documents and papers, all of which are valuable sources of information on James Boswell and Samuel Johnson as well as many of their contemporaries. The letters of Edmund Burke and John Wilkes, who both died in 1797, are especially illuminating on aspects of late eighteenth-century history. The two Whig polemicists were controversial figures in their day and Boswell's letters to them are invaluable comments on the political scene. How regrettable that the whole collection has now been bought by Yale University and a great part of Fettercairn's heritage has been lost to us.

Lord Monboddo and Robert Burns

Having arrived at the edge of Fettercairn by the Clatterin' Brig road, it might be advisable to loop back up the B966 and come back down again by the A94(T). The B966 runs through the real farm land of the Mearns, the red land, and the circuit from Fettercairn round and back to Fettercairn encloses some of the best farms in the district. Up at the top end, just beyond the B966/A94(T) junction at Abbeyton, lies the estate of

Monboddo with its revamped Monboddo House with outbuildings now made into dwelling houses. The estate had belonged to the Burnett family since 1675 and when James Burnett (1714-99) was raised to the Bench of the Court of Session in 1767 he assumed the title of Lord Monboddo. Lord Monboddo is known to us as the friend and kindred spirit of R. Burns, poet and *bon vivant*. Because of this association, it is commonly assumed that Lord Monboddo was a typical Crochallan Fencible, a drinking, wenching, philandering waster. The belief is as erroneous as the belief that Robert Burns was no more than a loose-living ploughman with a gift for rhyming.

Lord Monboddo was a man of great intellect and great achievement. He lived in an age of enlightenment and he contributed much to the progressive thinking of his day. His book, *The Origin and Progress of Man and Language,* anticipates a great part of what Darwin subsequently proved in his *The Origin of Species.* It is natural that two men of such original genius as Monboddo and Burns should seek each other out when they were in Edinburgh at the same time. The bond between them was the shared humanitarian impulse that prompted Burns to send a token cannon to the French revolutionaries and Monboddo to lease his lands to an army of smallholders rather than an elite of farmers. They were both educated, cultured, original thinkers and if Monboddo was as abstemious as Burns was profligate, it was no bar to their friendship.

Burns himself was the son of a son of the Mearns. His father, William Burness, left the Mearns at the age of nineteen and a memorial cairn stands by the A94(T) today near the farm of Clochnahill where the grandparents lived. The memorial column was erected in 1968 by one Wm. Coull Anderson, an American descendant of the Burns family. It is probably no more than a coincidence that a cairn commemorating Robert Burns is built in simple, phallic, form.

Whilst such a totem might be justified, it should be borne in mind that Burns was a gentleman as well as a libertine: the two are not incompatible. Burns's attitude to women exactly reflected their attitude to him; when he met a lady, she met a gentleman. The beautiful Elizabeth Burnett was one such. The

The memorial cairn, Clochnahill. Robert Burns' father left here for Edinburgh and eventually Ayrshire.

youngest daughter of Lord Monboddo, Elizabeth was a beautiful, talented and cultured girl. Her natural beauty was accentuated and highlighted by the sparkling eyes and porcelain complexion of pulmonary tuberculosis. At the age of twenty-three, Elizabeth Burnett died of consumption. Burns had met and been captivated by 'the heavenly Miss Burnett' and on her death he wrote the 'Elegy on the Late Miss Burnett of Monboddo'. Her name also appears in his correspondence and he referred to her in his 'Address to Edinburgh'. This chaste friendship that he had with Lord Monboddo's daughter should be remembered and set with many others against the usual slanders that one hears about Robert Burns.

Changes in the Mearns

The stock that Burns came from and the Scotch folk he wrote about were recognisable ethnic types, scarce changed through centuries of gradual development. The conditions under which they lived, the food they ate, the countryside around them had changed little since the Picts rolled stones together and burrowed into the earth to find shelter. Only the twentieth century has brought major change. We may welcome it, we may deplore it; we must recognise it. There is little that is recognisably 'Scotch' – or even 'Scottish' – in our way of life today. The rate of change has accelerated rapidly since the Second World War and now we have to fight to preserve some fragments of our heritage.

Some of the last strongholds of our native culture are the cropping farms of the Mearns. The farmers, owner or tenant, form a yeoman class that has served the land and the community well. The Mitchells, Middletons, Milnes and Carnegies have husbanded their acres and augmented their patrimonies over the years. Branches have flourished, branches have withered but the root stock has survived. The history of the Mearns is the history of such families and yet the whole economy and social structure of the area is founded on the hard graft of nameless unsung heroes, the ploo chiels and bothy billies o' the ferm touns o' the Howe.

There lies one of the greatest of all changes in our way of life in the Mearns. The old days saw ten men with ten pair of horse working a farm together with orra men and halflins taking the workforce into the teens. Add on kitchie deems and the men's wives who outworked in season and you had a sizeable team. Ferm touns were so called because they were groupings of farm house, farm buildings, bothies and farm workers' cottages. Every farm was a self-contained community and the workers put great store by the comradeship of their work. It is the loneliest job on earth now. Where a farm worker used to have his mates and his horses, he now has himself and machines. For company he has his transistor radio.

The mechanisation of farms has had many repercussions, practical and social. The social aspect has gone, the practical has changed. Where farms used to enclose their fields with drystone dykes or hedges and keep shelter belts of trees strategically sited, they now make prairies. Drystone dykes are too expensive to repair so they are allowed to fall down. Hedges and trees take up too much room so they are ripped out. Grazing is controlled with electric fencing and more and more animals are being reared and fed indoors. This results in a change in farm building and an enlargement of fields. Where

The men of the Howe and the Strath. Outside East Denoon bothy door in 1905.

a farm steading used to have a stable specially built with cobbled floor, wooden stalls, hay heck and feed trough, there are now no horses. Where milk cows used to stand in paired stalls with neck chains, trough and grip, they now roam in self-feed silage courts with access to computerised milking parlours. Where carts used to stand in cart sheds with their shafts protruding ready for hitching, metal bogies now stand wherever there is room.

This change in farming practice has resulted in great changes in the appearance of our countryside and you can see it even in the Mearns. The lines of trees that used to mark field boundaries and farm tracks, are disappearing. The hedgerows that used to harbour birds and animals have gone. The dams that long since used to power the threshing mills are dry. Our scenery is changing. The new look is that of factory farming. Custom-built buildings of mellow local stone have been replaced by big sheds; huge, roofed, metal hangars with as much unobstructed floor space as possible so that internal adjustment can be made as required. Alongside the big sheds are the silos, grain or feed storage silos that rise like factory chimneys from the bare earth around them. Fortunately we still have some trees left and public opinion is being swayed to plant more. The balance between modern farming practice and our traditional environment has not yet been completely upset. The Mearns still looks more like the Mearns than the intensive farming that is being conducted here might lead one to assume. There is hope that a realisation of the essential need for mankind to empathise with Nature might be about to dawn.

Driving down the dual-carriage race track carved through the Mearns, with cars crashing into each other at all angles, one wonders. Then one pulls off the A94(T) and meanders down the B966, B967, B9120, B974 or any other of the maze of feeder roads linking them and sanity is restored.

There is one loop off the main road here, up the hill through Mains of Kair farm and past Kair House, that goes right through a Roman camp. The Romans made few permanent settlements in these parts and this was a staging post for troops heading north, probably from Inchtuthill. We know a lot more about the Romans than we do about the Picts, whose artefacts decorate Angus and the Mearns, and this camp can be identified as a marching camp of the army of Lucius Septimius Severus. Lucius the Severe visited Scotland around 200 AD and organised some notable repair work on Hadrian's Wall. He is known to have travelled north with his army before returning to York where he died in 211. The camp at Fordoun is one of his.

Fordoun

A camp was always known to have existed at Fordoun but it took the marvels of aerial photography to define it. Detailed photographs now show the outline of the whole camp and the layout of the principal features of a typical *castrum*. It is a deserted spot now with the wind soughing through the trees and one can readily imagine the dejection of the Roman sentry hunched into the wind as he paced the *vallum* and cursed Pict, Scot, Norseman and the duty *signifer* alike.

Farther down the A94(T), and just off it since it has been bypassed, lies Fordoun village; an undistinguished hamlet. Fordoun retains the name of the parish of Fordoun but would

Easter Meathie, a fower-pair place in 1918. The workforce was older and younger than it should have been. The War had thinned the ranks.

probably have done better to have assumed the name of Redmyre, its neighbour village. Redmyre has more claim to original fame and Fordoun parish has more relevance to Auchenblae than to Fordoun village anyhow, but there it is. There is not a great deal to be said about Fordoun once one has noted that the trains no longer stop there and the main road has been taken away. However, one might add that James Beattie (1735 1803) was schoolmaster here before moving to Aberdeen University as Professor of Logic and Moral Philosophy. He was famous as the author of the *Essay on Truth,* a defence of the Christian faith against the forces of materialism and anarchy. It might stand a reprint today. He also achieved fame as a poet, especially of *The Minstrel.* A friend of Dr Samuel Johnson, he was painted by Sir Joshua Reynolds.

I imagine that Fordoun must now be enjoying a resurgence of spirit and a rekindling of hope. The community life of the place can once again focus on the wee village hall and the square now that the thundering menace of the A94(T) has been removed.

CHAPTER 7

From Laurencekirk to Brechin

Next stop down the road from Fordoun is Laurencekirk, also safely bypassed and recovering its identity as the agricultural capital of the Howe. Laurencekirk was originally called Conveth but by the eighteenth century both names were in use and gradually Conveth was dropped and now appears only as a farm name at Mains of Conveth on the outskirts of the town. The old Conveth was the nearest settlement to the site of St. James's Fair, one of the great fairs held for centuries up on Garvock hill.

Garvock hill is the massive rampart above Laurencekirk with one of the best viewpoints of the Mearns on its flank. Garvock is quiet today but it has known rumbustious times. St. James's Fair was one of the most important of its kind, a four-day spree of horse and cattle dealing with all the concomitant razzamatazz. No-one knows why it was held on the top of the hill when the nearest settlements were miles below but anyone can see why they didn't build their villages up on top of the windswept expanse of Garvock.

The most usual historic reference to Garvock is as a hunting ground of the Keiths, the Earls Marischal. One tale is always trotted out as soon as hunting on Garvock is mentioned and here it is. It seems that the Sheriff of Kincardine, John Melville, was murdered on Garvock in 1420 by some of his fellow lairds. The fact is verifiable, the legend is not, for legend has it that Melville was murdered then boiled in a pot and his murderers each drank from the brew. As conclusive proof of the deed there is a hollow over by Brownieleys farm entrance which is still called the Sheriff's Kettle. Added proof is furnished in the story of how the murder was planned. When the aforesaid lairds had complained to King James I about the conduct of John Melville in his capacity as Sheriff, the King had exclaimed, 'Sorrow gin the Sheriff was sodden and supped in broo!'

Royal commands were Royal commands. Melville was duly

invited to a hunting party on Garvock, murdered and boiled near Brownieleys. It could be true but I hae ma doots: it all sounds a bit too dramatic. When you go to the Sheriff's Kettle and find that it is just a vaguely kettle-shaped depression in the ground, the whole thing seems contrived. These old fables and folk tales are always the same. There is a core of fact, the basic story is true but the fact is then distorted out of all recognition. Whether it be the Dunnottar Crown jewels, the Fenella felony or the literal Lairds o' Garvock, the telling has taken over from the reality. It is all history now.

Down in Conveth life continued its uneventful way, punctuated only by a few riotous days each St. James's Fair, until Lord Gardenstone (1721-93) purchased the adjoining estate of Johnston in 1764. Lord Gardenstone had just been appointed Sheriff of Kincardine and was obviously intent on making his mark. As soon as he bought Johnston estate he set about reshaping Conveth into a model village. His aim was to provide good modern accommodation for all the residents and put up extra buildings to attract new industries.

For years the name *Conveth* had alternated with that of *Laurencekirk*. Lord Gardenstone settled for Laurencekirk. His new village was a success. Rents didn't go up as much as the residents had feared, the layout of the place was better and new industry was attracted. The best known of these was the snuffbox manufacturing of Charles Stiven. Chae Stiven had already made a name for himself as a maker of snuffboxes in his native Glenbervie before Lord Gardenstone invited him down to settle in Laurencekirk.

Charlie never regretted the move. He continued to produce his excellent snuffboxes but now they were called Laurencckirk snuffboxes. Their outstanding feature was the hinge on the lid which was of a concealed, integral, interlocking centre pin construction made to a microscopic tolerance. Charles Stiven was joined by his son Alexander who subsequently took over the Stiven business and by William Milne who married Alexander's sister. These were the three main producers of Laurencekirk snuffboxes but there were other less skilful imitators who cashed in on the Laurencekirk label. *Laurencekirk* is now accepted as the generic term for any snuffbox with the Laurencekirk-type hinge and they come in

horn, bone, wood, tortoiseshell or any combination thereof.
To the folk who knew him it was not surprising that Lord
Gardenstone should invite a snuffbox maker to set up business
in Laurencekirk. Lord Gardenstone was a snuff addict to such
an extent that he was reputed to go around with his clothes
powdered in the stuff. It is said that people talking to Lord
Gardenstone were able to help themselves to a sneeshin from
the surplus snuff caught in the folds of his clothing.

It was Lord Gardenstone's initiative that established the new
Laurencekirk and set up its flourishing linen trade and snuff
mull manufactory but that was at the end of the eighteenth
century; a long time ago. In 1965 a small boy at Laurencekirk
school, Bill Kerr, read about the snuff mulls in his school
geography book and wandered the streets for hours looking
for the shop that made them. When he finally asked for
directions he was ridiculed and laughed at for not knowing that
snuffboxes hadn't been made in Laurencekirk this century.
Laurencekirk was famous for snuff mulls. It is no longer
famous. It is busy right now getting back its original role as the
market town of the Mearns.

Laurencekirk is just one more little town that is happily
recovering its identity now that the traffic has been diverted.
The Laurencekirk bypass that leads the howling banshee past
its perimeter has restored a measure of dignity to the town.
Fearful accidents happen regularly along the length of the dual
carriageway but Laurencekirk is spared the pestilential
disadvantage of traffic jams and polluted air. Cars still block
the mile-long main street but they're in no hurry to get
through now and the drivers know each other and wave. As
you leave Laurencekirk at the south end you will see Lord
Gardenstone's quaint little village green and pagoda-like
shelter that reflects the present tranquillity of the place. It is an
unexpected feature for a Mearns market town, and a delight.

If Laurencekirk is not to be saddled permanently with its
reputation for linen stuffs and snuffboxes, we must look for
better means to remember the place. Thomas Ruddiman,
schoolmaster in Laurencekirk, might suit our purpose.
Ruddiman (1674-1757) was a classicist and noted grammarian
whose *Rudiments of the Latin Tongue* became the standard
textbook for the teaching of Latin, for centuries. He became an

outstanding publisher in Edinburgh, as well as Keeper of the Advocates' Library there. He reflects fully as much credit on Laurencekirk as Chae Stiven and his fancy snuff mulls.

Down the B9120 from Laurencekirk one comes back to Fettercairn by a different road. The little village of Fettercairn marks the end of the lush lands of the Luther Valley and the start of the climb up to Cairn o' Mounth. Five roads meet at Fettercairn and it is still a quiet little village. The last time anything happened in Fettercairn, barring the annual Cattle Show, was on 20th September 1861. That was the night Queen Victoria and Prince Albert spent, *incognito,* in the Ramsay Arms.

The best description of that visit can be found in Queen Victoria's own *Journal of Our Visit to the Highlands* and makes good reading. The whole point of the exercise was to allow Victoria and Albert to spend a few days alone together away from all the fuss and protocol. Her diary tells how the two intrepid travellers roughed it alone with only two manservants and a wench to serve their dinner in the Ramsay Arms. After the meal the pair went for a walk round Fettercairn accompanied only by 'General Gray, Louis and Alice and Lady Churchill'. It was a lovely quiet moonlit night when 'Suddenly we heard a drum and fifes! We were greatly alarmed, fearing we had been recognised, but Louis and General Gray who went back, saw nothing whatsoever'.

That was a near thing and no mistake. When the party went back to the hotel to find out what was going on, 'Albert asked the little maid and the answer was "It's just a band" and that it walked about in this way twice a week. How odd!' Queen Victoria records her belief that 'The landlord and landlady knew who we were but no-one else except the coachman and he kept the secret admirably'. Aye, weel, that's as may be. When the party left in the morning, 'The people had just discovered who we were and a few cheered as we went along'.

It is possible that Fettercairn didn't know that it was Queen Victoria that night, but only just. The landlord knew and the landlord's wife knew. The landlord was Charlie Durward and it would seem a fair bet that at some stage of the visit wee Mrs Durward would feel the urge to nip out and tell somebody, but there it is. Maybe Fettercairn Band was in the habit of walking round the streets in the dark. Fettercairn erected a Memorial Arch to commemorate the visit and hinder traffic by the Ramsay Arms and the real significance of the Royal Visit is that they still talk about it in Fettercairn. That is the measure of the place. The other talking point in Fettercairn is the annual Cattle Show and Sports at the beginning of July each year. Fettercairn Show is the best of its kind. It retains all the old attraction of the traditional cattle show and country get-together without too much imposed modern trumpery. All that remains of native Scotch culture can be seen at Fettercairn Show in one way or another. The cattle, sheep and horses on show are equal to any similar livestock in the world. The Women's Institute tent with its fantastic display of baking, craftwork and produce is a revelation of the highest domestic skill and the local sporting events are village entertainment at its best. The professional 'heavies' with their hammer throwing and wrestling provide the essential spectacular for the crowd. Attending Fettercairn Show is a most reassuring experience when the old Scotch way of life is disappearing so rapidly around us. Fettercairn is holding on to its past.

'Scotch' is certainly the word in Fettercairn, for Whyte and Mackay's distillery at Nethermill produces one of the best of all Scotch whiskies. Most of their single malt output goes for blending but a limited amount is bottled under their 'Old Fettercairn' label, and a rare treat it is. The limited production means that Old Fettercairn is not widely known but it is well worth looking for.

Scotch single malt whisky as produced in Fettercairn is world-famous for its excellence. It is a pure natural drink made from malted barley and fresh spring water with just a leavening of yeast. The term 'Scotch' is the internationally accepted criterion of quality in whiskies. There are blended whiskies, de luxe whiskies, single malt whiskies and vatted malt whiskies; all Scotch and all different.

The best way to find out about whisky is to go along to Fettercairn Distillery and see their Visitors' Centre. It is new and excellent. They have a video room where you sit down to see a film of the whisky-making process, and whilst you are watching it a young lass comes in with a tray of glasses and

Kinnear Square, Laurencekirk.

hands round free drams. That fairly fixes your attention. When the film is over and the dram demolished a guide takes you round the distillery and shows you the whole process from start to finish. More folk should know about Fettercairn Distillery.

At one time there was only one way of making whisky and that was the pot-still, single-malt way as in Fettercairn; then in 1830 an exciseman called Aeneas Coffey invented the Coffey Still. Despite the quite ridiculous name for a whisky process it caught on. The Coffey Still with its continuous distillation method can make whisky out of malted barley, unmalted rye and, I hesitate to add, American maize. American maize is better known to older generations as hen beans. To the best of my knowledge the system has not yet been tried with old rubber tyres. The great bulk of Scotch whisky is now made in Coffey stills and is blended with just as much pot-still single malt as makes it drinkable. With enough Old Fettercairn added, even the distillate of hen beans can be made enjoyable. All the different grades of Scotch whisky depend simply on the amount of single malt added and the length of the maturation period allowed. Vatted malts are blends of different single malts and very few are produced. Old Fettercairn is a pure undefiled single malt and a lasting credit to the twelve men and a girl who make it.

When one visits Fettercairn of a morning with the sun shining and not a soul stirring in the square, one sees why Queen Victoria's visit is still a major topic of conversation. There is not a lot to see in Fettercairn once you've studied the mercat cross and Queen Victoria's Arch and bought sweets in the shop. Folk who go to Fettercairn these days are usually heading for Fasque House or the Cairn o' Mounth. That leaves Fettercairn to the *cognoscenti* who appreciate its tranquillity.

A side road from Fettercairn runs up past the Distillery to link up with the back road from Fasque at Thainston to come round by Balnakettle and Balfour and rejoin the B966 just above Gannochy bridge. This is one of the very many unspoiled side roads that take the perceptive visitor into the real Scottish countryside. The folk up here have only to switch off their television sets to be back in the natural unspoiled countryside of a hundred years ago where birds and beasts are free. This is a land where the changing seasons mark the drama of the year – where summer days drone by in torpid heat and autumn nights draw in to winter's chill. These are the varied impacts of the year. These are the things that make the country so superior to the town. As more and more of our population becomes town dwelling, so fewer and fewer of our children will ever know the fun of country living. Spring in Scotland should not be withheld from Scottish children. When the roadsides are dappled with snowdrops and the yellow heads of daffodils emerge to start the colouring of the year, children should be there to see. Towns are sterile playgrounds. Children should be loosed in the countryside in Spring to see, to hear, to learn and to be happy; that is their ideal environment.

The Most Beautiful Glen in Angus

Just before you arrive at Gannochy bridge the road to Glen Esk runs off to the right. Glen Esk is the most easterly and, by unanimous vote of the Glen Esk inhabitants, the most beautiful

Pot stills, Fettercairn Distillery. The heart of the whisky-making process.

of all the Angus glens. There is no through road from Glen Esk and visitors must return by the access road. It is a winding route that runs for some fourteen miles along the line of the North Esk to Tarfside village, then a further four miles to Loch Lee. Cars are allowed only as far as Lochlee Kirk but the road continues up to Loch Lee and tracks run further into the hills by Glens Lee and Mark.

At the start of the glen the river forms the boundary between Kincardine and Angus but Glen Esk is an Angus glen. It is the last of the series of similar and nearly parallel Angus glens that run from the Strathmore Valley into the hills. Its beauty lies in its variety of scene. Rocky ravine and white water torrent at the start give way to flat meadow land and a rippling stream half way up before returning to chasm and cleft and dark, turbid pool at the top. All the glories of Lowland and Highland are encapsulated in Glen Esk. You need go no farther.

Apart from its scenery, Glen Esk has other features to make it special. It has, for a start, a most active and self-sufficient native population. The old way of glen life is not far removed from the present way of glen life. Modern farming methods do not apply to hill sheep stations quite as they do to lowland cropping farms. Glen farms still look like farms with buchts and troughs and hens running about. The present Skene, Main, Myles and Littlejohn families still farm pretty much as their grandfathers did. The village of Tarfside is the hub of their community, a new shop has opened recently and the threatened Post Office has been granted a reprieve. What had seemed the inevitable demise of the Glen community has been arrested yet again.

The highlights of the Tarfside season are the Sheep Dog Trials and the Annual Games. The Games, held on the last Friday in July and their attendant dance in the Masonic Hall are the peak of the Glen season. They must be the last genuine Highland Games left in Scotland. Tests of strength, agility and stamina for the local lads, they are a source of much amusement for the folk. There is no professional element in Glen Esk. The pothunters give it a miss. When you hear a steward tell a competitor at the start of a race, 'Na na, loon, ye gin roon the back o' the wid syne up through the gate', you know you are in Arcadia. No cosmopolitan gloss cloaks the original patina of Glen Esk.

These are the native glen festivities; visitors look for the summer opening of the Retreat. For many of them the Retreat is Glen Esk. It is a Folk Museum, tearoom and craft centre a mile or so south of Tarfside and a gem of its kind. Folk Museums are thick on the ground these days, some of them

Fettercairn, late Kincardine, Cross.

more folk than museum, but the Retreat is different.

Back in 1955 before the Folk Museum bandwagon had properly started, a few of the Glen Esk folk were concerned about the depopulation of the glen, the influx of newcomers and the death of the old way of life that they and the glen had known. Amongst those people, fortunately for us, was Miss Greta Michie, the Tarfside schoolmistress. Miss Michie was a local lady who had all the attributes of your good rural school head. She knew all her pupils, she knew all her pupils' parents and she could badger folk – pupils, parents and passers-by alike – into doing what she told them. When Miss Michie took up the idea of a glen museum she made it fizz. In no time she had amassed a collection of glen memorabilia that threatened to engulf her. A Glen Museum Trust was hastily convened and an approach to Lord Dalhousie was immediately met with the offer of the Retreat, a private residence just off the main road a mile or so short of Tarfside, to hold it.

The Retreat is ideal for the purpose. When Miss Michie had installed all her bits and pieces, there was still room for a Highland Home Industries' shop and a tearoom. The tearoom has been a boon. Stocked, staffed and served by Glen Esk ladies whose home baking is legendary, the Retreat tearoom is a tourist target. On a sunny summer's afternoon it can be a close-run thing between the attraction of the river at Dalbrack bridge and the cream sponges at the Retreat. The Retreat usually wins because there is always the excuse of the museum to look at. Miss Michie's collection is a model of its kind. It holds just about everything the glen ever held. It has rooms laid out like glen rooms: pictures, letters, snuff mulls, glasses, guns and teapots. The way of glen life is clearly illustrated in the Retreat. It has articles of Queen Victoria's dress on show, for the good Queen herself came over to visit the glen from Balmoral in 1861. The Queen's Well marks the spot, somewhat ostentatiously one fears, where she paused for refreshment. In her entourage was one George Michie, a 'game herd' who tended her garrons.

George Michie was a grand-uncle of Miss Michie of Tarfside, and from him a number of the Queen's personal possessions eventually passed to Miss Michie. You will find them now in the Retreat. One which you will not find in the Retreat is a gold circlet with clear agates enclosing a sprig of white heather and inscribed 'From B, 1875'. 'B' was John Brown. In 1872 John Brown had overpowered a man, Arthur O'Connor, who pointed a revolver at the Queen as she entered Buckingham Palace. The weapon was subsequently found to be unloaded but no-one, least of all John Brown, knew that at the time. In gratitude for his bravery the Queen gave him a gold medal. One wonders, as always, about the closeness of the relationship that permitted John Brown to give the Queen such a gift a few years later. The inscribed and enigmatic brooch is not included in the Retreat display.

A view of Fettercairn before the traffic roundabout spoiled it. The
Ramsay Arms can be seen through Queen Victoria's Arch.

So many folk stream up Glen Esk now in summer that traffic
is becoming a major problem. For years cars have been stopped
from going right up to Loch Lee; now new car parks are
having to be provided at Lochlee Kirk to cope with the cars and
buses that have to stop there. One result of all this tourist
traffic is that the Brechin folk now picnic up Glen Lethnot
instead of Glen Esk. Where will they go when the emmets find
Lethnot?

Lower down the glen, a mile in from the B966, there is a
caravan park that must rate amongst the best. For a start you
can drive right past it without ever seeing it. All you see is a
discreet sign and an entrance into a wood. The whole park is
landscaped with trees so that the vans are all screened from the
road and from each other, with belts of trees. If all caravan
parks were made to conform to the same standards of site
concealment, a major eyesore could be removed from every
holiday resort.

Burn House and its Estate

Across the road from the caravan site stand the house and grounds of the Burn. Originally called simply Burn House, the definite article was a later addition. Burn estate was bought by Lord Adam Gordon, Member of Parliament for Kincardine, in 1780 and the house rebuilt between 1791 and 1796. Lord Adam Gordon died in 1801 and the estate passed through several hands until eventually it was bought by Mr Herbert Russell in 1921 and partly rebuilt by him between 1933 and 1935. Until the outbreak of war in 1939 the Burn was the Russell family home, then it was requisitioned by the Government. The original intention was to make the Burn into an emergency maternity hospital for Dundee. At that stage it was feared that every major town in Britain would be bombed immediately and alternative hospital cover was set up. When Dundee was not seriously attacked, the Burn was made into a military convalescent hospital.

At the end of the war when the house was returned to Mr and Mrs Russell, they decided to dedicate it as a memorial to their son who had been killed in Italy in 1944. Because the Burn had been such a happy home for the family when the children were young, the Russells felt that it should be used for the continued benefit of young people. After some tentative enquiries, an approach was made to the Dominion Students' Hall Trust and in 1949 the house was handed over with an endowment. History has demanded a change in name for the Trust and it is now known as the London House for Overseas Graduates Trust. The house is used as a holiday/study centre for overseas students and for study courses run by the Scottish universities.

The Burn house is fortunate in that it is still in use. So many similar houses in Scotland have been knocked down, blown up or simply allowed to fall apart that the existence of the Burn as a dwelling house – even a students' hostel – is encouraging. There may be hope yet for others. The Burn was designed in the Adam style, and although it was subsequently modified somewhat out of context, it is inoffensive *in situ* and well worth preserving. The gardens and policies have been allowed to revert largely to nature but the Herculean task of maintaining immediate grounds and driveways is still attempted by a minimal staff.

Along the bank of the North Esk skirting the grounds of the estate, there is a walk much used and enjoyed by the public that well merits a visit. It is approached by a door in the wall beside the Gannochy bridge. The original path was reputedly cut by French prisoners-of-war working for Lord Adam Gordon and doubtless that is so. Lord Adam Gordon was a very senior and successful soldier. The walk holds to the line of the river and leads up to the Rocks of Solitude, a precipitous ravine where the river slides smooth and peat-brown before dashing itself white through clefts in the rock.

If your visit coincides with either the Spring or back-end runs of the salmon you may see and share the romance of the running fish; when the primeval instinct, the atavistic urge, to spawn and procreate sends the broad deep-bellied salmon from the sea to fight the river. Time and time again you will see the torrent dash them back. Eventually they win through. When the leap seems least possible they will rise higher, fight harder and beat the flood to continue their compulsive journey to the smooth water redds below Loch Lee. Nothing in nature can outdo that scene. When you see the salmon run, you see the work of God. He is never far from you in Glen Esk.

The Village of Edzell

About a mile down from the Gannochy bridge is Edzell, a village of distinction regularly featuring in 'Best Kept Village' lists. Edzell owes its existence to the Brechin-Edzell railway, three custom-built hotels and a golf course, for Edzell is a product of the tourist boom. The tourist boom that came with the railway in the nineteenth century, that is.

The original and historic Edzell was built around Edzell Castle, a stronghold of the Lindsays one mile west of the present village. Old Edzell exists now only as the ruined castle, the old chapel and the burial ground which is still used for Edzell folk. When the parish kirk moved from old Edzell to the present site on Edzell common in 1818 it took the Edzell name with it. The old name for today's Edzell was Slateford. Little is heard of the old Edzell nowadays except amongst firearms experts and collectors of old Scottish pistols, for Edzell at one time in the eighteenth century rivalled Doune in Perthshire as a manufactory of steel pistols. The present Edzell is something of an anachronism. Built to cater for the better class of Victorian tourist, the *bon ton* of the nineteenth century, it has always provided a safe haven for retired gentlefolk. If the term is somewhat dated, so is the population of Edzell. They sell a lot of pink gins in Edzell Golf Club. The last of the Old Colonial Boys still meet in the Men's Bar and the Second World War is regularly re-enacted. Fewer in number as each new season opens, the present group has Bob Hall as doyen and mentor. Bob Hall is an ex-tea planter, ex-Indian Army officer and ex-ten handicap polo player who played with maharajas; in the days when there were maharajas. The pre-lunch pink gin is an acquired taste but the crack is worth listening to.

Edzell is far enough off the A94 to be spared the brasher elements of tourism, and with its broad main street, extensive recreation grounds and common – courtesy of Dalhousie Estates Ltd – its river and woodland walks and easy access to the hills, Edzell is a delight. The ceremonial archway at the south end of the village is the Dalhousie Memorial Arch, erected in 1882 by the Edzell folk in memory of the Earl and Countess of Dalhousie who died within a few hours of each other in 1881. The floodlights which have just been installed to light up the archway are an eyesore.

Less than a mile to the east over the river from Edzell lies Edzell airfield. Built just before the last war as a fighter station, it is now a top-secret American airbase. Out of respect and in deference to our American allies one does not attempt to breach their total security ban on disclosing its present function, but anyone in Angus and the Mearns will tell you all about it if you care to ask. They will also tell you, if you ask, that the American servicemen from the Edzell base are the best-behaved servicemen you will find anywhere. There are hundreds of them living on-base and off-base, and hardly ever do you find an American causing trouble. Over the years they have integrated so well with the local population that they have become indistinguishable except that they are better behaved.

Edzell Castle. Magnus Magnusson opening newly restored area in 1987.

The only complaint one might reasonably level against the Americans is that they have applied a kind of latter-day Clearance to the area. They keep marrying the pick of our crop of young lassies.

Along from the airbase is Luthermuir, a plain little clachan laid out in regimented lines. It served as a centre for handloom weaving at one time and the last of Scotland's genuine time-served, self-employed handloom weavers was Will Taylor, who still lives in the village. His last Jacquard loom is now installed and operating at the House of Dun as a tourist attraction.

Brechin – Ancient City and Modern Town

Next stop, down the A94 or rather just off the A94 since the by-pass was opened, is Brechin. When the upstart settlements of Montrose, Arbroath and Forfar were still struggling for recognition, Brechin was the cultural, commercial and ecclesiastical authority for the district. Brechin made the laws, Brechin gave the orders: any Brechiner will tell you.

Brechin first registered its name when it was visited by a party of evangelising Culdees from Ireland around 900 AD and they established a religious settlement on the brae above Skinner's Burn. Brechin Cathedral occupies the site today. The Cathedral of Brechin has been a Christian church in some form or another ever since. It started as an Irish Culdee mission house and is now the parish kirk; in the intervening years it has been Celtic, Pictish, Roman, Episcopalian, several kinds of Reformed Protestant and now Presbyterian. The cathedral building has been developed over centuries and the present structure is the result of a rebuilding in 1900 to correct a previous, unsatisfactory reconstruction in 1806.

Of necessity the architectural style is conglomerate, incorporating as it does elements of church building going back to the first century AD The resultant kirk is a very pleasing amalgamation of different influences, enhanced by some of the finest stained glass in Scotland. Brechin Cathedral is a joy to see when the sun streams in and the vibrant colours of its radiant windows light up the muted interior. Several Pictish carved stones are kept in the Cathedral and until recently there was a display of church silver and pewter. Unfortunately, the patens, tankards and ceremonial plate with all their deep significance for Brechin and the Cathedral were stolen after a break-in through one of the stained-glass windows. One pewter flagon was subsequently recovered from an antiques stall in a London market but nothing else has turned up so far. Even if any more is found now, it can never again be left on open display.

Brechin Cathedral was founded by King Kenneth II of Scotland in 971 AD, confirmed by King David I in 1150, subsidised by Robert the Bruce in 1338, suspended by the Duke of Montrose in 1645, sacked by Cromwell in 1653, visited by Bonnie Prince Charlie's men in 1746, the Duke of Cumberland's a week later and in 1764 suffered a riot by the Brechiners themselves. It has been sacked, levelled, rebuilt, knocked down and set up again a time or two, and if you examine the fabric of the building, it shows. It is no longer a

Dalhousie Arch, Edzell. The floodlights are less obtrusive in a photograph.

cathedral in the literal sense of being the seat of a Bishop; the See of Brechin and the Bishop of Brechin are now centred in Dundee, but Brechin Cathedral is still a living monument of faith. When you walk down the Chanonry Wynd to the Cathedral today, as ever, you approach the beating heart of Brechin. History is in the air, emanating from the memorial stones and all around you when you enter the precincts of the old monastic quarters, the Sang Schule and the Bishop's Close. Whatever your religion you must be impressed by the dedication of generations of Brechin's citizens in maintaining their positive testimony to the Christian faith.

The oldest surviving part of the Christian settlement of Brechin is the Round Tower, built by the original Culdee missionaries. It stands at the south-west corner of the Cathedral, a symbol and a totem for Brechiners worldwide. Brechin Round Tower is one of only two in Scotland, the other being at Abernethy. Round towers were built as sanctuaries and repositories for church valuables in time of danger. Their construction coincides with the period of Viking raids on Britain, particularly on the Angus coastline, and the Brechin Round Tower is a classic of its kind.

One hundred and six feet to its topmost point, the original

161

tower was eighty-six feet high. The pointed top was a later addition. Its base is fifteen feet across and its top thirteen, but the internal measurement is a regular eight feet for the whole of its length. Only the most sophisticated and exact skills of stonemasonry could effect such a construction. The stones at the base are three-and-a-half feet thick, diminishing as they rise in spiral courses to two-and-a-half feet at the top. Each stone is dressed to the curve and fractionally narrower, giving a gradual taper to the top whilst preserving the perfect circle. When one thinks of all the attendant problems of stone quarrying and transporting, scaffolding and jib crane rigging, manoeuvring each stone into position and checking for curve and taper, the Round Tower becomes a marvel. It is just a pity that no record exists of the Culdees' agreements with their stonemasons on working hours, incentive schemes, danger money, bonus payments and number and length of statutory piecey-times. That would be history worth reading.

Across Skinner's Burn from the Cathedral and the Tower, on the adjoining hill, is Brechin Castle, one of the oldest inhabited dwellings in Scotland. Much modified and altered over the centuries, it is now the residence of the Earl of Dalhousie of the family of Maule-Ramsay. With all the rumbustious goings-on that regularly punctuated the litanies in the Cathedral's peaceful precincts, it is obvious that over the years Brechin Castle would be rather more than just a rustic retreat for the Maules. Its most notable entry in the history books is probably the occasion on 10th July 1296 when John Baliol surrendered the Scottish Crown and Kingdom to England and had the Great Seal of Scotland smashed in front of him 'in a very humiliating manner'. I'll say.

Just after that, in 1303, the Castle was besieged by King Edward I's army for three weeks before it fell. It probably wouldn't have fallen then but for a wee bit of bravado by the Governor, Sir Thomas Maule. It happened that the English had brought with them the latest thing in hi-tech weaponry: an engine of war they called the 'War Wolf'. This was a catapult of prodigious strength to hurl stones at fortified positions and break down castle walls – the ultimate deterrent of its day. The War Wolf had just papped a bool up on to the castle wall when the bold Sir Thomas stepped forward and dusted the spot with

Brechin Cathedral and Round Tower.

his kerchief in a gesture of defiance. Aye, weel, his defiance was short enough lived, for the very next chuckie hit him square on and killed him.

Neither Brechin Castle nor Brechin Cathedral is immediately visible to the passing stranger. The Cathedral is hidden by shops and houses, the Castle is screened by trees. Many casual visitors to the Ancient City of Brechin, arriving by the Forfar road, are in some doubt as to whether they are looking at the Castle or the Cathedral. In fact they are looking at the Mechanics' Institute. Well do they then say amongst themselves, 'If this is their Mechanics' Institute, what can their Cathedral look like?' Pause, passing stranger, and find out. Park your car in the Church Street car park and walk.

The Mechanics' Institute that fronts the Forfar road is the imposing building that looks like a cross between a cathedral and a castle. Donated by Lord Panmure and opened in 1838, it comprised a school, a library, a mechanics' institute as the name indicates and a public meeting hall. It is now run purely as a meeting hall administered by a committee of dedicated local people who have had to fight hard to save and maintain it. Brechin is well served by its citizens, for the Cathedral has its Society of Friends of Brechin Cathedral which exists to help, support and generally assist in the running of the Cathedral. They do good works.

In the eighteenth and nineteenth centuries Brechin was a handloom-weaving centre like all the other Angus towns, but Brechin became more industrialised and set up bigger factories earlier than the others. By the end of the nineteenth century, Brechin was a thriving manufacturing town producing jute, linen and woollen fabrics, paper, whisky and machine tools. Day and night twenty factory chimneys belched smoke into the clear air and the workers' lives ran to the scream of factory whistles. Where tourists now play pitch-and-putt by the riverside there used to be great bleachfields and factories. The factories bore the names of the Brechin folk who owned them – Dukes', Lambs', Smarts', Dakers' and Greigs'. These are the remembered names. Nobody now thinks of Annabella Dear, Maggie Cooper and Janet Williamson who worked their looms.

Of the old textile mills, only Smarts' Valley Works still functions. The firm has been successively taken over by Don and Low and Shell Industries and now produces broadloom polypropylene for carpet backing and furnishing fabrics. The high-grade linen and the bleachfields have long gone. The Valley Works and Glencadam Distillery are the only two of the old Brechin industries still operating but new enterprises are being established all the time to replace them.

One can hardly refer to the Coventry Gauge and Tool Company as a 'new enterprise' in Brechin, for they came during the Second World War and stayed on, but in terms of Dukes, Smarts and the Cathedral, they are not old. 'The Coventry' produces precision instruments and fine-gauge machine tools and provides a major part of Brechin's economy. Other 'new' industries include a Venetian blind factory, a light engineering company, a cartridge-loading concern and a package-making firm. The weekly cattle auctions have ended but an ultra-modern, hi-tech animal processing and meat-packing plant is working to capacity. That is a euphemism for saying that the slaughter-house is doing well. Of all its new industrial developments, the one that would seem to be most likely to take over as a staple industry for the future is Anglia Canners. They put locally grown soft fruits, vegetables and potatoes into tins. With the vast resources of Angus agriculture behind them, they would seem to be providing a service of unlimited potential. Recent expansion of the firm's premises and workforce appears to confirm this.

Brechin is an ancient city and a modern town. It has long enjoyed a commanding position in Angus and the Mearns – and rightly so. Its streets are redolent with history and tradition, its people are couthy and kind. In the circumstances it is inevitable that the foul fiend of jealousy should, on occasion, have cast covetous eyes on such an Elysium. How else can one explain that tale of the First World War when a German Zeppelin ventured over the coast near Montrose and came to Brechin? As the dastardly dirigible circled the city the crew studied the Castle, the Cathedral, the Round Tower, the ruined chapel of Maisondieu and all the old houses of the High Street. Just when the bomb aimer was making the last fine adjustment to his sights, the Captain called out to him 'Hold it, Fritz, we've been here already', and they floated on . . . one blushes to repeat such calumny.

Whilst it is true that at one time Brechin did have a somewhat dilapidated air about it, the maintenance and repair of its historic buildings is now well in hand. The Friends of the Cathedral, the Mechanics' Committee, local government departments and other bodies are all actively engaged in preservation projects. In addition, beavering away on his own, is Brechin's one-man restoration and rebuilding agency, Bill Cook.

Willie Cook is a phenomenon. A non-smoking, non-gambling teetotaller, he works harder than it seems possible for any one man to do. He has restored buildings in Brechin, Montrose and Aberdeen all by himself and won awards for his work. In Church Street, Brechin, there is a plaque on one of the walls recording his awards from the Civic Trust and the Regional Council. The standard of his work is the highest possible and he works obsessively.

Visitors to Brechin have been known to pity this honest labouring man endlessly pushing his barrowloads of old stones and new bathroom suites around derelict properties. They need feel no such emotion. The more perceptive among them might note that he whistles classical music whilst he works, his bonnet is set happily on the back of his head and it is the knees of his dungarees that are worn out, not the backside. Willie

Cook relishes his work. He is a cultured gentleman with a wicked sense of humour and but one obvious self-indulgence. His car is a brand-new, straight off the production line Rolls Royce.

The Satellite Settlements of Brechin

As the old administration centre of Angus and without the sea or the hills to restrict its influence, Brechin has always had a number of satellite settlements. One mile to the north lies Trinity village, so called because the Cathedral of Brechin is the Cathedral of the Holy Trinity. Trinity village – 'Taranty' in the local patois – was the site of one of the great mediaeval fairs and livestock markets. Taranty Tryst is now no more than a travelling fun fair with a two-day stopover but it still has a powerful significance for Brechin. There are still old Brechiners who remember the days of the horse copers, the boxing booths, the hobby horses and the genuine gold watches. Auld ferm chiels wha first went to Taranty Tryst as bothy loons now escort grandchildren who spend more siller in half an hour than the old boys saw in a twelvemonth. Taranty Tryst is deep-bedded in the Brechin psyche.

Nowadays, Trinity Muir is a popular golf course run by Brechin Golf and Squash Club. When the Tryst is on in June the first fairway and the eighteenth green are roped off for the duration of the fair and golfers lose these two holes for a few days. Centuries of tradition, use, wont, habit and custom shape the folk festival that is Taranty Tryst. It features in the annual migrations of the travelling folk; it is part of Brechin's heritage. The young bloods of the Brechin Golf and Squash Club want the travellers' wagons banned from *their* golf course.

In the days before the reorganisation of local government, when Brechin still had a Town Council and a Provost, Brechin also had a Town Officer. The last full-time incumbent was the late James Leiper. James was a valued adjunct to the Brechin scene. Dressed in his formal attire of red coat, white waistcoat, black trousers and black top hat, James Leiper lent authority and dignity to any gathering. He led all the civic processions and attended all Council meetings and formal assemblies. One

Maisondieu Chapel, Brechin.

of his many duties was the auctioning of sites for stalls at the Trinity market and he did it all with meticulous formality. James Leiper was a living tradition. He carried a ceremonial staff as emblem of his authority and Jim was not at all averse to administering a poke with the halberd to any of the lieges who didn't get out of the way smartly enough. Brechin's Town Officer didn't just look like a circus ringmaster, he performed like one.

The bypass road which has helped Brechin so much has also allowed Trinity village to breathe again. The road still cuts the golf course in two but a bridge connects the two halves with only a short walk between. Walking over the bridge lets you see the terrifying speeds reached by traffic on the bypass. Trinity golf course is pleasantly sited. It has too many parallel fairways for golfing comfort but it has some lovely viewpoints. The second half, over the bridge, slopes down in a smooth tree-girt expanse towards Murlingden with the ramparts of the Caterthuns and the mass of Wirren providing an imposing backdrop.

The White and the Brown Caterthuns are the first line of the Braes of Angus, the foothills that mark the edge of the great Strath. On top of each is an Iron Age settlement. The Brown Caterthun was the earlier and has been eroded much more, leaving only residual traces of defensive works ringing the top of the hill. The White Caterthun still has the remains of massive stoneworks crowning its top with defensive wall-and-ditch works below, just discernible in the heather. The White Caterthun is one of these primitive sites, like Callanish or Stonehenge itself, which induces moods of deep contemplation in the visitor. It is the spirit of the place. To stand on the White Caterthun of a November forenicht under a louring sky with the wind whipping ice-rain pellets at you, or to sit on the warm stones of the White Cater on a May morning when the air vibrates with larksong and soft breezes waft the scents of broom and heather down Lethnot and over the Strath, is to experience one emotion. A sense of wonder: a stirring of folk memory: a transcendental instinct that prompts prayer. That is what the White Caterthun does to you.

Below the Caterthuns and back on the Brechin road, you come to Little Brechin. Plenty of folk have gone through Little Brechin and not realised it but they have put up name plates now which should help. The old houses and pendicles of Little Brechin are set back off the road and the centuries have dealt lightly with them until now. Little Brechin is now being developed. Old cottages are being rebuilt and refurbished and you want to walk pretty quickly past some of them. The walk from Brechin, past Langhaugh, West Park, the Pittendreichs and back to Brechin used to be a favourite Brechin walk in the days when folk went for walks.

Continuing the circle round Brechin one comes to Careston, with church, school, castle and little else, which makes for a most delightful unspoiled rural parish. Careston Castle is still inhabited and is a development of a very old foundation much altered and replaced over the years. The Careston road, which branches to Fern, Farmerton and Noranside, is one of the quiet byways that probe the heart of Angus – the arteries that carry the lifeblood of the clachans and the ferm touns of Strathmore – the roads that lead to the quiet places. Fern village, where the kirk and school stand sequestered in a timeless wooden den, is the quietest of places.

Farther along the Kirriemuir road from Fern is Noranside, once a country house and estate but now an open prison. In between times it was a sanatorium, in the days when pulmonary tuberculosis was rife and the only known treatment was fresh air and sunshine. It is easy now to forget how recently that was. The original Noranside House is now the nucleus of a residential unit, and with staff housing, social club and all the constituent buildings of such a place, Noranside is quite a village.

Returning to the Brechin area and continuing the circle to the south-east from Careston, one comes to the main Forfar-Brechin road, the A94(T). Finavon, now a hotel, filling station and fast-food joint, was once renowned for the Castle of Finavon, home and stronghold of the Earl Beardie. The Earl Beardie, so called because of his great unkempt beard, was the Earl of Crawford, a notorious member of a notorious clique. The various Earls – of Douglas, Crawford, Ross, Huntly, Moray and their fellows – were prone to fight. They fought to establish their sovereignty, they fought to establish their places in the order of precedence; they fought because fighting was what Earls did.

Earl Beardie was renowned as a fighter even amongst Earls. When the Earl of Douglas was murdered in Stirling Castle in February 1452, Earl Beardie immediately undertook to avenge the deed for the Douglases. He made an alliance with the Earl of Ross to oppose the King, and in the month of May, when the Earl of Huntly was on his way down at the head of his army to support King James II, Earl Beardie intercepted him. At Huntly Hill near Brechin a battle ensued and the Tiger Earl started a hot favourite. He had the form, the breeding, and he knew the course. When the battle started at 11 a.m. on 18th May 1452 and Earl Beardie had his men entrenched on the top of the hill and the Earl of Huntly was approaching unawares, you couldn't have found a bookmaker in Brechin to quote you a price.

It should – and would – have been a walkover for the Tiger Earl had not skullduggery intervened. The Laird of Balnamoon was in command of one of Earl Beardie's crack units, a company of heavily armed spearmen that stood poised to swing into action and win the day. At the crucial moment, when the battle was equally balanced and the intervention of Balnamoon's men was all that was needed, they swung into action on Huntly's side. Balnamoon had suffered some minor slight from Earl Beardie the day before and in retaliation he changed sides and won the Battle of Brechin for the Earl of Huntly. Not many folk even know that there *was* a Battle of Brechin. Earl Beardie's castle of Finavon is now a ruin, the Victorian castle beside it is now let off in flats and Earl Beardie is a footnote in the history books.

The A94 crosses the South Esk by the Finavon bridge and the only other road bridge between that and the venerable Brechin bridge is the Stannochy bridge on the B9134. There is a third bridge, the Image bridge, so called because of the statues incorporated in its structure, but that is inside the grounds of Brechin Castle and is not accessible to the general public. The B9134 is the old Brechin-Forfar road still favoured by the locals in preference to the madness on the A94. The old road runs level out to Netherton, then starts the climb up the Aberlemno and Finavon hills, and the lay-by at the top of the first rise is one of the popular viewpoints of Angus. Even better views can be had from the heights of the old Pictish/Roman fort farther along the ridge of Finavon hill but few folk ever take that quiet side road that drops down from Aberlemno to Finavon – I'm glad to say.

Aberlemno village was once three little clachans of Crosston, Flemington and Aberlemno; now it is one. The main points of interest in Aberlemno are the four sculptured Pictish stones, the interesting little church and the proximity to a Roman camp. It has all happened at Aberlemno at some time or another. The stones are now kept covered up in winter to save them from further erosion, but in spring, summer and autumn they stand untrammelled. The field dyke snakes around the three by the road, the fourth stands alone in the kirkyard.

The wee kirk is compact and unusual inside. The painted wooden box-pews, which are not the most comfortable to sit in, fill the floor area, and three galleries leave little free space. The Pictish stone outside the west wall has the unusual addition of a hole bored through it, adding further confusion to the interpreters of Pictish symbolism.

Just by Aberlemno is the ruin of Melgund Castle, the imposing edifice built by Cardinal Beaton for his wife/mistress/ just good friend Margaret Ogilvie. As the daughter of Lord Ogilvy of Airlie, Margaret was used to the good life and she certainly enjoyed that at Melgund with all the luxuries the

Carved Pictish stone, Aberlemno kirkyard.

carnal Cardinal heaped upon her. Whether they were ever married or not is not clear from contemporary records but it seems a bit hard on the lass to refer to her, as most of the records do, simply as his 'bawd', 'mistress' or 'chief lewd'. It is possible that they were married before Beaton took holy orders but there is no doubt that he paid scant attention to clerical celibacy thereafter.

Back towards Brechin on the Pitkennedy road is Aldbar estate, notable as an example of the vandalism perpetrated by present-day society, Aldbar Castle was a sound, solid, inhabited building, levelled and carted away in the 1960s. It was an updated sixteenth-century castle which had been the family home of the Chalmers of Aldbar since 1740, yet twentieth-century fiscal policies and tax laws made it essential to destroy it, rather than donate it as a nursing home, hospital, school, college, hotel or whatever. Surely the wanton destruction of such a valuable, existing amenity should be declared a criminal act. A civilised nation's laws should make provision for retaining such national treasures. It was a triumph of man's achievement to create such a treasure and the measure of his barbarity to destroy it. The main gates of Aldbar Castle are now broken down, the west gatehouse has gone, the driveways and policies are overgrown and weeds thrive on the castle site.

The Chapel of Aldbar, which still stands in the Den, is a Victorian building on an ancient foundation – as was the castle. Aldbar Chapel housed the Aldbar Stone before it was removed to Brechin Cathedral. The chapel is so overgrown now that in high summer you won't even see it without hacking your way through the undergrowth.

There are roads linking all these places round Brechin, easy enough to find on the ground but difficult to describe; let us hark back to the Ordnance Survey. At grid ref. 626557 you will find Farnell Castle. This is definitely an offshoot of Brechin as Farnell Castle was built by the cathedral court as a retreat for the Bishop and a residence for important visitors. It appears in the cathedral records as 'Palatium Nostrum' in 1512. It suffered periods of neglect and abuse over the years but has now been refurbished and is again a dwelling house. Its most notable feature today is the delicate shade of pink with which it is now coloured.

Kinnaird Castle and the House of Dun

Nearer Brechin again, at 638572, you find Kinnaird Castle, the residence of the present Earl and Countess of Southesk. Kinnaird Castle has the great merit of looking like a castle. Over the centuries it has been enlarged, altered, rebuilt and renovated like every other castle, but Kinnaird was totally rebuilt in 1790 and then totally rebuilt again in 1854. The present building is an ornate structure on the lines of a French

Melgund Castle, Cardinal Beaton's present to Marion Ogilvy.

chateau standing in a thousand acres of walled grounds. The wall extends for over four miles in an arc from the South Esk river, which forms the remaining boundary, enclosing policies, gardens and an inner deer park, still with its resident deer.

Kinnaird Castle is the ancestral home of the Earl of Southesk and his family, the Carnegies. The story of Kinnaird Castle itself is written in *The History of the Carnegies of Southesk* which was compiled by the incumbent Earl in 1867. It records the first reference to a castle at Kinnaird in 1401 and traces the line of ownership right up to 1867. When one delves into the tome and reads that 'By a Charter dated 21st February 1409 the Regent conferred the lands of the half the town of Kynnard and superiority of the brew-house thereof upon Duthac de Carnegy and his heirs to be held of our Lord the King and his heirs in feu and heritage for ever', one is inclined to leave the rest to the historians.

Like nearly all our once-stately homes, Kinnaird Castle is suffering from twentieth-century neglect. Where armies of foresters and gardeners used to tend the grounds and teams of servants kept the castle, a depleted band now maintains an uneasy balance. The estate has been sold off to an insurance company and the castle is now administered by a Trust Fund.

Fortunately, the twentieth century has also seen the dawning of a more enlightened attitude to our national heritage, and no better example exists than the House of Dun. The beautiful House of Dun, home of the Lairds of Dun, the Erskines, is along the road from Kinnaird over the Bridge of Dun. For many years a hotel, the House of Dun was bequeathed by the last of the Erskines to the National Trust for Scotland and in 1989 was opened to the public after having been restored to its original William Adam design.

The House of Dun is a classic. Designed and built by William Adam, it sits on a rise above the Brechin-Montrose road and is an example of the Adam adaptation of the work of Andrea Palladio, the Italian architect of the late sixteenth century. This interpretation of the Palladian style was to become the hallmark of the Adam family. William Adam (1689-1748) was the son of a Kirkcaldy stonemason and he grew up to run his father's building construction firm. To the skills of building he added the arts of design and architecture. Had he not then sired his four sons, Robert, John, James and William, much more would have been heard of William Adam Sr. The lads became so successful and indeed famous – Robert in particular – that they gave the Adam name to a style, a movement and a period. Old Wm. Adam has since been largely ignored and he deserves better.

The House of Dun is one of the best remaining examples of William Adam senior's work. Built in 1730 for David Erskine, one of the long line of Erskines, Lairds of Dun, it really is a gem. Returned to its original architectural state and furnished with authentic period furniture – most of it original and genuine – the house is now a treasure chest. Essential structural alterations have been made in the past but the house has now been restored as far as possible to the original. With its full complement of furniture and fitments it gives an insight into the lifestyle of eighteenth- and nineteenth-century landed gentry that is quite fascinating.

One of the features of the House of Dun is the relief plasterwork that dominates the main saloon and public rooms. Extravagant swags and figures decorate the walls, though the effect is just a wee bit overpowering for me. I could do with a smaller helping of plaster. Most folk seem to like the general impact but I find it obtrusive. It detracts from the purity of line and balance that is the Adam hallmark. That, of course, is just

Kinnaird Castle, Brechin. Seat of the Earl of Southesk. A view from the old Valentine's picture postcard series.

my opinion. The plasterwork was done by Joseph Enzer and the guide ladies at House of Dun make much of the fact that he was paid £216 for doing so in 1742. They do not specify whether they consider the sum to be excessive or insufficient, and without a familiarity with the going rates for decorative plasterers in the first half of the eighteenth century and the comparative rates today, one feels ill-equipped to comment.

Other than a suggestion of excess in the plasterwork, the House of Dun is beautiful. The National Trust for Scotland is to be applauded for the meticulous work done in presenting the House as it is today. In addition to the immaculate state of the main building the Trust has restored grounds and gardens and even included, in the courtyard, a hen house, a gamekeeper's workshop, a potting shed and – who would have guessed? – a tearoom. When visiting the gamie's bothy it is worth your time to stand aside in the shadows for a moment to hear the comments from the folk who come in, addressed to the shirtsleeved, moustachioed, gamekeeper busy mending his traps at the table. That is until they realise that he is a very, very lifelike dummy gamekeeper.

In the courtyard complex there is also a weaving shed and a shop where their woven linen goods may be purchased. The looms are not Dun looms but it is good to see them there. They

House of Dun. Entrance to stable yard.

come from Luthermuir where Will Taylor, whom we have met already, worked them all his life in the shed at the bottom of his garden. Will has retired now – he still lives in Luthermuir – and whilst it would have been uneconomic for the business to try to carry on from Luthermuir, no doubt it can succeed with all the visitors to the House of Dun.

Whilst the great impact of the House of Dun is made by the architecture, the symmetry of its plan, the fittings, furniture and plethora of *objets d'art et de vertu* on display, there are other fascinating features. Look at the shower bath. In the dressing room adjoining the red bedroom there is a free-standing shower bath that equals anything we can produce today. The Lady Augusta was able to enjoy a hot, temperature-controlled shower with unlimited hot water shooting from a nozzle the size of a soup plate driven by an unlimited power supply. All she needed was the team of servants she already had, to carry up the hot water, top up the tank and pump the water up to the head. The only significant difference between the Lady Augusta's shower and your latest all-electric, *en suite,* contrivance is the power source. The Lady Augusta knew no power cuts.

House of Dun, north entrance. Now a National Trust for Scotland property.

Behind Dun House there is an interesting area along the back road to Brechin on Damside of Dun farm. The centre of the area is Dun's Dish, a natural pond which is now a bird sanctuary. Dun's Dish used to be famous as a curling and skating pond before the days of artificial ice rinks; right up to the 1950s the Brechin folk used to up sticks and head for Dun's Dish whenever the word went out that 'she's beerin' '. Flemish painters could have made an easy living out of Hunter Small and his entourage of young Brechin demoiselles cutting fancy figures on Dun's Dish. These were the old folk festivals that communities lack nowadays.

Stracathro Hospital

Further round, to complete the circle, one rejoins the A94 at Stracathro. Stracathro has a school, a kirk and a hospital but no town or village of the name. It does not need any. Stracathro is known worldwide as the teaching hospital that has sent nurses to every corner of the earth. Built in the grounds of Stracathro House, the hospital started as an Emergency Medical Services Hospital in 1940. Appropriately enough, the first patients to be

Stracathro House, now a staff residence for the hospital.

admitted were the casualties from an air raid on Montrose. No
doubt the German High Command had heard about Montrose
airfield. It was no surprise to Montrose that the Luftwaffe went
straight for the jugular.

When the first patients arrived at Stracathro hospital they
were met by Col. Millar, the Medical Superintendent, and Miss
Clark, the Matron, in person. Lorries full of equipment and
medical supplies queued up behind the ambulances. From this
accelerated start the hospital raced on. As the war progressed,
casualties started to come in from the Middle East and Europe
and special techniques were developed for treating war
wounds. Specialised departments were set up to deal with skin
grafting, orthopaedics and rehabilitation and much pioneering
work has been done at Stracathro in these fields. Orthopaedic
surgery in particular and a hi-tech surgical appliance unit have
made Stracathro famous. Patients from all over the land now
come to Stracathro for treatment.

Visitors who do not know the military background to
Stracathro hospital sometimes wonder why it was built out
there 'so far from everywhere'. Apart from the implicit insult

to Brechin there are very good reasons for hospitals being built out on their own. When air pollution in towns is such a threat to normal healthy people, how much worse must it be for city hospital patients? The air at Stracathro is a balmy blend of the perfumes of whin and broom and new-mown hay: of wood smoke and wet cypress, raspberry fields and country gardens. Wafting down from the heather braes of Angus, it is a specific in itself.

South again from Brechin on the A94 the road holds to the flat lands below the Finavon, Turin and Carsegray hills. On the west side is Oathlaw, a most attractive little dorp with hens foraging in the road and Shetland ponies standing knee-high in buttercups. The loudest noise in Oathlaw is the babble from the school playground at piecey-time. Below Oathlaw is Battledykes where only the name remains to speak of a violent past. There, in the rural pleasance, are the vestigial remains of a Roman camp. History tells us that it was a staging post for 26,000 legionaries at a time, on the great north trek of the Roman armies in Scotland. Peace be with them.

CHAPTER 8

Forfar, Glamis and Kirriemuir

Forfar is the county town of Angus. At one time it was the eponymous county town of Forfarshire, and Forfar saw no reason for its being changed, but there it is. Forfar now administers the county of Angus. Forfar is a happy little town – happy in the knowledge of its superiority. Other little towns (*pace* Montrose) strive to be bigger, better, prettier, superior; Forfar is perfectly happy as she is. Her satisfaction was epitomised for me when I met a Forfarian who turned out to have been in Rangoon about the same time as myself. 'Was it not fantastic', I enthused, 'to wake up each morning with the rising sun striking rays off the Shway Dagon pagoda and to . . .' He cut me off with a look. 'Forfar,' he said, 'is good enough for me'. That is the Forfar way. It is not narrow-minded or parochial: my friend had seen the world and come back. He knew Forfar was best.

A more parochial view was expressed by the Forfar lad, one of two from a patrol of the Fife and Forfar Yeomanry cut off in the Western Desert during the war. As they crawled hopelessly towards the horizon, one of the pair paused and raised his eyes to the sky. 'Peem', he said to his companion, 'd'ye ken fat day this is – it's Farfar Games.' His exhausted mate croaked his reply through blackened lips. 'Aye', he said, 'an' they're gettin' a braw day for it.'

There is no criticism of Forfar in these tales, they merely illustrate the Forfar conviction of her place at the top. The same sentiment was expressed more directly by Forfar urchins in the early days of the century. At that time a Forfar man, John Killacky, was Champion Cyclist of Scotland. Also at that time the Dundee Young Ladies' Christian Cycling Club undertook a day's cycle run to Forfar, the return journey to be by train. As the intrepid band of pioneers – two of them in bloomers – cycled triumphantly down the East High Street to the Cross the Forfar folk clapped politely. Not so the Forfar youngsters. 'Awa' ye go', they yelled, 'ye couldna' bate Killacky'. The

Killackey's cycle and motor shop, Forfar. A nostalgic shot.

youngsters were right. The ladies could never, ever, have beaten Killacky, and the little lads were true Forfarians.

Such a conviction of superiority makes for a happy Forfar community. There is no enervating self-doubt to qualify the vigour of the town's confidence. Forfar has a booming economy because Forfar folk make it so. Local lads who have gone furth to seek their fortunes have returned to Forfar to find them. The leading Forfar business names today are Bonnyman, Callander, Dalgety, Jarvis, Webster and a cleckin of others. They are Forfar loons (Forfar's word) who run Forfar and make it hum. Forfar thrives because Forfar folk believe in it.

Forfar is also writ large in the history of Scotland but Forfar makes little of it. The Scottish Parliament met in Forfar in 1057. Early Scottish kings were regular residents in Forfar Castle. Robert the Bruce was a weel-kent face. You hear little of that in Forfar now. Lesser towns proclaim their historic importance; Forfar just gets on with the job. Ask to see Forfar Castle, the scene of so much significant action for Scotland, and you are directed to a shop, to get a key, to open a door in a wall, to go up some steps and see where Forfar Castle used to be. Forfar Castle was a noble pile, much favoured by kings, usurpers, warring factions and invading English armies. The English held Forfar Castle at one time. Robert the Bruce

181

fought with the English against John Baliol. When William Wallace set up against the English, Bruce joined him. Forfar Castle changed hands as regularly. In 1302 Robert Bruce swore allegiance to the English once again, then he had John Comyn murdered in Dumfries and rejoined the Scots. It took Robert the Bruce a long time to make up his mind.

All the time that this jougery pawkery was going on, Forfar was having its Castle besieged, stormed, occupied and forfeited. The Forfar folk found this tedious and Forfar blamed it all on the castle for being there. With that pragmatism for which they are still noted, the Forfar men knocked the castle down. No invading army demolished it, no avenging liege lord levelled it. The Forfar men with their carts – and their womenfolk to do the heavy lifting – dismantled their own castle stone by stone and took it away to build houses and kirks and an auction cattle mart. Because Robert Bruce was the last to inhabit the castle, he is sometimes credited with its destruction, but not so. It was the toon's men that did it and they were dead right. Forfar has hardly entered the history books since.

Books could be written on the history of Forfar itself. The Picts settled in Forfar, then the Romans displaced them. The Picts returned, then the Northumbrians displaced them. The Picts – now Christian – returned, then the whole clamjamfry, less the Romans who had gone home, set up the tribal wars that are still going on – and maybe the Romans didn't all go home, for Forfar has always had a fair quota of Diplexcitos, Soaves, Iannettas and Macaris as long as I have known it. Historic relics abound but Forfar lets them be. St. Margaret's Inch on Forfar Loch is the site of Queen Margaret's Palace and Forfar Sailing Club keep their boats on it. Forfar is much more interested in the future.

The town is a thriving, bustling county capital with diverse industries, busy shops and happy folk. The old County Buildings still manage to give employment to large numbers despite regionalisation or whatever, the Auction Mart is one of the most important livestock markets in the country, and there are shops in Forfar that defy the creeping blight of innovation. Dalgety's and Roberts's shops in the East High Street and Jarvis's in Castle Street are run as shops should be run: for the

On the spot where Forfar Castle stood.

benefit of the customer. They are traditional shops that give the appearance, the substance and the service of traditional shops because they serve a traditional clientèle. The customers in Forfar shops are Angus wifies. Women who know what they want and know where they'll find it. Strangers who call at Forfar shops are surprised and delighted and go away twittering their appreciation. The Angus womenfolk take their shops as they take their country: for granted.

All kinds of industry flourish in Forfar. It has been a manufacturing town since the Picts started to wear shoes and came to Forfar to get them. For generations the Forfar folk were bynamed 'Souters' because of the importance of their cobbling trade. When mass-produced shoes took over, Forfar moved into the linen trade. When jute displaced linen, Forfar switched to jute. When polypropylene replaced jute, Forfar changed immediately to the man-made medium and installed Schultzer looms to make carpet backing and broadloom packaging materials. They even built a polypropylene factory of their own. This combined manufacturing and weaving operation was so successful that the big multinational companies were attracted and the biggest of the old Forfar firms, Don and Low, was taken over by Shell Industries. The other great Forfar industry is the Auction Mart. Situated as it is in the middle of the great Vale of Strathmore, Forfar has always been the centre of livestock trading in the area. As fashions in farming and food production have changed over the years, Forfar has seen the rise and fall of fortunes. When the Clydesdale horse powered the farm, Forfar was a Clydesdale stronghold. When the Ayrshire cow supplied the country's milk, Forfar supplied the Ayrshires. In the great Aberdeen-Angus days, the nation's butchers came to Forfar, and it is good to know that the butchers are still coming and that the rising tide of exotic breeds has been stemmed. The Aberdeen-Angus is making headway again. Bigger and maybe rougher than he was, but able again to compete as a crossing component with the Continental influx. Forfar Mart sees them all, but even more interesting than watching the cattle in the ring is to watch the faces *round* the ring. There you see all the blood lines of Angus clearly defined. The small, square, black-jowled Celt; the lank blond Scandinavian; the clear-skinned, red-haired Highlander. What lessons in genetics are to be learned round the No. 1 ring of Forfar Mart – on either side of the rails?

It is the cattle market that has kept Forfar close to its roots. The polypropylene operators are international whizzkids jetting off to the Continent and speaking German, but the Angus farmers meet in the Forfar Mart and speak the Angus tongue. It does your heart good to hear it.

There is no doubt that the great attraction of Forfar is its rugged individuality. Each and every wave of invasion that has flowed over Forfar has receded, up to and including the Polish forces who sought sanctuary during the Second World War. Forfar has assimilated Pict, Scot, Roman, Dane, Northumbrian, Saxon, Pole, a handful of Brechiners, and put her stamp on them. Forfar schools may list foreign-sounding names on their rolls but the Forfar loons who bear them will fume if you call them anything but Forfarians.

Ask any of these same Forfar loons what their home town is famous for and they will shoot sidelong glances at you. They will suspect a con. They know what their town is famous for and they know that the World knows and you must know too:

the Forfar Bridie. What the little folks do not know, and neither do I, is why this delicious helping of prime Angus beef encased in crisp short pastry should be called a 'bridie'. There are two popular theories.

Many, many, years ago before television had supplanted our native culture, it was a local custom to have a special kind of pie made for a bride on her wedding day. By obvious connection these became known as 'brides' and with the addition of the habitual Forfar diminutive suffix, 'bridies'. To signify good luck to the bride the pie was made in a horseshoe shape which has been maintained with only slight modification to this day. You can take that or leave it.

The alternative suggestion has rather more to it. The records of Forfar Town Council show that one Margaret Bridie came in from Glamis to the weekly Butter Market in Forfar to sell 'a product'. It is known to have been a comestible, a pie of some sort, which became a 'Bridie'. That seems reasonable enough and when you go out to Glamis kirkyard and see Margt. Bridie's (d.1835) gravestone, it makes sense.

The bridie today is big business. Four firms make them in Forfar and one firm alone, McLarens (est. 1893), sell the prodigious number of five thousand bridies per week. I find that staggering. On a Saturday they sell two thousand. No wonder McLaren's shop bears a sign 'THE Bridie Shop'. Today's bridie is made with prime Angus beef and onions in a short pastry case. A few are made without onions and still fewer with puff pastry. These have to be asked for specially. Ask for a 'bridie' and you get the short-crust-with-onions variety. At one time they made different grades of bridie and a 'special' was made with top-quality beef and sometimes even with added kidney. Now they are all made with top-quality beef and all are special. The standard bridie has two ventilation holes in the top, the non-onion specimen has one.

Anyone enquiring about the nutritive values of the Forfar Bridie is referred to Strathmore Rugby Club. Strathmore Rugby Club trains on bridies and the sight of the Strathmore pack executing its rolling maul at Inchmacoble any wet Saturday afternoon in November tells you all you need to know about the dietary qualities of the bridie.

McLaren's, THE Bridie Shop, is another of these friendly

Forfar shops – as indeed is Sandy Saddler's in the East High Street, that other leading bridie manufactory. They are examples of the old-style, old-established, family businesses for which Forfar is so famous. The present McLaren – young Bill (fifty this year) – is the great-grandson of the founding William who ran a tea and coffee shop along with his bakery. His back shop was subdivided into two sections, one for coffee, one for tea. Young Bill frequently ponders over what happened when a young lad brought his lass in and she wanted coffee when he wanted tea.

Armed with the history of the Forfar Bridie and a nodding acquaintance with Strathmore Rugby Club, there is only one further shibboleth needed to ensure your final acceptance in Forfar. That is the old Forfar description of a favourite Sunday afternoon perambulation of the town:

> East ee toon, Wast ee toon,
> Roon ee Spoot an hame.

No matter how you say it, the Forfarians will hear you with amused tolerance and correct you. Only a Forfarian is allowed to get it right. You will, however, be well on your way to being accepted.

The town sits comfortably at the head of Forfar Loch in the lee of Balmashanner. Sailing dinghies colour the grey gloss of the Loch, a thriving Leisure Centre crowns its head, Strathmore Cricket Club practise their arcane arts on the green sward of Lochside Park. 'Forfar will be Forfar still, when Dundee's a' dung doon' – so runs the old jingle and so says Forfar today. The finest poetry an expatriate Forfarian can ever hope to hear is the roup roll of an Angus Auction Mart sale:

> Baldardo, Turwhappie
> Kirkbuddo, Drumgley
> Lour, Tulloes, Clochtow, Ballindarg.

It is poetry, pure poetry; say it out loud. These are the names of Angus farms with Angus sounds that can carry the snell nip of Angus to the farthest prairie, veldt, maidan or outback – where Forfar loons have colonised the world.

Furth of Forfar, should anyone ever want to go further, the

main road thunders down to Dundee. You can be out of Angus in fifteen minutes down the A929 if you so desire, but that is not our way. Let us first wander the perimeter roads of the toonie. It has long been the belief of the Forfar fowk that all roads lead to Forfar. A glance at the position of Forfar on the map of Angus will justify their conviction. By George, all roads *do* lead to Forfar . . .

The B9128 comes in from Carnoustie, and just over a mile out of Forfar a side road cuts in from Dunnichen and Letham. Dunnichen House was the home of George Dempster, the great agricultural improver and entrepreneur of the eighteenth century. George Dempster was the son of a wealthy Dundee businessman and young George went in for politics and duly became an M.P. His electioneering system was the tried and tested method of the day: widespread bribery of the voters. Unfortunately for George his election coincided with a Government campaign against electoral malpractice and he was taken for dishonesty. What others had been doing for years with impunity was levelled against George Dempster as a major crime. He was fined the colossal sum of £30,000 and known to the public thereafter as Honest George.

Dunnichen Kirk sits at the crossroads just below the grounds of George Dempster's old Dunnichen House. The Letham folk have recently erected a memorial there by the roadside. This is not in memory of Honest George Dempster M.P., but to commemorate the Battle of Nechtansmere.

Nechtan was a king of some of the Picts. He was accepted into the Christian Church and was baptised at Restenneth Priory. He led an uprising against the Northumbrians, possibly under King Ecgfrith, who had held the eastern lowlands of Scotland for many years. That would then of course have been Pictland. The unidentified battle of Nechtansmere is reputed to have ended the Northumbrian occupation. These are the suppositions of history.

It is not known where Nechtansmere was, nor which of the Pictish kings fought there, nor are there any facts about the supposed battle other than a suggested date of 685 AD, but lots of wild guesses have been made over the centuries. Letham has apparently decided now that Dunnichen moss was Nechtan's mere, that the putative leader was Nechtan and to have appropriated the whole episode as a fact of Letham life. They have as much right as anyone else to do so, but since they have grafted on a midsummer 'Pictish' festival of equally spurious validity – and definitely doubtful taste – they could be going too far.

Whatever the circumstances of his election, George Dempster served as an M.P. and made a considerable mark. Contemporaries as disparate as Dr Johnson and Robert Burns have left comments – as disparate as themselves – on G. Dempster of Dunnichen. He was a character, a progressive thinker and a schemer of schemes. His ideas on improved agricultural methods and better conditions for agricultural workers were well ahead of his time and he started innovative projects all over Scotland. Letham village was one of his better ideas. It was planned as a spinning and weaving centre and the village was laid out accordingly. George Dempster set out to rival Dundee and founded a whole range of flax-processing plants to do everything from retting to weaving. For a time Letham was a boom town but very soon the rivers Dighty and Tay together proved too much for the Vinney. Letham's manufacturing industry withered and died and in 1818 George Dempster did likewise. He is buried at Restenneth Priory. His father, John Dempster, 'who died from a fall from his horse, much lamented. The 2nd of November 1753 in the 49th year of his Age', is buried in St. Vigeans Kirk.

The next strand in the spider's web of roads leading into Forfar is the A932 coming in from Arbroath and Friockheim. Now there's an old Scotch name for you! Friockheim. It is actually something of a fraud. It was named as recently as 1824 by the Laird, John Anderson, for some unknown reason of his own. Previously it had been simply Frioch. I like to think the name was suggested to him by Flemish flax workers he had imported to teach the locals how to work flax.

Friockheim was a successful early flax-processing place but it failed to find an alternative source of income when the flax trade died. It is now a dormitory village with its old cottages modernised and altered out of recognition. The village is oddly wedge-shaped with two main streets running divergently eastwards from the kirk, linked by five cross-streets. It is a busy little place, well served by its own shops and pubs.

Just off the A932 on the way into Forfar, the clachan of Guthrie clusters around Guthrie Castle and the old disused railway settlement. Guthrie Castle, once home of the Guthries of that Ilk, is now in American ownership. It sits in beautiful parkland and used to have a most original southern gate. That ornate entrance incorporated one of the railway bridges of the old Arbroath-Forfar railroad, constituting a triumph of expedient compromise. The gate has gone with the railroad.

Between the A932 and the next road into Forfar, the B9113, the lochs of Balgavies, Rescobie and Fithie lie along the Lunan Valley which opens out into the big Strath at Forfar. Balgavies (pronounced Balg-eyes) Loch is a Nature Reserve with an observation point and car park beside the A932. It is balm to the spirit to sit on the grass at the observation point and watch the water birds at Balgavies. Round the year you can see vast numbers of residents and visitors, and should you happen on the grebes you are sure of a laugh. The grebes are clowns.

Next loch down from Balgavies is Rescobie but Rescobie is better approached from the B9113. The A932 skirts it on the south side and runs on past Forfar Golf Club at Cunninghill to Forfar. Forfar Golf Club has known fame, hosting the Scottish Professional Championship on occasion and producing a host of good golfers over the years. Sandy Saddler of Forfar won many honours in the game before playing three times for Britain in the Walker Cup against America. He is better known in Forfar as the baker of the Saddler Special Bridie from Saddler's bakery. Bill Callender of Forfar Golf Club is presently a high heid yin in the Royal and Ancient Golf Club of St. Andrews. His current job is to give rulings when golfers refer impossible happenings on golf courses to the R. and A.

Forfar Golf Club has a good name but other names are often applied to their course. Many of the fairways of Forfar Golf Course are traversed by ridges, undulations, parallel hummocks and raised banks that break the smooth surface of the ground. A ball driven across these mounds is arrested in its forward momentum and may end up on a nasty downward slope that necessitates under-clubbing for the second shot. There speaks a victim: may it never happen to you.

Forfar claims that the course was built on old flax-growing ground and that the ridges were made for cultivation purposes.

That could be true but the course was rebuilt in 1923 by James Braid, and he should have known better. Golf is quite bad enough without corrugated fairways.

The next spoke in the wheel round Forfar is the B9113 running in from the Brechin-Arbroath direction, a continuation of the A934 and the A92 from Montrose. The B9113 leaves the A933 at the edge of Montreathmont (Montrimment) moor along the line of the old Cadger's path from Ferryden and Usan: the path that was used by cadgers carrying fish to the kings in Forfar Castle.

As the road approaches Forfar, the mass of Turin hill rises on the right and Rescobie Loch lies by the roadside to the left. Rescobie is a much-used loch these days. There is a Rescobie Loch Development Committee which organises things. What used to be a casual, informal, friendly affair conducted from a gamekeeper's cottage and a dilapidated boathouse is now a super-efficient, streamlined leisure activity. The fishers of Rescobie are now fully organised.

Between Rescobie and Forfar the ruined chapel of Restenneth sits in the trees with only the spire visible from the road. The old Priory is a noble ruin now, and to wander round it on a still summer's morning when the sun burnishes the old red sandstone pile, dark shadows fall from the crumbled aisle and somnolent cattle stand tail-twitching in the field, is to experience true peace. We live in times of rapid change when rural Scotland is being destroyed at an alarming rate. Places like Restenneth Priory must be cherished when we encounter them and savoured for what they are and what they represent: links with our past.

Restenneth Priory is one of the oldest Christian churches in Scotland. It is not known who founded it. It has been attributed variously and over centuries of time to Celts, Picts, Romans and visiting Saxons. The nearest we can come to fact is to say that it was an existing, functioning church in the time of Nechtan. That a Roman missionary called Bonifacius met and baptised Nechtan at Restenneth in 710AD. That David I (1124-1153) made a grant to the Prior and Canons of Restenneth and that after the Reformation from Popery (c.1559) Restenneth became the parish kirk of Forfar.

Whatever its history, Restenneth Priory has served as a

Restenneth Priory, near Forfar.

religious retreat and a spiritual sanctuary since the earliest days of Christianity in Scotland. It is a hallowed place, and to stand in the grass-grown cloister of Restenneth and ponder the meaning of existence is to approach, as near as we are allowed, to understanding.

On the approach road to the Priory there is an oddly architectured building labelled 'Restenneth Library'. This was commissioned by the Graham Hunter Foundation Inc., an American Trust Fund donated by George Graham Guthrie Hunter's family from Restenneth. The Library was built to accommodate a large assortment of Scottish history books and books of antiquarian interest collected by the Hunter family. It sits uneasily by the roadside and incorporates a wall and a mock gateway with Grecian urn finials. It is quite out of place. Restenneth Priory should have nothing to intrude on its space.

The next road into Forfar, the B9134, is the old Brechin-Forfar road that runs down from Aberlemno village which we have already visited. The road sweeps down a long incline with a view over Forfar into the setting sun. One hastens to add that no metaphorical connection is intended. Rich farmland succeeds the upland rock here and the great granary of

Strathmore stretches out in front. Lunanhead is on the B9134 just before it reaches Forfar, and Lunanhead owes its origins to plague and insurrection. It was the spot chosen for an isolation hospital when plague hit Forfar in the Middle Ages, and subsequently it was a huge army camp for Government troops during the times of civil disturbance, Young Pretenders and all that. There are still old folk who refer to Lunanhead as 'the Berrecks'. Old Forfar flattened its 'a' vowel into 'e'. Lunanhead today is suffering serious bungaloid contamination and is no more than a suburb of Forfar.

The A94 bypasses Forfar and takes the worst of the traffic screaming past, hell-bent. The quiet land at the foot of Forfar loch has been cut off by the new road. Where the Dean Water leaves the loch and herons used to fish undisturbed in the weed-bound shallows, culverts and embankments now conduct the stream efficiently away. It is a microcosmic example of what is happening all over the land. We are being built over, pavemented and cased in concrete. Towns are spreading over the countryside; villages are dying and their skeletons are being colonised by urban parasites. So sayeth Jeremiah: a more optimistic view would rejoice in the unspoiled bits we still have – especially in Angus. We can still wander a mile off the A94 and find quiet byroads with arched avenues of trees and bird-burbling hedgerows. There are still quiet places where the buzzard and the peregrine hunt alone. The threat we face is from that other peregrine, the tourist.

The A926 comes in from Kirriemuir via Padanaram, not a place to detain one long. The name Padanaram is one of many in Angus – Zoar, Garth, Jericho, Turin, Egypt, Rome *et al* – that carry a vaguely religious connotation for no apparent reason. Padanaram was a little village with all the appurtenances of a little village until country folk got cars and started shopping in towns. That left Padanaram as a wing of Forfar.

Glamis and its Castle

Back on the A94 south of Forfar the road leads in from Glamis, now safely bypassed. Glamis and its castle must be the

The Castle of Glamis, seat of the Earls of Strathmore, home of Elizabeth Bowes-Lyon who became Queen of George VI, and birthplace of Princess Margaret.

best known tourist target in the land. There can be few houses in the country that have not sported a Glamis Castle tea towel at one time or another. The castle of Glamis is the seat of the Earl of Strathmore and Kinghorne and is one castle that leaves no room for doubt. It looks like a castle. You may go to Stirling or Edinburgh and from three sides see castles that look like nothing more than tenement blocks, but not at Glamis.

Glamis Castle sits in an extended parkland with streams and lawns and avenues, pheasants and deer. It is approached by driveways from impressive gates with coats of arms and caryatids – and figures above the west gates that are manifestly not caryatid. Or at least they were not, until the Kirrie lads chucked stones at them on Saturday nights and broke off the definitive bits. The tourist appeal of Glamis Castle is based largely on its close connection with the Royal family. It was the seat of the Bowes-Lyons whose daughter Elizabeth became Duchess of York before becoming Queen and latterly, Queen Mother. The present Queen and her sister, Princess Margaret, lived at Glamis as children, and Princess Margaret was born there. The Royal connection goes back to the earliest times, for

Glamis has always been owned by the Scottish crown. It is recorded as having been a Celtic missionary post when St. Fergus lived and preached there, but even then the ownership records all list the Crown as proprietor. Originally the castle was built as a hunting lodge down in the low ground by the Dean Water. Reference to buildings and towers on the site go back to the fourth century, but the first mention of a royal castle at Glamis comes with King Malcolm II in 1034. When Malcolm was wounded in the nearby battle of Hunter's Hill, it was to Glamis Castle that he was taken and in Glamis Castle that he died. In 1372, Sir John Lyon was made Thane of Glamis by King Robert the Second and in 1376 he married the King's daughter Joanna. He then rebuilt the existing castle of Glamis into the core of the building that still stands.

In 1537 King James V occupied Glamis Castle and lived there until 1542. During this time the castle was enlarged and modified as a royal residence. King James V's daughter Mary (Queen of Scots) subsequently visited and spent some time in the castle. Glamis has always had this royal connection. In 1606, additions were made and the castle began to look rather as it does today. Much of the present building and its decorative plasterwork is dated 1621. From 1798 to 1800 major alterations were made and an entire wing was rebuilt to accommodate a new dining room. This section was again altered in 1854, and with only minor modifications subsequently, the present castle was complete.

From May to September the castle is open to the public and conducted parties are shown round. As might be expected, you get a better class of guide in Glamis than in your ordinary, run-of-the-mill castle. Our last one was a mature, cultured gentleman with a Regimental necktie and highly polished leather. He knew his subject, he described it clearly and comprehensively and he spoke, not surprisingly, the Queen's English. It was a pleasure to be conducted round Glamis Castle.

On occasion there are fêtes and junkets held in the grounds. Annually the Strathmore Vintage Vehicle Club holds an Extravaganza when vintage car buffs gather frae a' the airts. The Glamis Extravaganza is now one of the main vintage vehicle shows in the country and they produce some pretty

The village green, Leysmill.

impressive old cars every year. They also produce rows of stalls and booths that make the castle grounds look like a mediaeval fair. Wandering round the Glamis Extravaganza lets you see just what the old-time hucksters were at. The goods they offer may have changed, from hand-made wooden toys and uninspired sweetmeats to remote-controlled transistorised scale models and sticky pink candyfloss, but the vendors are the same. Every degree of humour, cunning, cupidity – and occasional generosity – is there. The elder Brueghel painted the folk at the Glamis Extravaganza.

Glamis village stands in the shadow of the castle and over the years the livelihood of the village depended largely on the castle's patronage. It is less dependent now. The village slumbers on and its most active industry is the Folk Museum. This is an excellent example of its kind. Appropriately housed in a row of old cottages, the Glamis Folk Museum offers a comprehensive collection of bygones and local artefacts to keep us in closer touch with our roots.

In the grounds of the manse there is a Pictish stone with the usual Pictish carvings on it, including the Christian cross. The Glamis stone is a bigger example than most, standing some ten feet high, and for Pictophiles it should be of particular interest. Standing as close as it does to Glamis Castle, it has attracted more than its share of myth and invention over the years. It used to be known as King Malcolm's Stone and a web of folklore was spun around it. The locals can still come up with some pretty far-fetched fallacies. Fortunately it is too far from Dunnichen for the Letham boys to incorporate it in any of their whimsies.

The Glens of Angus are usually taken to be the great glens running into the Grampians, but with the distribution of high ground over the county there are little glens running everywhere. One such is Glen Ogilvie, which starts just south of Glamis and is approached from the A928 at Milton of Ogilvie. The road runs below the hills of Berry, Carlunie and Ark and gives access to farms that are as remote as any in the land. This is the homeland of the Angus folk, the byways beyond the dual carriageways where the verges stay uncut and grass grows in the middle of the road.

Having followed the main route up the coast and down the middle, let us meander through some of the side roads that cut across the body of the county. Start at Inverkeilor, or from the new bypass round Inverkeilor, and take the B965 for Friockheim. At the Chapelton crossroads go straight along the road signposted 'Leysmill' and be prepared for a surprise.

Leysmill is not like other Angus villages. It is more like a Cotswold village after the developers have been through or an early attempt at a set for Brigadoon. It is neat, clean, tidy and out of place. It has an extensive village green owned by the villagers – the only one in Angus, they claim – and it is the green that makes the village so distinctive. At one time Leysmill green was a roughish bit of spare ground with trees and a burn bubbling through it, footpaths cut across at random, and litter lay in the long grass. Leysmill village green is now a smoothly cropped expanse of lawn with a stone-chip pathway and a children's play area with environmentally friendly educational activity fixed units conforming to standard safety regulations. The channelled burn is now a wimpling stream.

All would seem to be well with Leysmill, but a crack with a few of the Leysmillers makes you wonder. The present inhabitants of the village, barring an architect and the owners

Rev. Patrick Bell's reaping machine. Designed to be pushed rather than pulled.

of the Old Folks' Home, no longer work in Leysmill. In the old days they worked in the quarry and the flax mill. Now they are mostly Service personnel from H.M.S. Condor and teachers from surrounding schools. There is no Leysmill community of Leysmill-born folk. The Leysmill Village Amenities Association is a committee elected by incomers, Scots, English and Irish. Without its Association, Leysmill would still be a crumbling relic.

On the surface all is smooth and untroubled but there are undercurrents. The Scots appear to resent an assumption of superiority by the English, the English seem to dislike the insularity of the Scots, the Irish cannot distinguish Scots from English and in any case they are leaving, but between them they manage to collaborate quite well. Leysmill is either a happy example of the viability of the democratic principle in action or a hotbed of nationalistic, racist, rivalry. Whichever way you interpret it, you have to laugh. The village is certainly a good example of practical co-operation, and the best thing about it is that, because of an inadequate drainage system, no more houses may be built. There's the stuff of a play in Leysmill for somebody.

Before leaving Leysmill finally and reluctantly, one might just nip back to Chapelton and go along the Arbroath road as far as Letham Grange. Letham Grange is that modern phenomenon, the historic old country house that has been tinkered into a hotel. Two golf courses have been built in the grounds and an ice rink tacked on at one end. Bungalows are now erupting like a rash in every available space and the whole is an apt reflection of our contemporary Scottish culture. Probably an even truer reflection of our contemporary Scottish culture is that Letham Grange has just been sold, irrevocably, to the Japanese.

Back to Leysmill, one takes the road to join up with the A933 and crosses straight over to meet the B961 and turn left. This road climbs gradually up the side of Boath hill to coast gently down into Redford. Redford is the main village in the parish of Carmyllie. The lesser settlements of Greystone and Milton of Carmyllie are just a rickle of houses and a farm by a road junction respectively. There are really only two things for which Carmyllie is famous: paving stones and reaping machines.

The paving and building stone from Carmyllie quarries was used all over Britain and exported worldwide. Because it was shipped from Arbroath it became known as Arbroath stone and knowledgeable guides in Cologne Cathedral today will proudly show you their Arbroath stone. You know better now.

The reaping machine was invented in Carmyllie in 1826 by the parish minister, the Rev. Patrick Bell. No doubt his parishioners reckoned at the time that he would have been better employed with his kirk duties than with suchlike new-fangled contraptions – and what was wrong with a good sickle anyhow? Somebody was bound to have called it the Devil's work but the Rev. Bell just kept going with his experiments and eventually came up with the reaping machine. The old original horse-driven contrivance with triangular toothed alternating cutting blades working against a fixed edge; the reaper that made the first great stride into farm mechanisation. The name of the Rev. Patrick Bell should be known and lauded universally but the most he got out of it was a stained-glass window in Carmyllie Kirk. Very few folk today are aware that the Carmyllie minister of 1826 was the greatest pioneer of farm mechanisation there has ever been.

Airlie Castle, seat of the Ogilvies.

From Redford a road runs over by West Hills to join up with the B9128 into Forfar. A mile down the B9128 is Upper Tulloes, farmed by the Greenhill family. Upper Tulloes is a mixed farm with a difference: they breed Clydesdales. One of the biggest changes in farming, after Patrick Bell's reaper, has been the demise of the Clydesdale horse as the agricultural power unit. Tractors and powered implements have taken over and the horse has gone. At Upper Tulloes it is a surprise and a joy to see Clydesdale horses in the fields and in the loose-boxes. The Greenhills have bred horses for generations. They breed them because they have always bred them and now they show and sell and export them. Canada takes a surprising number of Clydesdale horses from Scotland each year and it is good to know that breeding Clydesdales is still a good business proposition.

The Redford road, the B961 which we left only to see the horses, runs down through lush farmland to cross the B9128 above Crombie Mill. The road dips steeply down to the Mill there and sharply up again to Crombie reservoir. The reservoir has been there a long time, but the surrounding ground has now been laid out as Crombie Country Park. It is a clean little park with pleasant walks round the loch and picnic spots for family picnics; altogether a good place to go, even if the anglers do complain about being disturbed.

From Crombie Country Park the B961 leads on past Kirkton of Monikie, where the farm straddles the road, to Craigton and Monikie Country Park. Monikie looks a much less natural reservoir than Crombie. It is mainly built up above the ground line and lacks the wealth of trees and shrubberies. From the edge of the water one does get panoramic views over Dundee and the Fife coast, and that's about it. The whole area south of Monikie comes under Dundee District's aegis and Dundee's tentacles are reaching out ever further. The whole area has a suburban look about it and the density of population is high.

Recoiling from the twin assaults of Dundee to the south and Perthshire to the west, one seeks sanctuary in the Angus lands of the Ogilvies and their Castle of Airlie. On a spur of land where the Melgam joins the Isla, Airlie Castle sits overlooking the twin ravines which run together at this point. Apart from providing a classic site for a castle, these river dens have proved a fruitful source of geological and botanical research. Eminent Angus men, Don, Lyall, Osborne and Sherriff – and at least one eminent Angus woman, Mrs Sherriff – explored and studied the Airlie gorge before proceeding to more exotic locations. The views from the upper windows of the castle into the river vales are breathtaking at any time of the year.

The Ogilvies are listed high in the muster rolls of Angus. The history of the Ogilvies is pretty much the history of Angus: successive chapters of violence and intrigue. The Castle of Airlie dates from about 1430 but the present building dates from a reconstruction of 1793. It was sacked by the Covenant forces under the Marquis of Montrose in 1639 and subsequently by the Covenant forces under the Duke of Argyll in 1640. In the interval the Marquis of Montrose had changed sides. It is remarkable how often this phenomenon occurs in Scottish history. From the days of the original Picts when Nechtan became a Christian and began fighting his own folk, through Robert Bruce, a Norman knight who fought for England then for Scotland then for England again then for Scotland to become King of Scotland, on to the Marquis of Montrose in 1638. The Marquis fought for the Covenanters in 1638, then against them from 1644 on. It is hard to keep track of all the back stabbings.

The original Airlie Castle was destroyed by the Duke of Argyll and his Covenanters in that stramash of 1640. Apart from the devious politics of the period, there was a longstanding feud between the two families, the Ogilvies hating the Campbells. That in itself is not surprising – most people did – but in this case it generated a reciprocal antipathy, and when the Duke of Argyll attacked the Ogilvie castle he burned it to the ground and set about the smouldering ruins with a hammer. There's Campbells for you.

Marshall, in his *Historic Scenes of Forfarshire*, quotes the Duke as having 'taken the hammer in his own hand and knocked down the hewed work of the doors and windows till he did sweat for heat'. That was the end of the old castle. Marshall adds that the memory has been preserved in 'The Burnin' o' the Bonnie Hoose o' Airlie' which he reckons to be one of the finest of our Scottish lyrics.

Whatever its provenance, Airlie Castle is now a worthy example of a dwelling place of the nobility. Angus and the Mearns is littered with dwelling places of the nobility. The whole area is rich in castles and forts and the 'big hooses' of the wealthy. It is less well endowed with the houses of the poor. For the very good reason that the houses of the poor quickly deteriorate, fall down and are blown away in the wind. There is only one group outwith the aristocracy whose houses have survived for centuries intact until today: the farmers. If Angus and the Mearns is rich in castles, it is abundantly affluent in farm houses.

From the eighteenth century, when legislation was enacted to improve agricultural practice and stabilise the leasehold of farms, the building of steadings and farm houses developed rapidly. In the old, open-pasture, free-range days, farm buildings consisted of a thatched cottage for the farmer with stable, byre and shed tacked on at the gable ends for the farm. Under the influence of the great farming pioneers, farm design and building burgeoned into a craft and an art form in itself. Angus and the Mearns today hold some of the finest examples of agricultural architecture in the country. Unfortunately, the demands of modern mechanised farming have rendered the old custom-built steadings unnecessary. The great stalled byres of the dairy farm have been replaced by the big sheds with milking parlour and self-feed silage yard. The stables and cart sheds of the cropping farm have been outmoded by the tractor and the agricultural machine. Modern farming demands the maximum available free space permitting internal adjustment as required.

It is just one more unfortunate fact that now the old practical, natural, beautiful farm steadings of our childhood have been vandalised by amateur do-it-yourself mutilation. Graceful old cartsheds with open ports and grain lofts that were beautifully designed entities of mellow local stone and slate are now unrecognisable conglomerations of deformed building. Stone and breeze-block, slate and perspex, wood and plastics are incompatible. The old farm steading was a balanced structure of natural material which enhanced the natural scene. The present practice of grafting big sheds on to dilapidated, crumbling, farm steadings has resulted in visual hurt and spiritual deprivation.

As you move around Angus and the Mearns today, look for the old farm buildings and cherish them when you find them. Search for the unaltered cart shed, the pristine horse mill, the original bothy. Seek out the friendly farm house detached in its dog-draped backyard and apple-tree'd garden and savour the spiritual solace that such an environment provides. Angus and the Mearns is the last sanctuary and stronghold of the Scotch folk. I say that quite without prejudice, of course.

Back towards Kirriemuir from Airlie, the B951 skirts Kinnordy Loch, a renowned bird sanctuary. Kinnordy is not one of your great open expanses of sparkling water with boats, more of a bog hole with birds. There are two observation points with hides and the area is under the management of the Royal Society for the Protection of Birds. It is an enthusiast's loch, a good selection of birds is usually present, but there are no ospreys as yet. Maybe by the time the trees have grown a bit higher the ospreys will come, and by that time they will no doubt be classed as vermin and culled. In the meantime, two or three pairs of great crested grebes frequent the reserve.

Kirriemuir

Kirriemuir is the next stop on the B951 – and on the main A926 Blairgowrie road – and a pleasant little stop it is. Opinions differ as to the exact meaning and derivation of the name 'Kirriemuir'. One authority says 'Cell of St. Mary', one says 'Large hollow' and one 'Main quarter'. They offer a pretty wide choice. There are thirty-six different spellings of the name on official documents over the centuries, and any one could provide a different derivation. There is also a Northmuir, a Southmuir and a Westmuir. It seems to me that Kirriemuir might just possibly have meant Eastmuir, but apparently not. Place names are not derived as easily as that.

Whatever its meaning, Kirriemuir has been there for a long time. Its origins are lost in the black hole of time, but earth houses and graves have been excavated, a crannog and primitive canoes found and the sites of standing and rocking stones marked around Kirriemuir. Little is known of the successive civilisations which created these relics but they leave no doubt that the area of Kirriemuir has been a homestead and a manufactory since the beginning of time.

The present town grew from two nuclei, the Gairie Burn and the Hill. Two small communities developed and were subsequently joined by roads running up and down the hillside. The result is today's pleasant little town. The old buildings, which replaced the even older wood and wattle hovels in the seventeenth century, were of native red sandstone and the summer sun setting on the heart of Kirrie still makes a picture of warmth and charm. Inevitably these older buildings are going and a rash of modern building is spreading over Kirriemuir. The outskirts are being consumed by the dreaded bungalows of suburbia and many of Kirriemuir's 6000 inhabitants are now commuters to and from Dundee.

The centre of the town is the Square where the old Town House still stands. In its lifetime it has served as Tolbooth, Courthouse, Police Station, Weights and Measures Office, Post Office and, latterly, chemist's shop. Repeated attempts have been made to remove it but fortunately the climate of public opinion has turned to conservation and now it seems safe. The last serious attempt to demolish the Town House was in the 1970s when the top of Bellie's Brae – and there's a name to savour – was being widened. Fortunately again, wiser counsels prevailed and the street was widened on the other side. The original Town House was built in 1604 and is the oldest building in Kirriemuir. Its present shape was defined in 1862 when an outside stair was demolished and a tower added. The 'little' town clock was installed in this tower, whereas the 'big' town clock is in the steeple of the Barony Kirk just over the way. The Town House belongs to the family of Douglas – the Earl of Home's branch – and their coat of arms is displayed on the front wall of the building. It is as well to note that, because wind and weather have all but obliterated the carving on the stonework.

The rest of old Kirrie was a jumble of little houses built at odd angles around a maze of narrow streets and wynds. These old houses all held handlooms, and although every Angus town used to have its handloom weavers, Kirriemuir existed by them. It has been a thriving centre of cottage industry through the centuries. The trade developed and expanded after the '45 and it increased until in 1792 Kirrie's production of woven cloth was worth £38,000 – a formidable figure in the eighteenth century. By the beginning of the nineteenth century, Government records show that 25,000 webs of cloth were being produced annually. As a web measured 146 yards in length, you can see why they called Kirrie the weaving town. In 1833 there were 3000 citizens of Kirriemuir engaged in the weaving and ancillary trades, 52,000 webs being produced that year. Kirriemuir linens and Osnaburghs were known all over Britain and the Continent. By the end of the century two million yards were being Government stamped annually.

One particular aspect of the trade is worth noting. The old Town House is listed as having been a 'Weights and Measures' office. Its real function at this period was to act as a measuring and stamping centre for the town's weavers. Every bolt of linen produced in Kirriemuir had to be examined and passed by a board of local inspectors at the Town House and certified as being of good quality and of the correct length before being stamped as fit for sale. We are inclined to think, nowadays, that 'Quality Control' is a relatively new phenomenon introduced by the fiendishly efficient Japanese. When you hear that the weaver producing any such sub-standard material was thus financially crippled and publicly humiliated, you begin to appreciate the height of excellence they maintained.

The history of the early years of Kirrie's weaving industry is one of steady expansion, but by 1839 the trade was undergoing periods of fluctuation, and during one recession the employers announced that the price for weaving a web was to be cut. Now, men who practised such rigorous self-discipline as the Kirrie weavers were not men to be readily disciplined by others. They were up in arms immediately – and literally. They armed themselves and marched against their employers. The employers called in the Law. The weavers chased the Sheriff and his constables off the street and troops were summoned from Dundee. Martial law was proclaimed and the weavers' leaders were arrested and charged in the High Court of Edinburgh. Prison sentences closed the incident.

There is still a weaving industry in Kirriemuir, but nowadays they weave jute and polypropylene in the two modern factories of Messrs J. & D. Wilkie's Kirriemuir Linen Works and Messrs Ogilvy & Stewart's Gairie Linen Works. 'The thrums – threads – that used to hang on the end beam of every loom and gave young Jimmy Barrie an idea for a name, are no longer necessary.' The day of the handloom has gone and the muted clack of the shuttle can be heard now only in hyper-efficient, air-conditioned, Board-of-Trade inspected factories. It is interesting to think back on the days when every cottage in Kirriemuir was a factory and ask oneself if the improvements in efficiency and hours and conditions of work have been reflected in an equal improvement in individual happiness. It is too easy to equate leisure with happiness. When you read the history and tales of old Kirrie, it is surprising to find how much time they spent laughing.

The other main traditional industry in the town is milling. The old Angus Milling Company is now incorporated into Hamlyn Milling but the company still produces oatmeal and oatflakes in Kirriemuir under the 'Peter Pan' label. The Peter Pan trademark was reproduced in a statuette by the artist Alastair Smart in 1972 and installed in the company's forecourt in the Glengate. Modelled on the familiar original in Kensington Gardens, London, the statue soon became a favourite with the Kirrie bairns. Almost inevitably, in these depraved times, it was attacked by vandals and smashed beyond repair. That was in 1982 but the feelings of the townsfolk were so strong that money was immediately raised and the artist re-commissioned to produce an identical model. In August 1983 the replacement statue was unveiled by the Countess of Airlie. It is reassuring to be able to report that it has remained unmarked during the intervening years.

The etymologist who translated Kirriemuir into 'large hollow' must have had his eye on the Den, for the Den is a very large hollow. It is Kirriemuir's Public Park, bought by money left to the town by George (Sydney) Wilkie, a Kirrie man who made his fortune manufacturing biscuits in Sydney, Australia. They say, in Kirriemuir, that George Street in Sydney is called after George Wilkie. It is a coincidence that a series of Kings of that name had streets named after them around the same time.

As a public park the Den of Kirriemuir is a centre of excellence. It has all that you could ask for in a public park and a lot more besides. A site of great natural beauty has been modified by judicious development into a comprehensive communal play area. Young children festoon the swings, older children run wild amongst the trees, senior citizens daunder down the grass, and courting couples court. It is fascinating to see, whenever you mention the Den to the Kirrie folk, how their eyes light up. The Den of Kirriemuir has seen more troths plighted than all your Loch Lomonds and Banks o' Bonnie Doon put together. Why else is the 'Ball o' Kirriemuir', that bawdy ballad of international renown, so famous? Every Ball that has ever been held in Kirriemuir has decanted into the Den:

> The Minister's dochter, she was there
> Richt popular wi' the men
> An when ye asked tae see her hame
> She led ye doon the Den . . .

J.M. Barrie

More acceptable to the majority of Kirriemarians is the town's connection with J.M. Barrie. Sir James Matthew Barrie

Sir James M. Barrie at the opening of the Barrie Pavilion, Kirriemuir, June 1930.

was born on 9th May, 1860 in Kirriemuir. His father was a handloom weaver who progressed from working his own loom in his house to working on the clerical staff of one of the factories. Due to a family tragedy, when his brother was killed in a skating accident at the age of seven and the subsequent illness of his mother, James went to live with his elder brother. For five years, from 1871 until 1876, James attended Dumfries Academy whilst the brother, Alexander, was an Inspector of Schools in that area. From Dumfries, J.M.B. proceeded to Edinburgh University in 1879 and graduated from there with an M.A.(Hons.) in Eng. Lit.

After a spell on the *Nottingham Journal* as a reporter, he came back to Kirrie to set up as a freelance writer. As soon as he had a few acceptances he took off for London to make his fortune. That he certainly did. In the year 1907 Barrie made £40,000. Judge that by today's values and remember that it was only one year's take and you will see that his total fortune was immense. Few people nowadays realise the fame accorded to Barrie during his lifetime. He was the confidant of the top people in the land from the Royal Family downwards. His reputation and standing during his lifetime were very much greater than they can ever be again, which is the exact opposite of the usual. Nowadays, Barrie is out of fashion. *Peter Pan* persists, *The*

Admirable Crichton was made into a film, and some of the plays are occasionally done on television but the rest is largely forgotten. When you try to evaluate Barrie's work, it is essential to remember to judge him in the context of his time. *A Window in Thrums* is sentimental and trivial nowadays but in its day it was realistic and progressive. If you ask me, I think *A Window in Thrums* and *Auld Licht Idylls* are the best of Barrie. As a child I was taken to Edinburgh to see *Peter Pan* and I thought it rubbish then. *Mary Rose* and *Dear Brutus* I think rubbish now. None the less, the insight and humour of Barrie's works are of the highest, and his delineation of character in his essays on Kirrie is masterly. It is just a pity he went a bit fey.

It is impossible to speak of Kirriemuir's attitude to Barrie because it varies with the Kirriemarian you speak to, but it is significant that they talk more of his cricket matches on the Northmuir and the Barrie Pavilion he presented to the town, than of his writing. To tell the truth, there are few folk in Kirriemuir today who have ever read a line of Barrie. His birthplace is marked by a National Trust for Scotland museum, the window in Thrums can still be seen overlooking the Commonty – although that was not the actual window – and there is a little rest garden in his memory beside the birthplace. The interest in Barrie now is purely as a magnet for visitors and Kirrie appreciates that. Around 200,000 people from all over the world have visited the Barrie birthplace since the opening of the museum in 1963. There is no doubt that Kirriemuir is proud of James Barrie, they are just not too sure why. A few years back there was a radio programme on Kirrie during which one of the Bailies of the town said in an aside – 'Aye, richt eneuch, ye've tae be shairp tae live in Kirrie'. Maybe J.M. wasna jist shairp eneuch.

On 7th June 1930, the Barrie Cricket Pavilion and Camera Obscura were opened and Sir James M. Barrie was made the first Freeman of Kirriemuir. The Camera Obscura is still sometimes in operation and well worth a visit. It is in an ideal position to give a panoramic view of the Angus glens and hills and amply repays the effort required to get access to it. It is not always open but a team of volunteers mans it in the summer and an enquiry down in the town will avoid disappointment if it is closed. The Camera Obscura is one of only three in Scotland, the other two being in Dumfries and Edinburgh. They consist of a rotating lens sited high up on a roof, projecting images through mirrors on to a viewing table inside the building. It sounds a prosaic enough implement but the picture it gives is one of heightened clarity because it is seen in the contrast of a darkened room and the effect is dramatic.

The older hamlets of Northmuir and Southmuir are now incorporated into the greater Kirriemuir, but Westmuir is still a separate entity a mile away along the Blairgowrie road. Fortunately, Kirrie is a designated Conservation Area and the hand of the vandal – if not his brother the developer – has been stayed. One of the more recent developments was the demolition of the old Reform Street school, built in 1874, with new buildings put on the site. Adjacent to this is the Town Hall, built in 1885 and happily still functioning as the social centre of the town – barring the Den, of course.

Since Reform Street school has been demolished the primary education of the Kirrie bairns is now catered for in the Northmuir and Southmuir Primary schools. The secondary school is Webster's High School, the Webster being one John Webster, a banker of Kirrie who left money for 'Instituting, erecting and maintaining a school in the town of Kirriemuir'. The school was duly built and named 'Webster's Seminary'. It lasted under that title until 1954 when they built the new Secondary school in the Southmuir and called it 'Webster's High School'. Since they kept the name Webster they could obviously have kept the Seminary. It was a delightful, antique, individual and acceptably pretentious name and thousands of old Webster's Seminarists must grieve with me that it has gone. Why were these nameless, faceless, office wallahs in Dundee allowed to do it?

In recent years Webster's has had an excellent record of academic and sporting achievement. It is a good school. It would have to be judged in the context of the day to know whether it has always been a good school. Reference to Webster's Seminary's Log Book, quoting the summary of H.M.I.'s Report for July 1875, makes one wonder: 'When we visited the school two years ago we formed pretty high expectations regarding it, we think not unreasonably. The accommodation was ample and convenient, there was a large number of intelligent looking pupils of a very respectable class; the staff was newly organised, powerful and liberally paid. 'We expected soon to see a school judiciously arranged, working out its plans in order and harmony. We expected to see a healthy tone of moral earnestness pervading the place: the pupils eager, vigorous, ambitious of success, innocently emulous of each other, the master strict, resolute, energetic, exciting the enthusiasm of the pupils, banishing levity and compelling respect by his own dignity, earnestness, extensive information and zeal.

'The picture presented by the school falls considerably short of our expectation. Mediocrity is the predominating feature of the pupils, some pass, some don't but there is not much difference between the one class and the other – Geography, History, Grammar and Intelligence are all pretty much the same. The Registers are not kept with perfect accuracy.

Mr Menzies	Headmaster
Mr Forrester	Assistant
Mr Anderson	Assistant
Stewart Crabb	Pupil Teacher
William Wilson	Pupil Teacher

School Roll – 102

'The pass on the whole is good and gives evidence of much honest and painstaking work. Much greater firmness in the Discipline is seriously wanted. Otherwise much intelligent work is thrown away. Simultaneous answering and talking in class, disorderly movements and, above all, copying must be checked.'

That is a wheecher of a report. A cursory reading of it might make one think that things were far from good in the school. It might seem that Webster's Seminary was not one of your better educational establishments, but to make that assumption one would have to see all the H.M.I. reports for Angus schools in 1875. That might show the school in a better light and the Inspectorate somewhat poorer. Maybe 1875 wasn't a vintage year for school reports generally.

The present Webster's High School was built in 1954 and is

being developed again. It will be interesting, too, to see what happens in the narrow Roods. The narrow Roods, one of Kirrie's main thoroughfares, is so called to distinguish it from the wider, upper Roods which crosses Reform Street and runs right up the hill to the Northmuir. The problem in the narrow Roods was traffic; Kirriemuir suffers just as much from it as every other little old mediaeval Scottish town. Its streets and wynds were never intended to take modern traffic. Various one-way systems have been tried, including the 'pedestrianisation' of the narrow Roods. I think there is a society against words like that.

The narrow Roods used to be a real street with traffic, then it became a one-way street, now it has been turned into a 'pedestrian precinct'. In the old days it was a canny wee byway with pavements and kerbs and a Starry Rock Shop and cars in the roadway and folks on the pavements and all the hustle of Kirriemuir going about its daily business. Now it looks a sad neglected sight – but, wait – I could be the fool, since I'm no bairn, who sees half-finished work. It may be better when it is finished. There must be more to come. My criticism is that the aesthetic appeal of the original architectural artistry and order of the tall buildings flanking the narrow passageway has been destroyed. The proportions have been upset. I fear that, as it now serves no useful purpose in linking the High Street with Reform Street and the Northmuir since nobody walks nowadays, so it will decay. I hope I'm wrong for Kirrie's sake – and at least the Starry Rock Shop is still there.

I hope I'm wrong with any criticism of Kirrie for it is a warm, couthy toon peopled wi' warm couthy folk and one of my favourite Angus places. It has a wide and varied social life catered for by a plethora of local societies. It is still small enough for all the native Kirriemarians to know each other, and that is the first essential for any community spirit; you have to know you belong to a community. From all its various clubs and groups I would select the Angus Strathspey and Reel Society as my favourite. Founded and conducted by Angus Cameron, the Angus Strathspey and Reel Society is a joy to listen to – and I have listened to it for nigh on twenty years.

The A.S. & R.S. started as a successor to the pragmatically named 'Angus Occasionals'. They met only occasionally. Angus

Cameron wanted a more formal orchestra, so he established the Angus Strathspey and Reel Society. The 'Angus' is the county, by the way, not the conductor. From Kirrie and environs he gathered together a team of highly qualified and accomplished musicians who play beautiful, haunting, traditional Scottish music. They also belt out foot-stamping, hand-clapping Scottish country dance tunes that have youngsters demanding to learn the fiddle and old ladies hoochin' in the aisles. The annual concert of the A.S. & R.S. in the Reid Hall in Forfar is a sell-out from the day it is announced each year. They always have a top professional performer to sing with them, but that is an extra. Connoisseurs of Scottish music go to hear the band. It is a delight.

If you think that teuchter tunes and cornkist ballads are just what you would expect from Kirriemuir, it might surprise you to learn that Kirriemuir has taken the art of Scottish music rather beyond that level. You may not know Angus Cameron but you have heard of Yehudi Menuhin and he has played with the Angus Strathspey and Reel Society on several occasions. Yehudi Menuhin has studied with the Society over a period and holds them in high regard for their musicianship. You don't need any better reference than that in musical circles.

Kirriemuir has this habit of being just a jump or two ahead of the field in most things. Even the highly dubious trade of second-hand car dealing has been raised to a fine art in Kirriemuir. This esoteric occupation is now one of Kirrie's major industries. It all started 'way back when a Kirrie lad, Joe Munro, came back from the war and started to deal in used cars. Cars had always been sold in Kirrie the same as anywhere else but Joe Munro came in just after the war when new cars were unobtainable and old cars were selling at highly inflated prices.

Joe Munro brought three things to the trade – hard work, personal integrity and an unconditional guarantee. He bought used cars, gave them a thorough overhaul and sold them with a six-month guarantee. If anything went wrong with one of Joe's cars then, it was immediately repaired at his cost. He bought carefully and overhauled completely before selling at a price which covered his work. As a result, Joe's name soon became a byword for honest dealing, he prospered and the trade which he pioneered is now firmly established as a Kirrie special. Joe has long given up the business but his spirit of enterprise continues and Kirriemuir is still a Mecca for the automobile faithful. Strangers who are unfamiliar with the Joe Munro dimension in car dealing are often taken aback by the scale of the operation in Kirrie, especially if they start up at the Southmuir where the Ewarts keep a showroom full of vintage Rolls Royces and Bentleys.

For those visitors with their own Royces – and even those few without – Kirrie offers a rare and special treat: the excellent home-made ice cream purveyed by Bridget Visocchi in her cafe in the Square. Bridget Visocchi's ice cream is the genuine old-fashioned kind that tastes like ice cream, and Bridget herself is a genuine, natural, old-fashioned character and personality. Originally from Italy and having spent all her married life in Kirriemuir, Bridget still speaks with a broad Italian accent superimposed on a broad Kirrie dialect. For thirty years and more Bridget has exerted a profound and beneficial influence on the Kirrie young who frequent her shop. Many's the potential miscreant who has been saved from greater sin by a daud ee lug from Bridget. It is a great regreat in Kirrie that Bridget Visocchi has just retired from the shop. May she long continue to prosper.

Any visitor to Kirriemuir would be well advised to start at Visocchi's, for there they will tell you all you want to know. From there go along to the Library and collect all the tourist literature. Circle the main area of the Square and call in at the Barony Kirk, built in 1786 and now known as the Parish Church and note the spire, an obvious afterthought, added in 1790 as a gift from Charles Lyell, Laird of Kinnordy. Check out the narrow Roods (and see if my fears were justified), investigate the old coaching inns of the Airlie and Ogilvie Arms and, above all, speak to some of the mahogany-hued patrons in deerstalker hats. They will tell you about Kirriemuir. They *are* Kirriemuir.

Go up to the Northmuir, then to the Barrie Pavilion, and if the Library has explained the opening hours to you, visit the Camera Obscura. See, if you are so inclined, the Barrie grave in the cemetery and remember what an old Kirriemarian told me: 'Aye, they thocht a lot mair o' him in London than we did here'. If you do go into the cemetery, look at the old Pictish stones there.

If you are more interested in the living than the dead, go along to Kirriemuir Golf Club and play one of the most beautiful courses in Angus. Just watch that great gaping hollow short of the eighteenth green: it ruins many a card. Above all, if you really want to delve below the surface of Kirrie, without using your clubs, buy a copy of Sandra Affleck's book, *A Guide to Kirriemuir and District*, and carry it around with you. You can buy it at James Norrie's shop at 39 High Street and it will tell you all you want to know and a bit more.

Remember one thing: it is common for neighbouring towns and villages to harbour fairly strong prejudices against one another, but Kirriemuir and Forfar have elevated their rivalry into an article of faith. They really work at it. If the subject crops up when you're in Kirrie, be prepared for the tale they will tell you about the Battle of Muir Moss. Kirrie beat Forfar there to claim ownership of the moss where they cut their peats, and shortly after the event the celebrated poet, Drummond of Hawthornden (1585-1649), was touring the area and was refused entry into Forfar. Plague was rife at the time and Forfar was taking no chances, as always.

Kirriemuir welcomed him and in gratitude he took their part in the feud. It happened that the Estates of Scotland were sitting in St. Andrews just then and Drummond contrived to send a messenger to the Provost of Forfar purporting to come from that body. The Provost hastily summoned his Bailies and they sat down to study the important missive. It turned out to be a polemic of particular pungency:

> The Kirriemarians and the Forfarians
> Met at Muir Moss.
> The Kirriemarians beat the Forfarians
> Back to the Cross.
> Sutors ye are and sutors ye'll be
> Fie upo' Forfar
> Kirriemuir bears the gree . . .

The 'sutors' refers to the fact that Forfar's trade was shoemaking, as Kirriemuir's was weaving, and the sutors of

Forfar and the weavers of Kirrie each nurtured a deep and satisfying hatred of each other.

I doubt if the lyric would make Top of the Pops today, but as an advertising jingle it certainly caught on in the seventeenth century. Forfar still smarts under its scorn. Kirrie thinks it's just great.

CHAPTER 9

The Glens of Angus

'The Braes o' Angus' and 'The Glens' are names that encapsulate nostalgia for expatriate Angus loons. For Angus residents they epitomise the essential appeal of the county. Add on 'Strathmore' and in those few words you create masterpieces of imagery. Long rolling fields of autumn gold, wooded hollows green in Spring, hill and dale, mountain and moor, all reflected in words. For Angus is a work of Nature's art and the braes, glens and Strath are Angus: there is no finer land. Where the foothills of the Grampian mountains rise from the alluvial plain, rivers have carved tortuous outlets through the native rock. The glens of Angus are the river routes of the North Esk, the West Water, the Noran, the South Esk, the Prosen and the Isla with all their myriad tributaries. They are the chisels that have carved the features of Angus. The Isla and its feeder streams seek the Tay and flow south to Dundee, the others cross Strathmore and find the Angus coast.

The boundary of Angus is the North Esk and its glen. Next to Glen Esk is Glen Lethnot, just over the brow of Wirren. It is a long trail by car down one Angus glen and up the next but no more than a few brisk hill miles by foot. Glen Lethnot is a quiet and dignified glen, regarded by the Brechiners as their own private backyard and reflecting the honour in its tranquillity. It is sparsely populated, the social centre being at Bridgend where the school and the hall are sited. The eponymous bridge is a structure of surpassing ugliness, high-sided, metal-built, and as offensive to the eye as it is obstructive to the view. Its predecessor was washed away. Roll on the flood. The road up Lethnot is good, if narrow, and goes as far as Hunthill Lodge where it ends. Through the end gate a track runs on up the glen to peter out eventually at the Shieling of Saughs.

This is the scene of one of the great folk tales of Angus, the Battle of Saughs. The battle figures prominently in local history and is much quoted as a major encounter of great significance. In fact it was a scuffle with a handful of

Highlanders, cattle rievers who had slipped down by the Water of Saughs and stolen a few Lethnot beasts. They arrived on a Sunday afternoon and on Monday morning were well away and were resting at the Shieling of Saughs when a bunch of Lethnot lads, led by young McIntosh of Ledenhendrie, caught up with them.

When the pursuers caught up, the robbers were just about to roast a calf and a somewhat embarrassing silence fell. It was broken by young McIntosh challenging them to fight, and in the general argy-bargy it was agreed that single combat between McIntosh and the chief thief should settle the issue. When the details were being arranged, one of the Highlanders fired a shot at one of the Lethnot men and killed him. That precipitated a general fight and the rievers' leader jumped on McIntosh and knocked him down. As the cattle-thief was just about to administer the *coup de grâce,* James Winter of Lethnot got behind him and hamstrung him. In spite of this appalling injury the leader 'fought on his stumps' until young McIntosh recovered and slew him. At the end of it all at least two robbers and one Lethnot man were definitely killed although Lethnot maintains to this day that 'the tradition is that not one escaped'.

Our authority for all this history is old man Marshall again. The only relevant detail he seems to have missed is that, in the heat of battle, the cattle wandered off and found their own way back down the glen. It was milking time.

No Highland marauders despoil the glen now – even on Sunday afternoons. Glen Lethnot is quiet to the point of torpidity. It is the place where frayed Brechiners go to ease the stresses and tensions of life in the Ancient City. There is a clachan of weekend huts behind the hill at Craigendowie above the Calletar burn where wise men go to meditate. The place would serve as a model for all others of its kind for no passer-by knows it is there. Hidden by the natural contours of the land, soberly painted huts strategically sited with the minimum intrusion on the natural scene provide havens for family retreat. Children play in the burn, parents walk by Nathro, Braco and the Calletar Den whilst grandparents doze in the afternoon sun.

Glen Lethnot is really a glen for autumn. The river from Stonyford down to Craigendowie is wooded with rowans and birches and the autumn colours with the pure gold of the bracken then, make it an artist's dream. The scenery varies as the hills close in or recede from the river bank but the whole glen is a charm. We are the last, favoured, generation to know the unspoiled rural delights of Scotland. Increased wealth and mobility are fast polluting the land with people. Commercial developers will destroy the countryside just as soon as they are allowed to: look around you. We should enjoy our unspoiled country whilst we may but be ever ready to defend it. A useful start could be made by opposing the intrusion of glitzy caravans and chromium-plated trailer homes that is already being made into Lethnot from the Drumcraig end. Glen Lethnot is too valuable to lose to Mammon. Trust it to the Brechiners.

Over from Lethnot the Paphrie and the Cruick burns cut niches out of the foothills before the Noran makes a major incision at Glen Ogil. At the foot of Glen Ogil the Den of Ogil reservoir lies deep in a cleft of the hills and is much enjoyed by the fortunate fishers of the Strathmore Angling Club. The other reservoir, at the top end of the glen, is the Glenogil reservoir and great is the confusion between them. The Glenogil reservoir is more remote and picturesque but percipient anglers know amongst themselves that it teems only with teensy little trout.

Glenogil serves as the base point for countless hill walks but do not venture into the Angus hills ever unless you are fit, well-booted and able to use map and compass. The braes are glorious places but never underestimate their danger: treat them with respect. Any one of the countless glens and dens of Angus can provide unlimited pleasure and every one of them can kill.

West of Glen Ogil is Glen Clova, approached by the side road that runs up through Cortachy village to join the B955 from Kirriemuir at 393596. Cortachy village is small, neat and dominated by the gates of Cortachy Castle. The castle has been an Ogilvy home since 1473 and their principal seat since Airlie Castle had a visit, as we saw, from the Campbells in 1691.

The setting of Cortachy Castle in the low land by the South Esk allows it to be seen to advantage through the trees from the Memus road. Set unusually low for a castle, probably because it was originally meant only as a hunting lodge, it certainly looks like a castle. Crowstepped gables, towers and pepperpot turrets decorate its Scotch baronial nucleus and it makes a pretty picture with lawns reaching down to the rock-girt river. The present structure owes most of its character to Blanche, Countess of Airlie, who had it rebuilt in the nineteenth century.

Up the hill from the castle, Dykehead is known mainly for its hotel – an old hostelry that has been the victim of some recent rather startling modernisation. Fortunately the customers have retained their pristine character. If you sift through the tourists, the visitors and the Sunday afternoon high-tea crowd from Forfar, you will still find the hill herds and the gamies, bred and reared in the glens: hert o' corn. Dykehead Hotel is strategically sited at the point where Glen Prosen and Glen Clova diverge – or converge if you are coming the other way. Glen Clova is the bigger and longer of the two and used to be one of the main routes through the Grampians to Aberdeenshire. Going up the glen, the road splits just at the Gella bridge and roads run up either side of the South Esk from then on. It is suggested, sensibly, that touring traffic should keep to the left road going up the glen and come back by the other. With the volume of weekend traffic now, that is definitely advisable. The roads join again at Clova where the hotel and church are and a single road carries on up to Braedownie. At that point the road peters out at a prettified picnic spot and car park. The famous Youth Hostel sits in the trees a few hundred yards further up and from there a track, Jock's Road, leads over the hills to Braemar.

The glen of the South Esk, to the east, leads one to the track over the Capel Mounth that leads eventually to Ballater but these walks are not Sunday afternoon strolls. Do not wander into the hills unless you are prepared and competent.

The White Water Burn from Glen Doll and the South Esk join at Braedownie. The South Esk springs from a profusion of hill burns running off the Moulzie and Bachnagairn slopes. Purists trace it right back to the little Loch Esk tucked away in the peat bog behind Bachnagairn. By the time you get that far you could have gone up half-a-dozen burns with equal authority. The South Esk is a river of great diversity and nowhere more surprisingly than in the stretch down the length of Glen Clova. The birlin', roarin', spate-swelled burns that have joined up to form the South Esk before it meets the White Water at Braedownie, suddenly change. The South Esk flows slowly and sedately down Clova, more like a Hampshire trout stream. A few alders and willows on the bank would make it like the Itchen or the Test. Not at all what one expects from a mountain torrent.

Heavily used by tourist traffic now, the glen roads were at one time much favoured by the native Caledonii, Picts, Celts, Scots and assorted gangrel bodies. Braedownie was a main junction with tracks running in from Glen Esk, Ballater, Braemar, Glen Prosen, Glen Isla, Glen Shee and the Gella. Most of today's travellers, apart from a handful of dedicated walkers, simply trundle their cars up to Braedownie and back again. A few venture a mile or so up the hill tracks, only a very few travel on from the glen. Whatever the purpose of the visit, whether it be to follow the old trails over the mountains to the north, to picnic by a hill burn or simply to drive non-stop up one side of the glen and down the other, Glen Clova impresses the visitor. It holds rock cliff and heather slope, rowan tree and river meadow. It offers Angus and the Mearns in microcosm, and whatever day of the year you visit, it is majestic.

On the return journey the road crosses the river at Gella Bridge. There is a new bridge there now, a functionally simple structure of concrete and iron that serves the traffic better than the old humpbacked pack bridge ever could. Cars can pass each other on the new bridge and speed faster to and from, but just look upstream and appreciate the beauty of the old brig. Styled in a single perfectly proportioned arch of soaring symmetry, the old bridge stands as a reproach to the new. Built from the bools of the river bed and the quarry stones of Doll, the old bridge is a classic, linking art and utility. The men who made that bridge, from the designer who drew the plans to the stonemasons who dressed the coping stones of the parapet, were artists. The final insult of the new bridge-builders was to put their hi-tech highway so close to the old bridge that you can't even see it properly now.

There are car parks by the new Gella Brig, one on either side of the river with adjacent picnic spots. Farther down the Kirrie

road at the charmingly named Cullow Market there is yet
another and any one of them can be a delight on the right day.
The 'right day' depends on luck and the folk you follow to the
area. It is a pity but it is difficult to love all of one's fellow
creatures all of the time. Vandals who leave soft drink cans,
biscuit wrappers and crushed paper cups blowing in the wind
must somehow be corrected and educated into a closer
empathy with Nature.

There was a time when Clova would have found its own
immediate answer to the litter leavers, and no mistake. The
Lady Dorothea Maria Ogilvy of Clova and Airlie, a poetess of
no mean calibre would doubtless have had a word or two to say
on the subject. Writing about Glen Clova in 1889 in 'Willie
Wabster's Wooing' she said, and I quote:

> Oh barony o' Clova, green and grand, strinkled wi' spairgen
> strype and brattlin strand,
> The sweetest strath in a' my fatherland;
> Yet wi' the warld I whamle whan-a-bee, ramfeezled runt, I
> hirple owre the haugh;
> Nae worth for beef or broth or milk o' whey, a rail-e'ed rousy
> girnigo-gibbie.

- and that was a love poem. With her love of Clova and
command of the language one can imagine how she would
have reacted to the incursion of plastic-packed convenience
foods and Bermuda shorts into her glen. She would have
fettled the ramfeezled runts in a wanny.

On the high ground at the top of Tulloch Hill, between the
roads to Clova and Prosen is the Airlie Monument. It is a copy
of one of the towers of Airlie Castle and was erected in
memory of David Ogilvy, 11th Earl of Airlie, who was killed in
the Boer War. A further copy of the Airlie Tower was made
when Forfar Town Council erected their War Memorial on top
of Balmashanner after the First World War. The twin towers
are now landmarks for many miles.

In the records of the Ogilvy family it is listed that the young
David Ogilvy was killed leading a cavalry charge at the battle
of Diamond Hill in 1900. His last command was to his
squadron to follow him in the charge, his last words were as he
lay mortally wounded on the veldt, 'Moderate your language,

please, Sergeant,' he said . . . and died. There could be no
better *envoi* for an officer and a gentleman. The memorial
above Clova and Prosen commands the finest views in all
Angus and the Mearns. I say so. You can stand with your back
to the four sides of the tower and see breathtaking views on
every side. The Glens, the Braes, the Strath, the sea; Angus,
Perth and Fife. An unequalled series of beautiful vistas.
Glen Prosen is a quieter, more natural and attractive glen
than Clova. Hordes stream up and down Clova all summer,
destroying the very environment and atmosphere they claim to
seek. That, of course, is the first act of tourism: to destroy the
object that attracts it in the first place. Glen Clova is now a
tourist attraction. Prosen is still an unspoiled Angus backwater.

The start of Glen Prosen is beautifully wooded where it rises
from Dykehead, and right at the start there is a quiet secluded
woodland pool down on the left side of the road. There you
will always see stankies and jeuks busy about their seasonal
chores with little concern for passers-by. As the road leads out
of the woods it takes a sharp turn to the right and on the
corner, hard by a wind-tossed eglantine, there is a pillar. This is
a memorial column in memory of Captain Scott the Antarctic
explorer.

Glen Prosen has always been a favourite glen for
discriminating visitors. Botanists like George Don from Forfar
and, more recently, Major Sherriff of Ascreavie have listed a
wide variety of alpine plants native to Prosen, Clova and Doll.
Glen Prosen was an area of special scientific interest long
before the phrase became a label. Amongst its more
enlightened visitors were Scott and Wilson of South Pole fame.
In 1910 and 1911 they visited Prosen as guests of the owner of
the bungalow at the entrance to the glen. It has even been
suggested that the idea of going to Antarctica first came to
them in Prosen but there is no particular evidence of that.

The monument is a solid structure of local stones and
cement, built to withstand the rigours of Glen Prosen winters
and the depredations of Glen Prosen motorists. Originally it
was a column and a horse-trough, then it was a column and a
modified horse-trough, now it is a replacement column and no
horse-trough. A succession of accidents reduced the original
monument to rubble. A plaque on the present edifice bears the

The memorial to Robert Falcon Scott and Edward Adrian Wilson.

original commemorative inscription to Robert Falcon Scott and Edward Adrian Wilson. It also bears a footnote which reads: 'This cairn was erected in 1981 on the site of the memorial fountain built in 1919 and accidentally destroyed in 1979'. It is confidently anticipated in the glen that the next man to hit the Scott fountain will stand a much better chance of being destroyed than destroying.

Round the corner from the memorial is an opening on the right which is the pathway up to the Airlie Tower. On a good day you can walk quietly up the hill to the monument and hear birdsong and windcroon. On a bad day you will coincide with young lads on motorbikes who roar up and down the path, over-revving their under-capacity engines to the scream of tortured metal and the utter discomfiture of the lieges. May you always strike a good day.

The view up the glen can be confusing from different points. Glen Cally, Glen Uig, Glen Logie and a host of other side shoots branch off on both sides and obscure the main glen. The road carries on up the east side of Prosen Water as far as Spott where there is a bridge linking the east and west roads.

On either side they continue: the east a few hundred yards to Glenprosen village and a private road to Balnaboth, the west road a couple of miles to Glenprosen Lodge and Runtaleave. Glenprosen village is a huddle of houses on a flank of the Hill of Spott with a telephone booth and a coffee/craft shop to justify the name of village. It is an unspoiled clachan and a joy to visit. The Kirk sits snugly under the hill in the trees at the foot of a track called 'The Minister's Road' leading over the hills to Clova. The Angus hills are lacerated with Ministers' Roads and Priests' Paths hereabouts: perambulation must have been an occupational hazard of the Cloth at one time.

The farm of Spott is famous locally as the home for many generations of the Whyte family and for their success in stock breeding. Go there in October when the Perth sheep sales are on and you will see Blackface tups such as you have never imagined. The young rams are brought in for washing and preparing before they go to the Sales and these are the finest specimens of the breed you can see anywhere. Larger, close-up, than one imagines a Blackface sheep to be, they have heads of monumental grace. The head of a Spott two-year-old tup is the kind of head you would only ever expect to see, silver-mounted, holding snuff at the President's end of a Regimental dinner table. Great spiralled horns make one grateful that the Blackface tup does not have the nature of the Rottweiler dog. The head is strong, broad, firm-jawed and bright-eyed. The profile is that of a Middle Eastern potentate. Spott rams are aristocrats.

Over the bridge at Spott and past the steading, the road undulates down past Lednathie and Uig to cut back by Pearsie and Prosenhaugh on the one hand and West Kinwhirrie on the other. Eventually it comes out below Cortachy village again and you have left Arcady.

Next glen westward is Glen Isla, last of the line. It can be approached from Kirrie and it can be approached from Alyth which makes it border country. It can also be approached from Glen Shee to the north which is just a wee bit of an imperfection for an Angus glen. It has this through road. True Angus glens do not have through roads. You go into an Angus glen and you expect to come out of the same Angus glen at the same end. Glen Isla has through traffic.

At the south end the B951 from Kirrie cuts past Lintrathen Loch and heads straight up the glen. The B954 from Alyth holds to the west and joins up with the B951 where a side road takes off north to the Backwater dam. A link road at the south of the loch goes round to Kilry Post Office, meets the B954, and just beyond that a further side road runs up the west side of the Isla past Kilry school to join the B951 again at Brewlands bridge. This road runs up over the moor and gives a different impression of the glen before dropping back down past Wester Brewlands to the river.

Back at Kilry Post Office below the B954 where it crosses the river is the Reekie Linn. Aptly named, since a pall of mist often hangs over the fall and looks like smoke, it is an impressive sight when the Isla is in spate. The river narrows into a rocky channel, then shoots over the fall in a spectacular leap. For sixty feet it drops straight down to rebound off a ledge and crash a further twenty feet into a deep dark pool, the Black Dub. From the Black Dub the river is led through a narrow ravine to pelt in a further fall over the Slug of Achrannie. All very impressive. The Slug of Achrannie is the farthest that salmon or sea-trout can reach, which is hard luck for salmon and sea-trout, for the upper reaches of the Isla would make ideal spawning grounds.

In the triangle between the B954, the B951 and the link road by Lintrathen there is a large and well-maintained mansion, Fornethy House. This was once the property and sometime home of the Coats family of Paisley. They bequeathed it to Glasgow Corporation to be used as a holiday home for 'Deprived Protestant Girls' from Glasgow. As circumstances changed over the years the religious discrimination has been dropped and soon boys are to be accepted equally with girls. That is the way of society nowadays.

Fornethy House takes Glasgow Primary school girls for two-week courses to give them a break from problems at home. They come up tired, wary and apprehensive. The leave reluctantly. The Headmistress, Miss Pearl Fletcher, is a gem. With her sympathetic teaching and domestic staffs she makes the girls' stay a Girl Guide Camp, a Surprise Picnic and a Butlins Holiday Home rolled into one. Fornethy House memories are treasured by hundreds of wee Glasgow lassies

Brian Cocker, shepherd at Spott, checking a young ram for Show potential.

who have few enough memories to cherish.

The parishes of Lintrathen, Kilry and Glenisla still sustain as good a social and communal life as you will find anywhere these days. All over the world the old way of life has gone. Eskimos play basketball now and Angus hill herds ride three-wheeled motor bikes made in Japan but the Glen folk respect the old way of Glen life. Even though they themselves live a totally different life of comparative luxury and ease. The new inhabitants of the Glen may be incomers from the cities and the south who are able to outbid the locals for vacant houses but, once installed, they integrate.

If there is a problem, it is the impossibility of Glen folk buying Glen houses. Property values are such that southerners can always outbid locals and there are no longer any houses to rent. Workers who have lived and worked all their lives in Glenisla are forced to go and live in nearby towns whilst their houses become holiday cottages. That is a great disservice to the individual and to the Glen.

Kilry parish is a living, active, centre of social life, probably because it is near enough to main roads and towns. Glenisla rather less so. Kilry school has twenty-four pupils and two teachers; Glenisla eight pupils and one teacher. Each has a flourishing Women's Institute still carrying on the old traditions of the 'Rural' and each runs its entertainment from the Hall. Brewlands Hall, which caters for the Glen, is situated beside Brewlands bridge, a new construction which replaces the old single-span humped structure now mouldering in the trees a few yards downstream (cf. the Gella).

The upper reaches of the glen are dominated by Mount Blair (2441 ft.) and the B951 is forced to wind round it to enter Glen Shee. A side road which leaves the B951 just below Brewlands bridge follows the Isla up past Folda and Tulchan to Sheilin, right up in the Monega hills. This extended glen of the Isla runs in to the Caenlochan National Nature Reserve, one of the most remote of all Nature Reserves usually approached from Glen Doll and Jock's Road.

A loop off this side road leads back round to the B951, passing Forter Castle on the way. This is the Forter Castle that was stormed and burned by the Inverewe Campbells in 1640, the time they sacked Airlie and banished Lady Ogilvie from one or the other establishment and the utter confusion of song-writers. There is little doubt – but of course in history there must be some – that Lady Ogilvie was driven out from Forter Castle and not Airlie Castle. There is one little revealing sidelight on the Forter episode which is real history. The letter from the Duke of Argyll to his minion, Campbell of Inverewe, ordering the destruction of both castles is explicit. It is also extant. It gives detailed instruction on how to destroy and burn the castles and ends: 'Bot you neid not to latt know that ye have directions from me to fyere it, onlie ye may say that ye have warrand to demolish it; and that, to make the work short, ye will fyere it'. That is the kind of duplicity that could give the Campbells a bad name.

From the point where the Forter road rejoins the B951, the road dips down towards the river and the Glen Isla Games field. If one is concerned with the traditions of the Glen and the survival of old ways of life, it is reasonable to suggest that the Glen Isla Games at the end of August each year are as near to an orthodox Pictish Folk Festival as you are likely to find anywhere. Aye, and there have been some years when the

Hamish McDermott in action in front of the main grandstand, Glenisla Highland Games.

Games Ball could fairly have been said to be getting on for a Bacchanalia. The Games Field is a strip of flat ground in a bend of the Isla, as picturesque a wee cranny as you could imagine. It is maintained by the Glenisla Friendly Trust, a welfare fund from the days when charity was a necessity in the Glen. Now it serves only the Games. The Ball is held in Brewlands Hall.

Glen Isla Games are a genuine survivor of the old-style Sports Day for the locals. The whole Glen turns out on Games Day and the schools get a half-holiday. Do not confuse it with Braemar. The travelling circus of highly paid exhibitionists which migrates round the 'Highland Games' circuit ignores Glen Isla. The 'Games' charade exists only to attract tourists. The Glen Isla Games exist for the Glen Isla folk. Expatriate Glenners synchronise their visits home with the Games. Commercialism has not yet tainted Glen Isla – and yet – last summer's Games were shown on television so that may have been the death-knell. It will be a sorry day, indeed, when the reigning champions of Glen Isla Games, the Davidsons of Forter, *père et fils,* are ousted by subsidised professional entertainers.

The view from Forter Castle, which is presently being restored as a dwelling, down over the Games field and the Isla to the Braes, is one of the great joys of Glen Isla. It shows why Glen Isla is often referred to as the Green Glen. If Lethnot is an autumn glen, Glen Isla is for spring. The panoramic picture viewed from Forter on a Spring morning is predominantly green. The river banks, the trees, the burgeoning growth of leaf and branch and bracken is verdant. Glen Isla *is* the Green Glen.

The B951 disappears into the A93 in Glen Shee and the best way to avoid that is to come back down the Glen Isla road and go home. On your way down you will pass, if you must, the old Glen Isla Hotel and the newer hostelry, which used to be the manse, on the opposite side of the road. Both these establishments have just changed hands. The Ferriers have sold their Hotel to an English couple, the old manse has gone to an Isle of Wight pair. That about sums up the present and the future of Angus and the Mearns: *multum,* as my old man would have said with even less relevance, *in parvo.*

Further Reading

Christie, Elizabeth, *The Haven under the Hill (The Story of Stonehaven)*, Bruce, Stonehaven.

Edwards, D.H., *Around the Ancient City.**

Fraser, Duncan, *Discovering East Scotland.* Standard Press, Montrose.

Guthrie, J. Cargill, *The Vale of Strathmore.**

Hay, George, *History of Arbroath.**

Jervise, Andrew, *Memorials of Angus and the Mearns.**

Marshall, *Historic Scenes in Forfarshire.**

McBain, *Arbroath Past and Present.**

McPherson, J.G., *Strathmore Past and Present.**

Reid, Alan, *Picturesque Forfarshire.**

Simpson, W. Douglas, *The Ancient Stones of Scotland.* Robert Hale, London.

Tranter, Nigel, *The Queen's Scotland (The Eastern Counties).* Hodder and Stoughton.

Warden, Alex J., *Angus or Forfarshire.**

Watt, Archibald, *Highways and Byways round Kincardine.* Gourdas House, Aberdeen.

* These books are out of print but are all available from libraries.

Index